Retirement

Reasons, Processes, and Results

Gary A. Adams, PhD, is an associate professor and the director of the Masters of Science Program in Industrial and Organizational Psychology at the University of Wisconsin Oshkosh. His research has focused on retirement decision-making and bridge employment. He has been published in journals such as *Journal of Applied Psychology, Personnel Psychology, Journal of Organizational Behavior, Journal of Occupational Health Psychology, Journal of Personality and Social Psychology, Journal of Vocational Behavior,* and *Educational and Psychological Measurement.* He has presented his research at conferences, such as those sponsored by Society for Industrial and Organizational Psychology, American Psychological Society, and American Psychological Association.

Terry A. Beehr, PhD, is a full professor and the director of the Doctoral Program in Industrial Organizational Psychology and professor at Central Michigan University. His research has focused on topics such as occupational stress, employee motivation and morale, team building, employee turnover, and leadership. He has authored over 85 journal articles, books, and book chapters. His publications have appeared in such journals as *Journal of Applied Psychology, Journal of Business Research, Journal of Organizational Behavior, Journal of Vocational Behavior,* and *Personnel Psychology.* He has served as a member of the editorial review board of *Journal of Organizational Behavior* and *Academy of Management Journal.* Currently he is on the editorial review board of *Personnel Psychology.* He has received many honors including the Presidents Award for Outstanding Research and Creative Activity at CMU, Honorary Faculty Initiate Phi Kappa Phi National Academic Honor Society, and numerous research grants. His research has also been presented at conferences including the Society of Industrial and Organizational Psychology and the American Psychological Association. He is also a fellow of the American Psychological Society and the Society for Industrial and Organizational Psychology.

Retirement

Reasons, Processes, and Results

Gary A. Adams, PhD
Terry A. Beehr, PhD
Editors

 Springer Publishing Company

Copyright © 2003 by Springer Publishing Company, Inc.

Springer Publishing Company, Inc.
536 Broadway
New York, NY 10012-3955

Acquisitions Editor: Helvi Gold
Production Editor: Sara Yoo
Cover design by Joanne Honigman

03 04 05 06 07 / 5 4 3 2 1

Library of Congress Cataloging-in-Publication-Data

Retirement : reasons, processes, and results / Gary A. Adams, Terry A. Beehr, editors.
    p. cm.
   Includes bibliographical references and index.
   ISBN 0-8261-2054-7
   1. Retirement—United States—Decision making. 2. Retirement—United States—Psychological aspects. 3. Retirees—United States—Psychology.
4. Retirees—United States—Attitudes. 5. Retirees—United States—Economic conditions. I. Adams, Gary A. II. Beehr, Terry A.

HQ1063.2.U6R47 2003
306.3'8—dc21
                                  2003050393

Printed in the United States of America by Maple-Vail Book Manufacturing Group.

To our families, Carmen, Benjamin and William Adams
and Dana, Matthew and Alison Beehr

Table of Contents

List of Figures

Contributors

Janet Barnes-Farrell, PhD, is an associate professor and director of the Doctoral Program in Industrial/Organizational Psychology at the University of Connecticut. Her primary fields of expertise include performance appraisal and concerns associated with aging and work. Dr. Barnes-Farrell has been conducting research on issues related to our aging workforce for over a decade. She has presented and published over 20 papers on topics ranging from age discrimination to early retirement decision processes. Her research has appeared in a number of professional journals, including: *Experimental Aging Research, Journal of Applied Psychology, Human Resource Management Review, Organizational Behavior and Human Decision Processes, Personnel Psychology, Psychology and Aging,* and *Work and Stress.* Dr. Barnes-Farrell is a member of the editorial board for the *Journal of Applied Psychology* and coeditor of an upcoming special issue of *Experimental Aging Research.*

Dennis Doverspike, PhD, is a full professor of Psychology, a fellow of the Institute for Life-Span Development and Gerontology, and director of the Center for Organizational Research at the University of Akron. He holds a diploma in Industrial/Organizational Psychology from the American Board of Professional Psychology. He is a coauthor of the books, *Affirmative Action: A Psychological Perspective* and *The Difficult Hire.* He is also the author or coauthor of over 70 professional publications. His research has appeared in journals such as *Journal of Applied Psychology, Personnel Psychology, Journal of Business and Psychology,* and *Public Personnel Management.* Dr. Doverspike has over 20 years of consulting experience and has formerly served as executive vice president of Barrett & Associates, an international, human resources management consulting firm. Currently, he maintains an independent, private practice that serves state and local governments, the federal government, and major private employers.

Daniel C. Feldman, PhD, is the Synovus chair of Servant Leadership and the director of the leadership research consortium at University of Georgia's Terry Colleges of Business. He has authored over seventy-five articles and five books on career development issues in management. His most recent book, *Coping With Job Loss: How Individuals, Organizations, and Communities Respond to Layoffs,* was named one of the four outstanding books of the year by the Academy of Management and has been cited in T*he New York Times* and *The Wall Street Journal.* In 1997 he was the recipient of USC's Educational Foundation Research Award for being the outstanding researcher in the professional schools. He has also won a J.L. Kellogg Research Professorship for his work on socialization, a CIBER Fellowship for his work on expatriates, a Riegel and Emory Fellowship for his work on downsizing, and the Addison-Wesley Best Paper Award from the Academy of Management for his work on early retirement.

Robert E. Gibby, MA, holds a master's degree and is a doctoral candidate in industrial-organizational psychology at Bowling Green State University in Bowling Green, Ohio. Mr. Gibby's present research focuses on measurement issues related to testing and the assessment of job attitudes. He was awarded the 2002 Top Student Award by the Institute for Psychological Research and Application.

Martin M. Greller, PhD, is a full professor of Management at the University of Wyoming, where he has served as MBA director. Prior to joining U. W. he taught at Baruch College, City University of New York and at New York University. Dr. Greller is a psychologist licensed in New York and New Jersey. He was a senior consulting psychologist for RHR International and director of human resources planning and development for The New York Times Company. He earned his PhD from Yale University for work in organization behavior. He currently is on the editorial boards of *Journal of Vocational Behavior* and *Human Resource Planning,* and served as chair of the Careers Division of the Academy of Management. Since his 1989 book with David Nee, *From Baby Boom to Baby Bust: How Business Can Meet the Demographic Challenge,* his work has explored how organizations and older workers can foster work life continuity.

Charles B. Hatcher, PhD, is an assistant professor in the Department of Consumer Science of the School of Human Ecology at the University of Wisconsin Madison. He has been recognized nationally for empirical work focusing on personal financial decision making. His doctoral thesis on the economics of retirement planning decisions was chosen by the American Council on Consumer Interests (ACCI) as the best dissertation of 1997. His article, *A Model of Desired Wealth at Retirement,* was chosen as best journal article of 1997 by the Association for Financial Counseling and Planning Education (AFCPE). Dr. Hatcher received his BS, MS and PhD Degrees from Cornell University in 1993, 1995, and 1997, respectively. Dr. Hatcher is currently conducting research examining rural versus urban differences on rates of return on housing stock through a grant with the United States

Department of Agriculture. Other current research projects include work on optimal investment portfolios for retirement, life insurance adequacy of United States households, and the financial planning strategies of low-income American households.

Kène Henkens, PhD, is a Researcher at the Netherlands Interdisciplinary Demographic Institute (NIDI) in The Hague where he has studied issues concerning the aging labor market for more than ten years. He has studied female labor supply, macro consequences of an aging labor force, and retirement decisions. To study retirement, Kène carried out a number of large surveys among older workers and supervisors in the Dutch civil service, industrial and retail sectors. Currently he is involved in a study on flexible retirement funded by the Dutch Management Studies Foundation and in research on employers' views on older workers. He is joint head of the social demography department of NIDI. He has published his retirement research in journals such as *Research on Aging, Journals of Gerontology: Social Sciences, European Journal of Population, Journal of Applied Social Psychology, Ageing and Society,* and *European Sociological Review.*

Jerome Kaplan, PhD, is senior fellow, elderhostel coordinator, and nursing home administrator program coordinator with The University of Akron Institute for Life-Span Development and Gerontology. Prior to joining the Institute, he was executive director of Mansfield (Ohio) Memorial Homes and an adjunct professor at The Ohio State University, coming from Minnesota as special assistant on aging to its Governor. He has advised a U.S. Vice President on gerontology and the Comptroller General of the United States on nursing home policy. He is the founding chairman of the Ohio Research Council on Aging. He is honorary editor-in-chief of *The Gerontologist* and past president of The Gerontological Society of America. In 1978, he was selected to represent the Western Hemisphere at the World Congress of Gerontology in Tokyo. He is the author of over 300 publications and has received numerous honors.

Kenneth S. Shultz, PhD, is a full professor of Industrial/Organizational Psychology in the Department of Psychology at California State University, San Bernardino (CSUSB). He has been at CSUSB since 1992, moving from assistant to full professor. He also served three years as director of the Master of Science Program in I/O Psychology at CSUSB. In addition, Professor Shultz spent the 1998–99 academic years serving as a National Institute on Aging postdoctoral fellow at the Andrus Gerontology Center at the University of Southern California. Professor Shultz has been studying aging workforce and retirement issues for almost a decade. He has presented and published over 25 papers on aging workforce and retirement issues and has made a number of invited presentations on these issues. His research can be found in journals such as *Journal of Vocational Behavior, Journal of Occupational and Organizational Psychology, International Journal of Organizational Theory and Behavior, Public Productivity and Management Review,* and others.

Harvey L. Sterns, PhD, is a full professor of Psychology and the director of the Institute for Life-Span Development and Gerontology at the University of Akron. He is also a research professor of gerontology in Community Health Science at the Northeastern Ohio Universities College of Medicine. His research and many publications have focused on topics such as changes in perception, motor function, intelligence and problem solving with age, adult education, and industrial gerontology. Currently he is president of Division 20 of the American Psychological Association and codirector of the Western Reserve Geriatric Education Center. He is a fellow of the Gerontological Society of America, the American Psychological Association, and the American Psychological Society. He has also received many professional honors, such as the Distinguished Service in Education, Research, and Communications Award, the Clark Tibbets Award from the Association of Gerontology in higher education, the Dr. Arnold L. Heller Memorial Award from Menorah Park Center for the Aging, and the Outstanding Researcher in Ohio Award.

Linda K. Stroh, PhD, is a Loyola University faculty scholar and professor of organizational behavior at the Loyola Graduate School of Management. She has published over 80 articles on issues related to organizational policy, both domestically and internationally. Dr. Stroh's work can be found in journals such as *Journal of Applied Psychology, Personnel Psychology, Academy of Management Journal, Strategic Management Journal, Journal of Organizational Behavior, Journal of World Business,* and various other journals. Dr. Stroh is coauthor of two books, *Globalizing People Through International Assignments* and *Organizational Behavior: A Management Challenge. The New York Times, The Wall Street Journal, The Washington Post, The Chicago Tribune, Fortune, Newsweek, U.S. News and World Report,* and *Business Week,* as well as various other news and popular press outlets have cited Dr. Stroh's work. Professor Stroh's research has been featured several times on *Tom Brokaw's Nightly News* and *CNN.* She is also a past chair of the Careers Division for the Academy of Management. Dr. Stroh currently serves on the editorial review board for *Journal of Applied Psychology, Journal of World Business,* and *Journal of Vocational Behavior.*

Maximiliane E. Szinovacz, PhD, is a research professor of Internal Medicine with the Glennan Center at Eastern Virginia Medical School. She has taught at several universities, including Penn State, Florida State, the University of Illinois, and Old Dominion University. Dr. Szinovacz's research focuses on retirement and family issues. She is currently working on a NIH-funded project on Marriage, Families, and Retirement. Earlier research, funded by the AARP-Andrus Foundation, was devoted to women, retirement, and grandparenting. She also conducted research on children whose parents are caregivers. Her research has appeared in various journals, including *Journal of Gerontology, The Gerontologist, Research on Aging, Journal of Marriage and the Family,* and *Family Issues.* In addition, Dr. Szinovacz recently edited several books including *Families and Retirement* and *Handbook on Grandparenthood.* In addition to her work at the Glennan Center, Dr. Szinovacz is privatdozent at the University of Vienna, Austria, and currently is engaged on a project with the European Centre for Social Welfare Policy and Research in Vienna.

Mary Anne Taylor, PhD, is a professor in the Psychology Department at Clemson University. Her research includes investigations into the prediction of retirement adjustment. Specifically, her work focuses on the role of social support, psychological readiness for retirement, and retirement planning as predictors of postretirement satisfaction. In addition, she studies the different techniques used by organizations to recruit older job applicants. She has published her work in outlets such as *Psychology and Aging, The Career Development Quarterly, Educational Gerontology, Human Resources Management Review, Public Personnel Management,* and *Group and Organization Management.* Her research has been presented at conferences such as the Society for Industrial and Organizational Psychology, the American Psychological Society, and the American Psychological Association.

Hendrick Van Dalen, PhD, is a researcher at the Netherlands Interdisciplinary Demographic Institute (NIDI) in The Hague, a senior researcher at the Research Center for Economic Policy of the Erasmus University in Rotterdam, and a research fellow at the Tinbergen Institute, a joint venture of the universities of Rotterdam and Amsterdam. He was formerly affiliated with the Scientific Council for Government Policy in the Hague. His research interests covers the economic consequences of aging, population economics, public sector economics, social security issues, the economics and sociology of science and the history of economic thought. He has been published in, among others, *Population and Development Review, Ageing and Society, Social Choice and Welfare, Journal of Policy Modeling, Journal of Law, Economics, and Organization, Public Choice,* and *American Economist.*

Michael J. Zickar, PhD, is an associate professor of industrial-organizational psychology at Bowling Green State University, in Bowling Green, Ohio. Dr. Zickar's research focuses on developing psychometric tools that help solve practical problems such as how to select and identify individuals who are misrepresenting themselves on job applications. His work has been published in top scientific journals, such as *Applied Psychological Measurement, Personnel Psychology,* and *Journal of Applied Psychology,* and he has presented at leading scholarly conferences such as the Society for Industrial-Organizational Psychology, the American Educational Research Association, and the Psychometric Society. He is on the editorial board of *Organizational Behavior and Human Decision Processes.*

Preface

The overall purpose of this book is to review, summarize and integrate current literature on the topic of retirement and to suggest areas for future research and practice. Demographic changes such as the increasing number of older adults and their decreased level of workforce participation have prompted considerable interest in the topic of retirement on the part of both researchers and practitioners from a number of different areas. Among others, these include researchers and practitioners in the areas of economics, sociology, gerontology, and psychology. This diversity of perspectives, theories, and approaches applied to the study of retirement makes it difficult to develop a coherent view of the literature. Developing such a coherent view is needed in order to better inform research on the topic of retirement and the management of the retirement process.

Audience

The book is aimed primarily at undergraduate and graduate students, academics, and researchers in gerontology, industrial and organizational psychology, developmental psychology, and organizational behavior and human resources management, and secondarily at those in the fields of labor economics and industrial sociology. Practitioners and consultants in these and related fields are also likely to find the book of interest.

Approach

Because the purpose of this book is to review, summarize, and integrate a diverse literature rather than adopt a specific theoretical orientation, the book will be structured around the retirement process as it unfolds. That is, in three phases: preretirement, retirement decision making, and postretirement. Within this framework the various chapters cover the economic, sociological, gerontological, and psychological theory and research. Taken together they provide a comprehensive review of the retirement literature in a single source.

Acknowledgments

A work such as this could not have been completed without the assistance of many talented people. We begin by acknowledging the contributing authors. We thank them for their very hard and very good work. Along these lines, a special thank-you goes to Ken Shultz whose advice and suggestions were appreciated throughout our editorial process. We also acknowledge Sheri Sussman and Shoshana Bauminger at Springer Publishing for their diligent behind the scenes efforts. Similarly, our thanks go to Emily Morgan, and Jamie Jacobson for their assistance with manuscript preparation. A hearty thank you also goes to our colleague Steve Jex, whose friendship and sense of humor has proven invaluable. Finally, but certainly not least of all, we thank our families, Dana, Matthew, and Alison Beehr, and Carmen, Benjamin, and William Adams, for allowing us the time and support needed to complete this work.

1

Introduction and Overview of Current Research and Thinking on Retirement

Terry A. Beehr and Gary A. Adams

Considering that retirement is something most people expect to experience in their lifetimes and that we have all seen people experience it, one would think we must know what it is. Inspection of written research and theory on retirement shows that the definition of retirement is somewhat elusive, however. To paraphrase what a now retired colleague of mine was fond of saying about psychology, perhaps "retirement are plural." There are many retirements, or at least many forms of retirement. Theory and empirical research give us retirement concepts such as bridge employment or partial retirement, voluntary retirement, social security (or pension) eligibility or receipt, perceived retirement, and early retirement. We thought we knew what retirement was until we tried to study it. Should we define it tightly and narrowly? Maybe not. Of course any one study must have a clear operational definition for its variables (including retirement), but retirement is really an individual, organizational, and societal or cultural construct. Understanding how varied its forms are is one of the first, most valuable insights that strikes many of us retirement researchers. This realization also gives us both a sense of excitement and trepidation when thinking about one's own retirement. On the one hand, there is the opportunity to choose the way I would like to retire; on the other, it becomes apparent that there are ways to retire that may not be attractive to me!

What will readers find in this book? In addition to discussions of the wide variety of types of retirement, several other issues catch attention in multiple chapters. Some are the aging of many societies and the implications of aging populations, the nature of retirement as a process that defies attempts to consider it in one manner only, the richness and confusion resulting from having multiple disciplines study and recommend applications for it, and the relative inaction of society and government even as we recognize some implications of an aging society.

Regardless of the research definition or the form of retirement we actually experience, it seems true that retirement is a process rather than an event or a state a person experiences at one point in time. Just like aging itself, retirement can unfold and change over time as employed people approach retirement, and retirement also changes after the experience of it begins. People's expectations about retirement before they experience it and their subsequent experience with it vary from person to person, and for any given person the decisions about and experience of retirement varies from one time period to another. As researchers, we may be able to predict what employed people will do immediately after entering retired life, but predictions about retired life farther into the future are as difficult as they are in any other behavioral domain. Conceiving retirement as a process implies change, but we probably have not done a good job of investigating changes over time in relation to retirement decisions and experiences.

Contributing to both the confusion about retirement and the richness of it as a research topic is the fact that several different disciplines are interested in the topic, they view it through the lenses of their own interests, and they tend to approach it from their own areas of expertise. Sociology, medicine, policy studies, psychology, human resources management, economics, and gerontology all have their views of the causes, or at least where to look for the causes, of retirement, and many of them also are interested in understanding the quality of life after retirement and how to improve it. Unfortunately, we may be more active early in our retirement than we are later. Maybe the applied lesson here is that we should enjoy our favorite retirement activities while we can! It bodes well that most of our conversations with recent retirees seem to indicate that they are happy they made the decision to retire when they did (and some say they wished they had done it sooner)!

Of course, as individuals, we all age continuously, but it might be somewhat of an historical anomaly that the overall populations of virtually all Western countries are aging. Our societies are experiencing aging in a way and at a pace that probably was not true for the societies our parents and grandparents knew. In the middle of the current century, scholars will look back and tell us what the effects of this aging trend were on the masses of individuals and on our societies and institutions. For now we can only guess. There are prescriptions and suggestions for action to improve our chances of maintaining a strong and healthy society and population, but thus far, we are not really doing much about the aging trend. Projections about the demise of the social security system in the U.S. have not yet led to very strong action by government. Aside from government, Americans as individuals have not been particularly good at saving for their financial future, and that bodes poorly for supporting themselves in their retired years. We could go back to a system where the young and middle aged took care of their parents (sometimes by living together, but now sometimes by supporting them financially). We could go back to working until we are closer to death (which formerly occurred at a younger average age). These might be the fallback solutions for taking no action as a society; we can even argue that they worked once, however, and so we surely could muddle through again. After all, at one time we thought of retired life as a short period that began when we could not work any more and ended when we died! We could return to that view of retirement from one that is now common in the West, i.e., retirement is a fairly long and well-deserved period in one's life when one is no longer required to pay attention to the demands of paid work). It is a long period of leisure to which we are all entitled.

How shall we consider this period of retirement, and what issues and variables are important in relation to it? It depends on who is answering this question. Retirement is interesting to people in many different disciplines, and each approaches it from the perspective of its own interests, areas of expertise, and tools. Even though we are all striving to see the bigger picture, disciplines and discipline-bound theories still tend to drive the thinking and research about the topic. Economics shows that money is important in people's retirement decisions, sociological theories indicate the changing roles that retired people play in society, psychologists look at perceptions of and reactions to retirement, human resources management considers organizational policies impacting people's retirement decisions and the impact of retirement on the company, policy studies take a similar approach but with a focus on societal policies and outcomes, and medicine pays attention to health before, during, and after retirement. Retirement is indeed one of those topics about which few people have all the information or consider all the ways of investigating. The chapters of this book, taken as a whole, indicate some of this diversity of viewpoints and provide insight into the whole process of retirement.

There is a major focus in retirement research on factors that predict or influence the decision to retire. The chapters also hint, however, at some relatively less studied but probably still important issues. Two of these are the effects of retirement on various parties (e.g., the retired individual, the former employing organization, and the larger society) and who pays for whatever it is that is done in the name of retirement. Both of these issues involve values questions. For the individual, two variables that are important in deciding to retire also may be important in the quality of retired life: health and finances. With these, retirement can be a valuable and enjoyable time in life. Without them, it might be much more burdensome. Less is clear about the effects of retirements on former employing organizations. We might speculate that organizations offering "early" retirement incentives expect organizational benefits to accrue. Do the organizations actually reap the expected benefits, and are they better off in all the ways that are important? It appears that researchers have not grappled with this thorny problem. What about society? We assert and assume that "too many" retirements are bad (e.g., consider economic projections about the financial viability of the social security system), and yet there have been depressed times when it appeared beneficial to get people (older people) out of the workforce so that others (younger ones) could get jobs. What is the "right" proportion of people for a society to have working versus retired? Does the answer really depend on the temporal variations in unemployment and other economic indicators? Less effort has been spent on serious research and theory about this issue.

The second issue that seems to lurk behind many policy debates is who pays for retirement. The societal and political debate usually sounds like it focuses on the questions of how we can pay for retirements and *can* we pay for retirements. These questions may really be thin disguises for the question of *who* pays for retirement. Do the individuals pay for their own retirements, do employers pay for their employees' retirements, or does society pay for its citizens' retirements? Arguments in the direction of a privatization of social security in which people might pay less social security tax but invest that money themselves in various ways are consistent with the value that individuals should pay for their own retirements. Any pressures on employers to provide for their former employees' retirements assume that organizations should pay for retirement, and attempts to shore up social security to make it more viable (including issues like increasing the age of eligibility and increasing social security taxes) seem to assume that society should be responsible for the well-being of its retirees. These are value-driven issues. Research directly conceived in these terms doesn't appear to have been conducted very often. For example, might we expect that people will take these ideological stances based on their own self-interest, e.g., would people who make or have the most money be the most likely to favor the ideology that people should pay for their own retirements, would organizational leaders favor anything but organizations being responsible, and would people who pay the highest taxes not favor certain societal responsibility approaches (e.g., increasing taxes)?

Overall, this concept of retirement seems to mean many things and take many forms. Although its definition needs to be broad, once we get to specific retirement types we are likely to discover that different forms of retirement are predicted by different variables. The variety of disciplines investigating retirement is fortunate because it helps give us a variety of perspectives. Taking them all into consideration will eventually prove useful for research, theory, and application. We believe that anyone wishing to learn about retirement and be challenged by new ways of thinking about it will find the following chapters to be stimulating.

2

Contexts and Pathways: Retirement as Institution, Process, and Experience

Maximiliane E. Szinovacz

The concept retirement refers to several distinct phenomena. Retirement as an institution implies societal structures that regulate older workers' withdrawal from the labor force and provide old age insurance for those who have left the labor force. As a process, retirement implicates decisions on and patterns of labor force withdrawal. The experience of retirement refers to the multitude of life changes brought about by retirement. These phenomena are interlinked and closely tied to other societal structures and individual life spheres. Retirement research has only started to address these complex linkages. For example, much has been written about the economic consequences of trends toward earlier retirement and of the aging of the baby boom generation, while information on implications for other societal institutions or families remains scarce. Similarly, we know a great deal about the influence of finances, health, and spousal employment on retirement decisions, but relatively little about the impact of career trajectories or family-related considerations on retirement transition processes. Research on retirement adjustment also lacks a contextual emphasis—many investigations have addressed well-being in retirement, but few examine how retirement experiences are shaped by societal or familial contexts. The main aim of this chapter is to explore retirement as an institution, as a process, and as an experience, with an emphasis on the complex contexts and pathways that shape these phenomena. The first section of the chapter, devoted to retirement as an institution, depicts elements of the institutionalization of retirement and then describes selected consequences of retirement for societies, organizations, and families. In the second section, I review current research on retirement decision processes. This section shows how the institutionalization of retirement, as well as other contexts such as labor markets, work history, or marital and family characteristics, impinge on individuals' retirement decisions and retirement pathways. The third section addresses the retirement experience, that is, how well individuals adapt to retirement and which conditions moderate the impact of retirement on individuals. The chapter concludes with recommendations for future research.

Retirement as Institution

Sociologists define institutions as established patterns that are supported by norms and sanctions (Hess, Markson, & Stein, 1993, p. 313) and sometimes marked by initiation rituals. The institution of retirement thus refers to distinct patterns of labor force withdrawal that are normatively accepted. Sanctions occur mainly through financial incentives or disincentives, but may also include social pressure. Initiation rituals tend to be limited and focus on retirees' past accomplishment in the labor force rather than on the retiree identity.

THE INSTITUTIONALIZATION OF RETIREMENT

Retirement as an institution is a fairly new phenomenon, dating back to the middle of the 20th century. It characterizes most industrialized nations, but many developing countries have yet to institutionalize retirement (Social Security Administration, 1999). The institutionalization of retirement in developed countries is reflected in the widespread exit from the labor force within a relatively short age span and often prior to the loss of individuals' physical or mental capacity to remain gainfully employed. Depending on prevalent pension and old age security regulations in different countries, most persons now leave the labor force permanently between ages 55 and 65. For example, the median retirement age for men between 1990–1995 was 62.2 year in the United States, 62.0 years in Sweden, 60.3 years in Germany, and 65.2 years in Japan. Women's median retirement age for the same period was 62.7 in the United States, 62.0 years in Sweden, 59.9 years in Germany, and 62.9 years in Japan (Gendell, 1998). In contrast, many developing countries are characterized by continued labor force participation well into old age, a clear sign that retirement has not yet been institutionalized (Williamson & Pampel, 1993). In the late 1990s labor force participation rates for men age 65 and over were 75.7% in Zimbabwe (1997), 58.7% in Guatemala (1999), and 58.1% in the Philippines (1998), compared to 14.7% in Poland (1998), 1.9% in Belgium (1997), or 16.5% in the United States (1998) (International Labour Office, 1999). Note: Trends in retirement age are easier to discern from men's labor force exits because some older women never worked.

Crucial for the development of retirement as an institution were employer pensions and state-funded old age security systems. These plans originally served as a supplement to personal savings and family supports but eventually became one of the main income sources for the elderly. In the United States, for example, 56% of the income of persons age 65 and over derived from Social Security benefits and private or government pensions in 1999. Furthermore, for 64% of aged individuals Social Security alone constituted at least 50% of their total income (Social Security Administration, 2001).

Despite its importance for the institutionalization of retirement, the implementation of state administered old age security plans was not the only force leading to retirement among the elderly. Costa (1998) estimates that labor force participation among U.S. men aged 65 and over was 78% in 1880 and dropped gradually during the later part of the 19th and throughout most of the 20th century. Industrialization, age discrimination in employment, health problems among older workers, and an increased demand for leisure all contributed to this trend. Furthermore, group- and firm-specific pensions date back to the late 19th century. For instance, pensions to Union veterans were granted as early as 1890. Nevertheless, widespread nonemployment in old age was clearly facilitated by the Social Security Act of 1935 (Costa, 1998; Graebner, 1980) and further reinforced by employer funded private pensions. Thus, the institutionalization of retirement per se and of an expected retirement age was made possible by the development of old age pension programs, but also was influenced by other societal trends such as labor market changes, employers' attitudes toward older workers, and individuals' preferences and needs.

THE NORMATIVE UNDERPINNINGS OF RETIREMENT

The normative underlining of retirement as institution derives, on the one hand, from formal regulations embedded in old age security and pension programs, and on the other hand, from social and individual expectations about retirement and retirement age. Social security programs mandate (explicitly or implicitly) that older workers should leave the labor force or at least drastically reduce work hours, and that they do so at a specified age. These rules manifest themselves in worker and employer expectations about when retirement should occur and are supported by sanctions pertaining both to the age of retirement and postretirement employment.

Social Security programs, as well as private pensions, provide windows for "normal or on-time retirement," that is, they define the age range during which retirement should occur and encourage retirement at specific ages (Blöndal & Scarpetta, 1998; Gruber & Wise, 1999; Kohli, 1994). For example, in the United States labor force exits abound around ages 62 and 65, corresponding to early and regular Social Security benefit eligibility. In addition, labor force exits are also common around age 55, mainly due to early retirement windows provided in private pension plans (Gruber & Wise, 1999).

There also is some attitudinal support for retirement and old age security programs. Expectations for retirement in the U.S. have been somewhat undermined by the abolishment of mandatory retirement in 1986 and considerable uncertainty and discussion about the future of Social Security (Reno & Friedland, 1997; Sherman, 1989). Nevertheless, most individuals approaching typical retirement ages who have any plans at all expect to either reduce work hours or to stop working altogether. Using data from the nationally representative Health and Retirement Survey, Ekerdt, DeViney, & Kosloski (1996) report that 21% of workers age 51–61 in 1992 anticipated stopping work altogether, 19.8 expected to reduce work hours, 9.1% wanted to change their work, 7.1% indicated that they would never stop working, and 43% had no concrete plans as yet. There also seems to be some notion that retirement should occur at a certain age. Settersten and Hagestad (1996) report that 54.7% of a small sample of individuals age 18 and over living in the Chicago metropolitan area indicated an age deadline for men's retirement and 46.8% indicated one for women's retirement. The modal age deadline for retirement was 65 years for both men and women, corresponding to the normal Social Security age, yet there was also significant variation in these age deadlines. Fewer than 30% mentioned the modal age deadline, but the majority placed the age deadline for retirement within the 60–65 age range. The clearest evidence for the normative underpinnings of retirement as social institution comes from opinion research on Social Security programs. Widespread support for Social Security programs has been documented both in the U.S. and Europe (Dekker, 1993; Rix, 1999). In the U.S., this support continues despite considerable concern about the future of the program (Reno & Friedland, 1997; Sherman, 1989).

Institutions are typically supported by social sanctions. In the case of retirement, these sanctions are in the form of social pressure and financial incentives or costs. Social pressure derives mostly from expectations that older workers should leave the labor force to make room for younger workers. It is not clear, however, how much social pressure older workers experience. Among respondents to the 1992 wave of the Health and Retirement Survey (Juster & Suzman, 1995), fewer than 15% felt that their coworkers "make older people feel that they ought to retire before age 65" (author computation). However, the reference to early retirement in the survey may have led to the low agreement with this statement. Indeed, coworkers' attitudes tend to be less benign in the face of firm downsizing or closings (Hardy, Hazelrigg, & Quadagno, 1996). Lack of social pressure on older workers to retire may also reflect contradictory norms. On the one hand , Social Security, pensions, and especially mandatory retirement regulations foster expectations that older workers should leave to provide job opportunities for younger workers. On the other hand, laws against age discrimination in employment, and more general norms pertaining to equal rights, contain a strong message that older workers have a right to keep working as long as they wish. These contradictions may lead to ambiguity in attitudes about continued employment among older workers. They may also render answers to surveys extremely sensitive to economic conditions and to question context. For example, in 1986 just over one-third of respondents to a Dutch survey agreed with the statement that "a person 65 years or older is just as much entitled to work as a young person," but in 2000, over half of respondents endorsed the same statement (Van Dalen & Henkens, 2002). The authors attribute this change to enhanced job opportunities in the late 1990s. Furthermore, a similar item in the survey "work done by workers of 65 and older deprives young people of work" yielded different responses. In 1986, half of respondents agreed, compared to just over one-third in 2000 (Van Dalen & Henkens, 2002), suggesting that question wording also influences responses. Thus, older workers are under some social pressure to retire, but this pressure is often ambivalent and contingent on labor market and other societal conditions.

More stringent sanctions (both positive and negative) are incorporated into both Social Security and private pension regulations. Old age security and pension programs include mandates pertaining to retirement age and postretirement employment. At least until recently, Social Security contained earning rules that sharply taxed earnings for beneficiaries (Graebner, 1980; Gruber & Wise, 1999; Hardy & Hazelrigg, in press). These rules reflect one explicit goal of old age security programs, namely their potential for opening jobs and promotion opportunities for younger workers (Kohli, 1986). Consequently, late retirement was traditionally associated with the cost of work at substantially reduced if any financial gain to the employee. Age-eligible workers who postponed retirement either lost a significant proportion of their benefits or, if employment exceeded a prescribed amount, had to forego benefits altogether (Gruber & Wise, 1999). Especially in the U.S. some of these regulations have been relaxed or abandoned in anticipation of worker shortages (Hardy & Hazelrigg, in press; U.S. General Accounting Office, 2001). However, mandatory retirement regulations remain in force in most European countries where unemployment rates have recently been higher than in the United States.

In addition, most old age security and pension programs enforce "regular" retirement age through benefit reductions for early retirement. These rules aim at protecting the financial viability of retirement benefit programs and at ascertaining workers' loyalty to their employers. The extent of these reductions, as well as the definition of the regular retirement age, is often driven by labor market and Social

Security financing considerations (Gruber & Wise, 1999). Recently, several countries have increased benefit eligibility age for future retirees or raised penalties for early retirement (Blöndal & Scarpetta, 1998; Schmähl, 1993; Hardy & Hazelrigg, in press). Most pension plans also include sanctions for too early retirement although even managers may not always be aware of these sanctions, especially for defined benefit packages (Woodbury, 2001). As in the case of Social Security, pensions are typically reduced when employees retire prior to a certain age or before reaching a specific number of service years. However, when companies strive for more retirements among their employees (e.g., during downsizing), these restrictions are often relaxed or replaced by early retirement incentives (Hanks, 1990; Hardy, Hazelrigg, & Quadagno, 1996; Woodbury, 2001). While some of the recent or still debated changes in Social Security and pension rules benefit workers (e.g., relaxation of the retirement test allows greater flexibility in postretirement labor force participation), others have potential negative effects especially for selected groups of workers. For example, delay of the regular retirement age and the move from defined benefit to defined contribution pension plans tend to be particularly detrimental to lower-income groups and minorities (Flippen & Tienda, 2002; Gonyea, 2002).

RETIREMENT RITUALS

Status transitions are often accompanied by initiation rituals. In the case of retirement, these rituals focus less on the entry into a new life stage than on the termination of the work career. This reverse focus of retirement rituals testifies to the ambiguity of retirement as a status and its attendant roles. Indeed, Rosow (1974) characterized retirement as a roleless role. While it is certainly not correct to assume that retirees are no longer productive or active (Freedman, 1999; Herzog, Kahn, Morgan, Jackson & Antonucci, 1989), it is true that the content of retirement activities remains largely undefined and prescriptions for the retiree role are few (Savishinsky, 2000). There is some expectation that gainful employment will be terminated or at least reduced and that, as long as they are able, retirees should remain "busy" (Ekerdt, 1986). This ambivalence leads to considerable incongruity among indicators of retirement status (Ekerdt & DeViney, 1990; Szinovacz &

DeViney, 1999). For example, some retired women consider themselves "housewives" rather than "retirees" (Adelmann, Antonucci, & Jackson, 1993; Belgrave, 1988), most likely because their involvement in household work continues well into the retirement years. Not only are retirement rituals focused on the past and retiree identities ambivalent, the formal ceremonies marking an employee's retirement are themselves often "formulaic, predictable, and clichéd" (Savishinsky, 2000, p. 54), leaving workers with little sense of acknowledgment or fulfillment. However, the very existence of these rites underscores the institutionalization of the retirement transition.

To summarize, retirement evolved as institution in the aftermath of industrialization. Its strongest societal bases are old age security regulations and benefits, but it is also supported by social norms and transition rituals.

Consequences of Retirement as Institution

What are some of the consequences of retirement as institution for societies, organizations, families, and individuals? At the societal level, institutionalization of retirement enhances age structuring, fosters the identification of productivity with gainful employment, and serves as a mechanism of social control. Organizations are influenced by the retirement institution through regulations pertaining to pensions as well as through the impact of retirement on work force planning, work force mobility, and labor costs. The familial impact of the institutionalization of retirement manifests itself foremost in the shift of old age support from families to society and employers. However, specific old age security regulations also affect other family behaviors. The influence on individuals is evident in retirement expectations, retirement decision processes, as well as the adaptation to retirement. These influences on individuals are addressed in later sections of this chapter.

SOCIETAL CONSEQUENCES

Social Security and pension programs define age-based windows for labor force exits in the later years. This led to greater segmentation and chronologization (divisions based on chronological age) of the later part of the life course (Kohli, 1986); that is, career and retirement phases became more distinct, the transition from work to retirement more abrupt, and the timing of retirement tied to chronological age rather than to the physical or mental ability to work. These trends culminated in greater age stratification and age differentiation at the societal level (Riley & Riley, 1994). Such age differentiation is evident in multiple societal phenomena and often implies hardships for those deviating from the normative, age-segmented life course . For example, many institutions are geared toward specific age groups (e.g., schools toward children, adolescents, and young adults, and workplaces toward young and middle-aged persons). This age segregation among institutions runs counter to such concepts as lifelong learning or mid-life career changes that require education (Riley & Riley, 1994). It also favors specific types of support systems. For example, employers have become more aware of the child care needs of their employees, but supports for elder care (which is probably seen as a later-life responsibility) remain scarce (Bäcker & Stolz-Wittig, 1997; Scharlach, Lowe, & Schneider, 1991). Age differentiation further permeates social policies. As Settersten (2003) notes, "(m)any policies are based on age, under the assumption that individuals at particular ages have a common set of needs and are "at risk" by virtue of their age" (p. 211f). Consequently, rights and duties are age-specific (e.g., children may not work), as is the allocation of resources (e.g., state-sponsored health insurance is limited to the elderly). Age stratification also contributed to ageism (e.g., assumptions about older persons' declined productivity) and furthered the predominance of gainful employment as basis for social status and value (Freedman, 1999; Riley & Riley, 1994). By the end of the 20th century, however, researchers observed some reversal of these developments especially in the U.S., resulting in greater individuation of the life course at least toward the end of life (Henretta, 2001). The abolishment of mandatory retirement in 1986, legislation against age discrimination in employment, changes in the earnings test for Social Security recipients, and the shift from defined to contributory pension plans by some employers opened greater opportunities for employment in the later years and allowed more flexibility in retirement transition processes (Hardy & Hazelrigg, in press). In most European countries, however, retirement transitions continue to be abrupt as mandatory retirement age has only been delayed but not eliminated (Blöndal & Scarpetta, 1998). Although the current impact of these policy and program changes remains debated, forecasts of greater demand for older workers and of substantial problems in financing Social Security once the baby boom cohorts reach retirement age are bound to encourage increased employment in later life both in the U.S. and in Europe (Henretta, 2001; Walker, 1999).

None of these developments alters the strong identification of employment with productivity and, implicitly, with social status and recognition. When retirement benefits are tied exclusively to employment history and earnings, they devalue other work such as family work or volunteering, two types of nonpaid work common among workers and retirees (Freedman, 1999). One step countering this association is the recognition of child rearing as societal contribution. In many European countries (but not in the U.S.) some of the time spent out of the labor force for child rearing purposes is credited toward Social Security benefits (Social Security Administration, 1999). However, these credits rarely cover the full loss in Social Security benefits due to maternal leaves (fathers are entitled to the same regulations but rarely take advantage of them), and generous paid leave programs for young mothers in most European countries encourage longer work disruptions (Prinz & Marin, 1999). Disrupted work histories, part-time work to manage work and family responsibilities, and continuing sex discrimination in wages all contribute to considerable gender disparity in Social Security and pension benefits (O'Rand, 1988; Prinz, 1995). Wives can rely on their spouses' benefits (Hieden-Sommer, 1993, 1994; Pampel, 1998; Rosenman & Winocur, 1990), but widows and especially divorced women may face a financially insecure old age. In the United States, for example, the 1998 poverty rate for women age 65 and over was 4.7% if married and 21.7% if living alone (U.S. Bureau of the Census, 1999).

The benefit regulations in the United States provide for a spouse benefit, that is, spouses of beneficiaries who have reached Social Security age are entitled to one half of their spouse's benefit, regardless of whether they were employed or not. Spouses who also have entitlements based on their own employment receive the higher benefit. For many women this is their spouse's rather than their own benefit. Currently, 37% of women receive benefits exclusively on the basis of their own employment history. This percentage is expected to rise to 60% by 2060 (National Economic Council Interagency Work Group on Social Security, 1998). This regulation negates the value of women's own achievements in the labor force (Holden, 1997). It also reinforces the traditional husband-provider model and women's economic dependence on their husbands. In other countries (e.g., Germany and Austria), women are entitled to old age benefits at an earlier age than men although most countries will eliminate this rule in the future. Because husbands are usually somewhat older than wives, women's earlier retirement age facilitates joint retirement of spouses, but it may force nonmarried women to exit the labor force earlier than they wish or can afford (Gonnot, 1995).

Old age security programs further constitute an important mechanism of societal control and order (Kohli, 1986). Because benefits are tied to earnings and length of labor force participation, Social Security encourages continuous employment and rewards occupational achievement. It thus imposes a control mechanism on individuals' lives that replaces older systems of family and community control. In the same vein, Social Security provides for social order by regulating labor force exits and thus the succession of workers in the labor market, once again substituting for older (preindustrial) succession avenues that relied on replacement of family members within households (Kohli, 1986).

Because these control functions are enforced through financial sanctions, those on the margins of the labor market, including minorities and nonmarried women, can face dire economic circumstances in their old age. Nevertheless, Social Security serves more as an economic safety net than other old age pensions because it involves a considerable redistribution of income, i.e., the replacement rate (ratio of benefits to earnings) is higher for lower income groups. The importance of Social Security as an economic safety net is, perhaps, most evident from estimates of poverty among the elderly if Social Security did not exist. According to Social Security Administration estimates, the overall poverty rate among older people in 1999 would have been 48% without Social Security compared to the actual 8% (Social Security Administration, 2001).

Although social security programs and pensions certainly do not guarantee prosperity in old age, they have contributed to a substantial increase in economic well-being among the elderly (Pampel, 1998).

By creating a new group of consumers, retirement thus serves as a "vehicle for economic development" (Laws, 1996). However, opinions about the general economic impact of Social Security are divided. Some argue that Social Security discourages saving for old age and thus reduces personal savings. Social Security expenditures and taxes also may reduce national savings. In addition, concerns have been raised about increased wage costs (due to employer contributions to Social Security) and resulting reductions in firm competitiveness in the global economy. However, the extent of these economic consequences may be quite small (Gramlich, 1997).

ORGANIZATIONAL CONSEQUENCES

The institutionalization of retirement, as well as specific Social Security regulations and pension programs, also have direct implications for employers. To date, such implications received relatively little attention in the literature and are thus difficult to assess. What little research is available suggests both positive and negative implications. Positive consequences for employers derive from the importance of retirement for workforce succession and retention. Negative consequences include costs associated with loss of valued workers due to retirement as well as the expenses associated with retirement benefits.

As noted above, Social Security provides for a succession of workers in the labor market and promotes labor force withdrawal at specific ages. Employers benefit from these programs because dismissal of workers entails considerably more negative connotations than their retirement (Woodbury, 2001). The institutionalization of retirement thus provides firms with predictable means to ensure succession of workers, both through new hires and through promotion within the firm. Such succession also reduces labor costs as long-term workers' salaries are typically higher than those of more recent hires (Van Dalen & Henkens, 2002). Furthermore, early retirement programs tend to attract weak performers and thus help firms rid themselves of less productive workers (Kim & Feldman, 1998).

The benefit regulations of Social Security and especially of pension programs (at least those based on defined benefit plans) also encourage loyalty to the firm. Defined benefit plans are usually not transferable when workers move and thus encourage worker retention.

Indeed, the mere availability of employer-sponsored pensions helps to attract workers. In some countries (e.g., Austria) employer contributions are integrated into the state old age security system, typically involving state-employer-union negotiations about benefit rules (Prinz & Marin, 1999). In this case private pensions become unnecessary and employers do not have to engage in competition over pension benefits to attract workers (Woodbury, 2001).

Although retirement serves foremost as a means of worker succession, it also provides a pool of latent labor. Retirees are available for nonwage labor (e.g., as volunteers) and constitute a source of labor supply in times of labor shortages (Freedman, 1999; Laws, 1996).

Retirement also entails costs for employers. The most obvious cost derives from mandatory employer contributions to Social Security and pension benefits. These costs include the benefit contributions themselves as well as the administrative apparatus required to meet federal and state reporting requirements.

In addition, workers' ability to retire can lead to labor shortages. It is anticipated that with the aging of the population, especially when the baby boom cohorts enter retirement age, skilled workers may be in short supply. Retention of older skilled workers may require special incentives that could be costly to firms, including job conditions and benefits that are specifically geared toward older workers (Judy & D'Amico, 1997). However, increased flexibility in retirement age also undermines the predictability of workers' retirements and thus hinders workforce planning.

There also is some indication that firms' retirement programs (especially early retirement incentives) may have latent costs. Such programs are typically meant to foster employee exits in times of low productivity and to encourage succession of younger and typically less costly employees. Because retirement incentives must be offered to all eligible workers, they can thus result in exits of those workers the firm would wish to keep. However, research suggests that the less productive workers are more inclined to make use of retirement incentives (Kim & Feldman, 1998). Moreover, retirement incentives also influence morale among those workers not eligible for the program. Mollica & DeWitt (2000) report, for example, that perception of too generous retirement incentives leads to increased turnover especially among more tenured employees. Such workers may be particularly hard to replace because their exits lead to loss of firm-specific talent.

CONSEQUENCES FOR FAMILIES

There has been considerable debate over the implications of Social Security taxes for families and intergenerational relations. Advocates for the privatization of Social Security especially argue that current social welfare programs provide an unfair advantage to the elderly, at the cost of children and young families (for critiques see Pampel, 1998; Williamson, Watts-Roy, & Kingson, 1999). However, historical research demonstrates that prior to the enactment of Social Security, elders accumulated family funds through contributions of unmarried children, forcing some children to delay marriage or to forego further education and thus the prospect of upward mobility. Those lacking family funds sometimes found support within their communities or from charities but were at considerable risk of poverty (Harber & Gratton, 1994; Held, 1982; Laslett, 1977; Thomson, 1989). In developing countries, many elders still rely on their families for economic support, but families are often not a reliable income source and some elders would favor economic independence from their children (Ngan, Chiu, & Wong, 1999). Old age security programs free adult children from most direct financial responsibility for their parents and enable them to direct their financial resources toward supporting their own children's upbringing and education (Szinovacz & Ekerdt, 1995). They also foster emotional ties that are not burdened by financial considerations and duties (Kingson, Hirshorn, & Cornman, 1986; Knipscheer, 1988; Quadagno & McClellan, 1989). Indeed, even though family members continue to provide for each other in times of need, their preference is for state-based support of the elderly (Treas & Spence, 1989). Of course, state old age security programs do entail an intergenerational contract, that is, benefits for the elderly are funded through taxation of current employees. However, the inherent redistribution of income within old age security programs (i.e., replacement rates are higher for lower-income groups) lightens the financial burden of those who would be particularly strained by economic supports of their elders. A shift to private retirement savings, on the other hand, would benefit higher income groups. It would also erode the intergenerational contract by shifting the old age security paradigm of interdependence and social cohesion toward a paradigm of independence and individualism (Walker, 1999; Williamson, Watts-Roy, & Kingson, 1999).

Another, not always unintended, consequence of retirement regulations on families derives from child care credits. As noted above, many European countries allow child care credits in the calculation of old age security benefits (i.e., some years taken off by parents are counted as if the parent had worked). Depending on how generous such credits are, they may entice childbearing. Indeed, Prinz (1995) offers a cost-benefit analysis for suggested social security policy changes in Austria (where fertility is currently quite low) that explicitly incorporates an "emancipatory and pronatalist pension scheme." Aimed at reducing both women's dependence on husbands' benefits and the pension costs associated with child rearing, this scheme provides for quite generous child care credits at the expense of survivor benefits. Prinz (1995) suggests that the resulting increase in fertility would, in the long run, increase the social security contribution/expenditure ratio and serve to maintain a stable size of the labor force. It is debatable whether the emancipatory intentions of this scheme would work. Pension coverage of child care years in conjunction with generous benefits for mothers (i.e., lengthy paid parent leaves) is likely to increase the time mothers spent out of the labor force. The scheme is thus likely to enhance women's own benefits and thus reduce their dependence on husbands' benefits but would at the same time undermine continuous careers.

The institutionalization of retirement has had far-reaching consequences for societies, organizations, and families. At the societal level, it contributed to age stratification, the identification of employment with productive activities, societal control, and old-age economic well-being. For organizations the institution of retirement provides a means of workforce succession and planning but also involves costs related to loss of skilled workers and old age pension contributions. Familial consequences derive foremost from the shift of old age support to the states and individual taxpayers, although specific pension provisions may also influence other family behaviors such as fertility or mothers' employment. At the individual level, old age security programs and pensions influence retirement timing and transition processes. These influences and other factors impinging on the retirement transition are discussed in the next section.

Retirement Transition Processes

Retirement is commonly viewed as an abrupt transition from employment to nonemployment at the precise time individuals meet Social Security or pension eligibility. Yet accumulated evidence suggests that retirement transitions are considerably more complex. They evolve from a variety of contextual influences and follow divergent pathways. Much of the existing literature on retirement transitions either explores how specific old age security and pension programs influence labor exit patterns (Blöndal & Scarpetta, 1998; Gruber & Wise, 1999; Kohli, Rein, Guillemard & Van Gunsteren, 1991) or how individual characteristics impact on retirement decisions and timing (Beehr, 1986; Hayward, Friedman, & Chen, 1998; Quinn & Burkhauser, 1990; Szinovacz & DeViney, 2000). This section takes a slightly different approach by emphasizing the multitude of contexts involved in retirement transition processes and by viewing exit pathways from a life course perspective.

THE RETIREMENT DECISION PROCESS

To understand the decision whether and when to retire, it is necessary to consider two sets of factors—those related to the extent of leeway individuals have in making the retirement decision, and those related to the various push and pull factors (the cost-benefit ratio) of retiring at any given point. Economic models based on rational choice theory tend to view barriers to retirement decisions within the cost-benefit framework (Leonesio, 1996). However, involuntary actions are not subject to cost-benefit considerations (Quinn & Burkhauser, 1990). The decision framework shown in Figure 2.1 implies the latter theoretical approach. Decision making barriers and opportunities constitute the most fundamental layer of the decision process. It is only when choice exists that cost-benefit considerations enter retirement decisions. Individuals who are struck by sudden illness or expelled from the labor force on the basis of mandatory retirement regulations have little option but to retire, regardless of their desire to do so or the financial and familial implications of the transition (Quinn & Burkhauser, 1990). Other scenarios may involve some, but only limited, choice. For instance, a life-threatening illness of one's spouse does not necessitate labor force withdrawal. However, professional home care service opportunities in the community may be such that the only viable alternatives for the couple are home care by the spouse or institutionalization. Some couples may not consider institutionalization as a true alternative, that is, the value placed on keeping the ill spouse at home will override all other considerations. Analyses of data from the U.S. Health and Retirement Survey support this conceptualization. Some wives who entered retirement with ill spouses viewed their retirement as a "forced" transition (Szinovacz & Davey, 2002).

CONTEXTS

The most important contexts involved in retirement transition processes are shown in Figure 2.1. These contexts are interrelated within as well as across macro, meso, and micro levels, and it is typically their combined influence that determines pathways into retirement. A thorough discussion of each of these contexts is beyond the space limitations of this chapter. I will consequently provide examples for selected contexts, especially those not addressed in previous chapters or in the preceding section.

At the societal level, contexts influencing retirement transition processes include population structures, modes of production and labor markets, norms, and the numerous state regulations pertaining to employment, old age security, and social welfare. Population structures determine the age structure of societies and thus the relative size of retiring cohorts. Small birth cohorts (low fertility), especially when followed by larger cohorts, and/or limited survival into old age (high mortality) produce low old age dependency ratios (the proportion of retirement-age persons relative to the number of individuals in their productive years). Under such conditions the societal burden of old age security remains relatively low (Bosworth & Burtless, 1998). The societal upheaval created by the reverse scenario, large cohorts with low mortality followed by smaller ones, is exemplified by the aging of the baby boom cohorts. In anticipation of difficulties in financing old age security programs for retiring baby boomers many states have altered social security regulations. For instance, in the U.S. the age of full Social Security eligibility was raised, several European countries

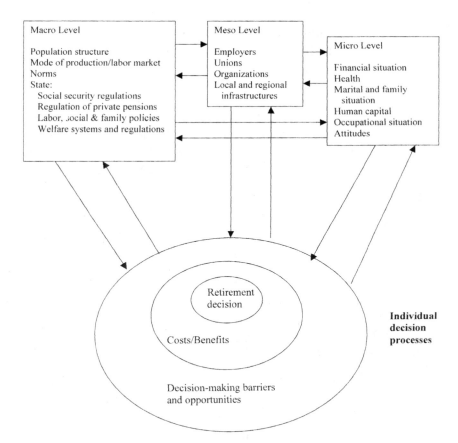

Figure 2.1 Retirement decision process.

abandoned early retirement schemes, and many countries strive to maintain older workers in the labor market (Bosworth & Burtless, 1998; Hardy & Hazelrigg, in press; Social Security Administration, 2002; Van Dalen & Henkens, 2002; Walker, 1999). However, the success of such rule changes is contingent on other contexts, including labor markets, employers, and individuals. Postponement of retirement can only be successfully implemented if labor markets can absorb more older workers, employers are willing to hire and retain older workers, and workers themselves are willing and physically able to remain in the labor force. One case in point is the impact of disability or illness on workers' retirement decisions. Even though life expectancy at age 65 increased considerably within the last decades from 77 in 1940 to 81.2 in 1998 for men and from 78.7 to 84.8 for women (National Economic Council Interagency Work Group on Social Security, 1998), some workers encounter health problems at the time of or prior to regular retirement age. Indeed, several studies suggest that early retirement is linked to ill health (Disney, 1996; Hayward, Friedman, & Chen, 1996) or to the anticipation that continued employment may have adverse health effects (Amann, 1989). Furthermore, disability or hazardous work conditions are distributed unequally among population subgroups. Minorities are more prone to retire for ill health (Hayward, Friedman, & Chen, 1996) and health-threatening work condition predominate among blue-collar and selected groups of service workers. These groups in particular can be negatively affected by policy changes that raise the retirement age. Disability may force such workers to leave the labor market early and thus be subject to benefit reductions for too early retirement, a situation that erodes the economic safety net Social Security is supposed to provide (Flippen and Tienda, 2002). In addition, workers who retire due to ill health are likely to die relatively early and thus to receive benefits for a shorter time period than healthy workers. This raises issues of equity as Social Security contributions are not tied to postretirement life expectancy.

There is also a close link between mode of production or labor markets and retirement transition processes. It is certainly not surprising that old age security programs emerged in the wake of industrialization and modernization. In agricultural societies farm succession was regulated within families and entailed provisions for "retiring" parents (Held, 1982). The support of older parents usually placed no undue burden on the younger generation because few people enjoyed a lengthy period of old age during which they were unable to work (Wolfbein, 1949, cited in Hardy & Hazelrigg, in press). Changes in the mode of production and in the employability of older workers raised the costs of parental support (see above). However, the birth of old age security programs and specific regulations within these programs were not only a response to these changes but also reflected the need to stimulate consumption (Graebner, 1980). Old age security programs and pensions certainly fulfilled this legacy. Today, "older Americans are increasingly being represented as a means to economic recovery and growth, especially, though not exclusively, for small communities" (Laws, 1996, p. 178). The success of luring older Americans into retirement communities is, of course, contingent on retirees' interest in migration. If they are economically dependent on their offspring, older Americans have neither the purchasing power nor the migration potential sought by economic developers.

Other than the economic paradigms underlying specific old age security programs, little attention has been paid to normative influences on retirement transitions. One example of such influences is the impact of filial responsibility expectations on the labor force behaviors of older persons. Ngan, Chiu, and Wong (1999) report that many retirees in Hong Kong (where a state old age security program was only recently implemented and is not yet accessible to most elders) are on the one hand receiving insufficient support from their children but on the other hand are dissuaded from seeking employment. Children discourage the reemployment of elderly parents "because they believe that it is a shame to the family that their aged parents have to work" (p. 44). Thus filial responsibility expectations prevent elders from late-life labor force participation even though children's supports are not always sufficient and the elders themselves would often prefer economic independence from their children.

Another example for normative influences on retirement transitions is the impact of gender roles on couples' retirement timing patterns. Although most middle-aged wives in today's society are employed, husbands are still viewed as the main providers. This image encourages retirement patterns where the wife either retires first or both spouses retire jointly. However, couples' desire for joint retirement is often at odds with their aim to maximize benefits. This dilemma is particularly pronounced when the age difference between spouses is large, leading couples to compromise solutions that balance unfavorable benefit prospects and unwelcome retirement transition patterns (Szinovacz, 2002). Couples who fail to follow this cultural mandate often experience some upheaval in their marital relations (Moen, Kim, & Hofmeister, 2001; Myers & Booth, 1996; Szinovacz, 1996).

The importance of social security and pension systems has been detailed above and in other chapters of this volume. However, other state policies also impact on retirement transitions and especially benefits. For example, family policies pertaining to parental leave or the supply of subsidized child care influence parents' (typically mothers') ability to combine child rearing and employment. As noted above, lengthy disruptions in employment can lead to significant reductions in Social Security benefits and are partly responsible for women's enhanced risk of poverty in their later years (National Economic Council Interagency Working Group on Social Security, 1998; Smeeding, 1999).

Mesolevel structures other than employers and unions may be less influential for retirement timing processes than for postretirement life styles. Local infrastructures determine what kind of leisure or volunteer activities are available to retirees and will contribute to retirees' decisions on whether to remain at the location of their former workplace or to migrate. Migration decision models suggest, for example, that decisions on whether and where to move are contingent on a variety of push and pull factors that include climate, environmental hassles, cost of living, or the housing market (Longino, 2001). Nevertheless, local and regional infrastructure can also impact on retirement decisions per se. For example, firm closings may lead displaced workers to retire permanently rather than to seek employment elsewhere when the community has few alternative job opportunities and the displaced worker is strongly tied to the community. Similarly, the availability of local organizations that help retrain and place older workers may impact on displaced workers' ability to obtain jobs.

Numerous studies have explored the personal factors or contexts that influence retirement decisions. Foremost considered in these models are individuals' age, financial situation (assets, pension wealth, earnings) as well as health (Leonesio, 1996). Other factors have received much less attention. I will focus on two of the less frequently considered contexts as examples. One of these contexts is the worker's career and job. Hayward, Friedman, and Chen (1998) demonstrate that characteristics of both the longest occupation held and characteristics of current position influence retirement decisions. Workers in long-term jobs demanding high social skills were less likely to retire as were those whose current jobs entailed high substantive complexity. Attachment to the firm or the job itself also influence retirement decisions. For example, workers in the auto industry who had long service records were less prone to accept early retirement offers, a phenomenon referred to as the "stickiness" factor (Hardy, Hazelrigg, & Quadagno, 1996). It is important to note that these work contexts are influential even after controlling for financial and health factors.

Another neglected context for retirement decisions processes is the marital and family realm. As noted earlier, spouses tend to favor joint retirement. However, other marital factors, including spouse's pensions, spouse's health, and the quality of the marital relationship have all been shown to impinge on retirement decisions (Szinovacz, in press). For example, married individuals in troubled relationships are less prone to retire, most likely because they prefer to spend their time at work rather than in marital disputes (Szinovacz & DeViney, 2000). Spouse's health has been tied to retirement decisions of both men and women. It is not clear, however, whether spouse's illness promotes or deters retirement. Apparently, caregiving responsibilities constitute a push factor toward retirement, while the financial costs associated with a spouse's illness may forestall retirement (Blau, 1998; Hayward, Friedman, & Chen, 1998; Honig, 1996; Hurd, 1990; Szinovacz & DeViney, 2000). Family financial obligations may also preclude retirement. Several studies indicate that workers with dependent household members (other than the spouse) tend to delay retirement (Hayward, Friedman, & Chen, 1998; Szinovacz, DeViney, & Davey, 2001; Beehr & Nielson, 1995).

Taken together, these examples demonstrate that retirement decision processes are affected by a variety of contexts at the societal, organizational, community, familial, and individual levels. Furthermore, these contexts not only exert a direct influence on retirement decisions but are often interlinked. Further understanding of these processes requires a life course approach and the exploration of pathways into retirement.

PATHWAYS

The concept of pathways into retirement conveys the notion that retirement decisions reflect long-term and sequential processes over the life course. The life course perspective further implies that divergent life spheres (e.g., work, family) are interlinked (Elder & Johnson, 2003; Settersten, 2003), suggesting that retirement decisions evolve not only from occupational and employment experiences but also from experiences in other realms. This dynamic view of retirement process-es contrasts with most microeconomic models that typically focus on preretirement workers' current situation. Although some preretirement characteristics (e.g., pension wealth) imply long-term career process-es, they rarely convey specific life course sequences. For example, research shows that individuals who experienced job interruptions and unemployment spells are more prone to retire (Hayward, Friedman, & Chen, 1998), but it is less clear whether the timing of labor force exits and unemployment spells or the reasons for these interruptions matter. In light of the scarce literature on retirement pathways, I offer a few examples from existing studies that can inform future research endeavors.

Workers who leave the labor force prior to Social Security and pension eligibility are not necessarily left without state support. Other social welfare programs, especially unemployment and disability in-surance, can provide economically feasible avenues toward early re-tirement. How attractive these pathways are depends on the specific regulations for these programs. In the United States unemployment and disability are subject to relatively stringent rules, so that early exits are mostly through employer retirement incentives. In contrast, several European countries offered quite generous and long-term un-employment and disability benefits that effectively provided early re-tirement windows (many of these programs have been abandoned or altered in anticipation of the costs of baby boom retirement). Some countries also provided specific programs such as a gradual retire-ment scheme in Sweden, an early retirement program in Germany, or contractual preretirement programs in the Netherlands (Gruber & Wise, 1999; Kohli, Rein, Guillemard, & Van Gunsteren, 1991) that facili-tated early labor force exits. According to Guillemard and Van Gun-steren (1991), the effect of these early exit pathways is more than just a "rescheduling of retirement" (p. 374). They alter the boundaries between work and nonwork and lead to the social reconstruction of links between welfare systems within the life course. Retirement exits become more individualized, the association between retirement and old age is broken, and ever-changing early exit programs may under-mine individuals' control over the retirement decision (Guillemard & Van Gunsteren, 1991).

Several investigations document the influence of early life course experiences on retirement decisions. One example is Pienta's (1999) study of the impact of women's childbearing patterns on labor force exits in later life. Her research indicates that among women age 55–64, those who delayed childbearing were more likely to remain in the labor force, whereas childless women were more prone to exit the labor force. Taking the influence of women's childbearing pattern one step further, Henretta, O'Rand, and Chan (1993) examined exit patterns of spouses' labor force exits after their partners' retirement. Their analyses show that women who continued to work during their child rearing years are more affected by their spouse's retirement (i.e., they leave employment more quickly) than women who interrupted work during child rearing. The differences in these findings can probably be attributed to variations in the analyses. Pienta (1999) controls for spouse's employment status (which is negatively related to wives' retirement), whereas Henretta, O'Rand, and Chan (1993) assess the effect of child rearing leaves exclusively for women whose husbands had already left the labor force (both studies control for other characteristics influencing retirement decisions such as health and pensions).

Taken together, these examples demonstrate that retirement decision processes evolve from a variety of contextual influences and lifelong experiences in divergent realms. The resulting pathways into retirement are thus highly individualized, and this diversity is reflected in the retirement experience.

Retirement Experiences

How well individuals adapt to retirement has been a focus of interest to researchers as well as to the popular media. Yet answers to this question remain vague and limited. Early research concentrated on the roles of retirees and postretirement activities as well as on characteristics or attributes that predict postretirement well-being. Many of these studies are tainted by conceptual and methodological limitations such as reliance on cross-sectional studies and insufficient attention to diversity (Calasanti, 1996b). More recent research is grounded in a life course perspective that stresses contexts, pathways, and interlinked life spheres (Elder & Johnson, 2003).

THEORETICAL FRAMEWORKS

Underlying these diverse emphases are distinct theoretical frameworks for the study of postretirement well-being (for reviews see Atchley, 1976; Kosloski, Ginsburg, & Backman, 1984; Ross & Drentea, 1998; Tornstam, 1989). Early approaches focused on the loss of the work role occasioned by retirement and suggested that this loss would undermine individuals' identity and lead to social withdrawal. Others suggested that retirement may not have such negative consequences provided the retiree could replace his former work role with other meaningful activities. Empirical evidence pertaining to the role loss and substitution arguments is limited, inconsistent, and dated. For example, it is not clear whether type, quality, or quantity of activities is most important (Mutran & Reitzes, 1981; O'Brien, 1981; Palmore, Burchett, Fillenbaum, George, & Wallman, 1985; Reeves & Darville, 1994). In an expansion of activity theory, Ross and Drantea (1998) argue that it is not retirement per se but involvement in fulfilling or alienating activities which influences well-being. Their analyses indicate that retirement leads to a loss of sense of control, mainly due to a reduction in problem-solving activities. However, retirees did not report more distress than full-time workers.

Countering the role loss and substitution arguments is Atchley's (1999) thesis that there is considerable continuity in identity and self concept over the retirement transition, and that this continuity contributes to retirement adaptation. That retirement does not necessarily constitute an identity crisis is upheld by accumulating evidence showing that, on average, retirees are satisfied with their lives (Bossé, Aldwin, Levenson, & Workman-Daniels, 1991; Calasanti, 1996a; Crowley, 1985; Ekerdt, Vinick, & Bossé, 1989; Herzog, House, & Morgan, 1991; Midanik, Soghikian, Ransom, & Tekawa, 1995; Palmore, et al., 1985; Reitzes, Mutran, & Fernandez, 1996; Wan, 1985). Nevertheless, a significant minority of retirees (estimates range from 10% to over 30%) report some problems in retirement or a decline in well-being after retirement (Bossé, Aldwin, Levenson, & Ekerdt, 1987; Ekerdt, Vinick, & Bossé, 1989; Hardy & Quadagno, 1995; Kim & Moen, 2002; Richardson & Kilty, 1991, 1995).

A more complex view of retirement adaptation derives from the life course perspective and its integration with selected assumptions from other theories (see Figure 2.2). The life course perspective draws attention to four concepts that seem crucial to understanding of postretirement well-being: (a) contextual embeddedness of life transitions, (b) interdependence of life spheres, (c) timing of life transitions, and (d) trajectories and pathways (Bengtson & Allen, 1993; Hagestad, 1990; Elder & Johnson, 2003; Settersten, 2003). Contextual embeddedness implies that the experience of life transitions will be contingent on the specific circumstances under which the transition occurs, including selected attributes, current and past statuses and roles, as well as societal context (which is not displayed in Figure 2.2). It is further assumed that life spheres are interdependent, so that experiences in one sphere (e.g., employment) influence and are influenced by experiences in other spheres (e.g., family). Furthermore, the experience of life transitions is contingent on their timing in terms of cultural deadlines, personal expectations, and occurrences in other life spheres. The notion of trajectories and pathways points to the historical context of life experiences (historical time), their development over time (trajectories), and the interrelationships among diverse life transitions (pathways). While the life course perspective provides a general framework for analyzing life course transitions, it offers few concrete hypotheses as to how and why specific life course transitions impinge on well-being (except, perhaps, for assumptions concerning on- and off-timing of transitions. (Hagestad, 1990). Insights from control, life transition (stress), continuity, and role theories can be used to identify the mechanisms through which life course transitions such as retirement influence well-being.

Individuals who are able to exert control over their environment and/or derive a sense of control from their actions enjoy enhanced well-being, whereas lack of control reduces well-being (Heckhausen & Schulz, 1995; Herzog, Franks, Markus, & Holberg, 1998; Herzog & Markus, 1999; Mirowsky & Ross, 1989; Ross & Wu, 1995; Schulz & Heckhausen, 1997; Seeman & Lewis, 1995). Life transitions such as retirement sometimes occur under circumstances that leave individuals little choice over the transition (e.g., poor physical health). Under such conditions, retirement may lead to reduced well-being.

The disruption of individuals' lifestyle and daily routines brought about by life transitions has been associated with stress (Burke, 1991, 1996; Diehl, 1999; Kessler, Price, & Wortman, 1985; Pearlin, Lieber-

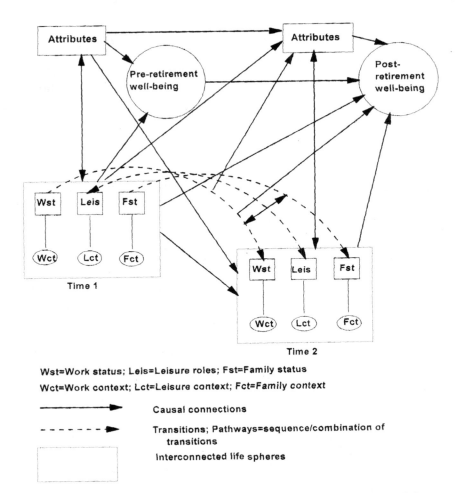

Wst=Work status; Leis=Leisure roles; Fst=Family status
Wct=Work context; Lct=Leisure context; Fct=Family context

Causal connections

Transitions; Pathways=sequence/combination of transitions

Interconnected life spheres

Figure 2.2 Theoretical model of retirement well-being. (Adapted from Szinovacz & Davey, 2001).

man, Menaghan, & Mullah, 1981). How stressful life transitions are is contingent on individuals' vulnerability, characteristics and meaning of the transition, and on the context of the transition (Kessler, Price, & Wortman, 1985; Thoits, 1991; Wheaton, 1990, 1996). Vulnerability derives from lack of coping resources or accumulation of life transitions (Turner & Lloyd, 1995; Wheaton, 1990). Traits of the transition (whether it is desirable, expected, identity-threatening or identity-enhancing, whether it concerns a salient or less important life domain, and whether it disrupts established behavior and interaction patterns) also influence stress (Atchley, 1989, 1999; Burke, 1991; Thoits, 1991). In addition, the context or meaning of the transition defines stress. Transitions out of stressful roles can be experienced as a "relief" and reduce rather than enhance stress (Wheaton, 1990).

Continuity theory emphasizes the importance of maintaining focal identities over life transitions such as retirement (Atchley, 1999). Thus, pronounced life style changes following retirement, as well as experience of simultaneous life events that lead to disruptions in salient identities, are likely to reduce well-being.

Role theory stresses human agency, that is, how social roles are constructed and enacted (Turner, 1978). Role construction may precede the actual assumption of a position (anticipatory socialization) and may entail reconstruction of experiences in past roles (Berger & Kellner, 1964). This implies that roles are dynamic and may change over time. Furthermore, the concept of role expectations points toward the importance of assessing postretirement well-being not only in terms of continued or new activities but also with regard to the implementation of activity plans. The theory also provides specific assumptions about role transitions. Role transitions are considered to have a stronger negative impact if they involve exits from salient and enduring roles, if there is a lack of anticipatory socialization, and if other salient roles are not available. On the other hand, role transitions are assumed to have a more positive impact if they reduce role conflict and if they involve entry into roles that are salient or enhance goal attainment (Burr, 1973).

The theoretical model outlined in Figure 2.2 attempts to integrate the assumptions derived from the above mentioned theoretical perspectives. It is clearly beyond the boundaries of this chapter to discuss each of the implied relationships in detail nor is there empirical evidence to substantiate many of the implied associations. Thus, I will rely on specific examples to illustrate the major assumptions and concepts shown in Figure 2.2.

ATTRIBUTES

The main attributes associated with retirement well-being are financial status and health (Kosloski, Ginsburg, & Backman, 1984). The impact of both health and finances on postretirement well-being reflects lifelong processes of disadvantage (Calasanti, 1988; O'Rand & Henretta, 1999). For example, there is little evidence supporting the common myth that health declines in retirement (Ekerdt, 1987). Rather, health problems predating retirement, sometimes reflecting long-term illness associated with discontinuous work histories, cause premature retirement (Hayward, Friedman, & Chen, 1996) and are bound to undermine retirement well-being (Bossé, Aldun, Levenson, & Workman-Daniels, 1991; Calasanti, 1996a; Crowley, 1985; Kim & Moen, 2002; Seccombe & Lee, 1986; Szinovacz, 1989). On the other hand, retirement from jobs involving hazardous work conditions may promote early retirement and retirement adjustment. A study of Austrian steel workers (Amann, 1989) revealed, for example, that these workers look forward to retirement. Having seen coworkers succumb to work-related fatal illness and feeling fatigued after long years in dangerous jobs, these steel workers hoped that retirement would bring a "few good years before dying."

Financial problems in retirement also reflect the marginalization of selected population subgroups, including those with discontinuous work histories, those in low-wage jobs, or those engaged in part-time work due to family or other obligations (O'Rand & Henretta, 1999). This marginalization culminates in reduced postretirement well-being (Bossé, Alduin, Levenson, & Workman-Daniels, 1991; Calasanti, 1996a; Kim & Moen, 2002; Richardson & Kilty, 1991; Seccombe & Lee, 1986; Szinovacz, 1989; Wan, 1985).

Other attributes have received less attention. There is some indication that the impact of retirement on well-being may differ among societal subgroups (e.g., gender and race). However, evidence on the association between gender and retirement well-being has been inconsistent (Carp, 1997; Slevin & Wingrove, 1995) and there is little research on race differences. These inconsistencies suggest that it is not gender or race per se that influence retirement well-being but rather gender and race differences in work experience, income, and other life experiences (Calasanti, 1996a; McIntosh & Danigelis, 1995; Szinovacz, 1991). Personality also may play a role in retirement adaptation but research is scarce. In line with the control thesis, some research suggests that goal continuity contributes to retirement well-being (Robbins, Lee, & Wan, 1994).

STATUSES AND STATUS CONTEXTS

How individuals experience retirement will at least partly depend on characteristics of their former work roles (type of occupation, hours spent on the job, work demands), the context of these roles (e.g., job attitudes, work commitment and salience, or performance), and their work history or career trajectories. In line with the theoretical assumptions outlined above, one would expect retirees to experience more adaptation problems if their work facilitated a sense of control and constituted a salient and dominant life domain. However, higher-level occupations that usually fit these criteria typically also provide individuals with more resources (coping skills, income) that reduce vulnerability to life event stress. There is surprisingly little research exploring the intricate linkages between work characteristics or contexts and postretirement well-being. Some studies investigating effects of occupational prestige or socioeconomic status render inconsistent findings (Calasanti, 1988; Dorfman, Kohout, & Heckert, 1985; Matthews & Brown, 1987; Richardson & Kilty, 1991; Szinovacz, 1989), and Reitzes, Mutran, & Fernandez (1996) found no impact of worker identity on retirement-related changes in self-esteem or depression.

The notion of interdependent life spheres points to the importance of nonwork contexts for retirement adjustment. Such nonwork contexts provide individuals with alternative salient identities after retirement and offer opportunities for postretirement engagement. For many individuals, marital and family relations constitute the most important of these spheres, and research confirms their importance for postretirement well-being. There is consistent evidence that individuals who are married and especially those who strongly identify with their marital role are more satisfied in retirement (Atchley, 1992; Calasanti, 1996a; Kelly & Westcott, 1991; Niederfranke, 1989; Reitzes, Mutran, & Fernandez, 1996; Seccombe & Lee, 1986). Retirement satisfaction is also fostered by congruence between spouses' evaluation of retirement (Buchmüller, 1996), by the other spouse's adaptation to retirement (Haug, Belgrave, & Jones, 1992), as well as by joint leisure activities and decision making (Dorfman & Hill, 1986; Dorfman, Heckert, Hill, & Kohout, 1988). On the other hand, marital problems enhance perceptions of retirement-related hassles (Bossé, Alduin, Levenson, & Workman-Daniels, 1991).

The assumption of linked life spheres implies not only that marital/familial contexts will moderate retirement experiences but also that retirement impinges on this domain, and several studies support this argument. Retirement has been shown to influence couples' division of household labor, the power structure of the relationship, and marital quality itself (for a review see Szinovacz, in press). For example, retirement seems to reinforce the quality of the marital relationship. Individuals who enter retirement in happy marriages tend to report further improvement after retirement, whereas unhappy marriages prior to retirement further deteriorate after retirement (Davey & Szinovacz, in press; Myers & Booth, 1996; Rosenkoeter & Garris, 1998). Entering retirement within the context of an unhappy marriage apparently enhances vulnerability to the transition either because unhappily married individuals lack another salient identity or because the combination of marital problems and life event stress resulting from the retirement transition leads to stress accumulation. Past research further provides some evidence that retirement may have negative consequences if it undermines individuals' sense of control in the marital relationship. Wives with retired husbands sometimes complain about the husband being "underfoot" or interfering in the household domain, and such perceptions, in turn, seem to be contingent on the husband's ability to develop meaningful postretirement activities (Dorfman & Hill, 1986; Ekerdt & Vinick, 1993; Schäuble, 1989; Szinovacz, 1989; Vinick & Ekerdt, 1991). It is notable that both studies of housewives and studies of retiring wives found indications of the "husband underfoot" problem (Keating & Cole, 1980; Szinovacz, 1980).

Retirement also can raise the saliency of family relationships (Niederfranke, 1991). Some retirees become more involved in interactions with grandchildren (Kremer, 1985; Niederfranke, 1991; Schäuble, 1989), and men may catch up on previously neglected contacts with their children (Niederfranke, 1991; Szinovacz and Davey, 2001). On the other hand, retirement may enhance stresses associated especially with financial family responsibilities. Financial support of children may strain retirees' financial resources (Kremer, 1985) and can contribute to enhanced postretirement stress (Marshall, Clarke, & Ballantyne, 2001).

Workers often expect significant increases in social and leisure activities after retirement, but many fail to implement these plans

(Beehr & Nielson, 1995; Bossé & Ekerdt, 1981; Vinick & Ekerdt, 1992). Indeed, there is no clear evidence of significant changes in the extent of social network contacts after retirement (Bossé, Alduin, Levenson, & Workman-Daniels, 1990, Bossé, Alduin, Levenson, Spiro, & Mroczek, 1993; Palmore, 1985; Wan, 1985). There is also little indication that enhanced involvement in leisure or social activities contributes to retirement adaptation (Wan, 1985). It may very well be that it is the disparity between expectations and actual experiences, rather than amount of leisure activities, that hampers retirement satis-faction. What seems to change after retirement is not so much the extent of social activities but the composition of social networks. Friend networks seem to be altered as coworkers are replaced with others, especially those who are bound to validate individuals' retiree identity such as nonemployed friends (Bossé, alduin, Levenson, Work-man-Daniels & Eckerdt, 1990; Bossé, alduin, Levenson, Spiro, & Mroczek, 1993; Francis, 1990; Van Tilburg, 1992). Such identity-validating friendships may ease the transition into retirement whereas other social contacts may not (Francis, 1990). Which types of social or leisure activities contribute to retirement satisfaction may also de-pend on the characteristics of other salient contexts, such as the mar-ital/family context. Szinovacz (1992a) reports, for example, that visits with relatives tend to enhance retirement adaptation foremost among widows, whereas married women profit from involvement in commu-nity activities. However, wives' involvement in outside social or com-munity activities can be detrimental to their husbands' adjustment in retirement (Dorfman, Heckert, Hill, & Kohout, 1988; Myers & Booth, 1996). Thus, identity-enhancing social activities on the part of one spouse may infringe on the salience of the marital identity on the part of the retired partner.

Much of the societal impact on retirement well-being is indirect. Old age security rules or age discrimination in employment regula-tions influence postretirement finances and the timing of the retire-ment transition, and finances and timing in turn relate to well-being. For example, the abolishment of mandatory retirement raises workers' control over the timing of their retirement, leading to higher satisfac-tion in retirement (Kimmel, Price & Walker, 1978; Peretti & Wilson, 1975). On the other hand, postponement of benefit eligibility increases the chances that retirement is entered in poor health, and illness-motivated retirement has been linked to poor retirement adaptation (Bossé, Alduin, Levenson, & Workman-Daniels, 1991; Calasanti, 1996a; Dorfman, Kohout, & Eckerdt, 1985; Hardy & Quadagno, 1995; Matthews & Brown, 1987; Seccombe & Lee, 1986).

TRANSITIONS AND TRAJECTORIES

Transitions constitute changes in statuses over time (e.g., retirement), and trajectories refer to careers within single contexts such as the work or retirement career. As noted above, it is often specific characteristics of transitions that predict stress rather than the occurrence of the transition itself. In the case of retirement, the most important characteristics appear to be the timing of and choice over the transition.

Transitions tend to be more detrimental to well-being if they occur off-time. Off-time transitions either conflict with cultural timing expectations (e.g., retirement prior to the socially institutionalized retirement age) or contradict individuals' own expectations and preferences. Because cultural norms pertaining to the exact timing of retirement are rather vague (Settersten & Hagestad, 1996), early retirement per se is unlikely to undermine well-being unless it is tied to adverse circumstances such as poor health. Considerable evidence indicates, however, that off-time retirement from the individuals' perspective contributes to postretirement stress (Marshall, Clarke, & Ballantyne, 2001; Szinovacz, 1989). Retirement adaptation is also hindered if the transition is outside individuals' control. Involuntary retirement (due to mandatory retirement or firm closings) undermines well-being (Crowley, 1985; Gall, Evans, & Howard, 1997; Hardy & Quadagno, 1995; Herzog, House, & Morgan, 1991).

Adaptation to life transitions constitutes a process, that is, the impact of the transition may change over time or in phases. In the case of retirement, several researchers noted a "honeymoon" effect, that is, initial enchantment followed by some disenchantment (Atchley, 1976; Ekerdt , Bossé, & Levkoff, 1985; Richardson & Kilty, 1995). However, the honeymoon effect may be more characteristic for men (Kim & Moen, 2002; Richardson & Kilty, 1995), and it may be contingent on preretirement well-being. Kim & Moen (2002) report, for example, that new retirees whose preretirement morale was low profited most from retiring. This finding is consistent with the notion that exits from stressful roles can be experienced as relief (Wheaton, 1990).

PATHWAYS

Pathways reflect combinations of life transitions or the dependence of life transitions on other statuses. The pathway considered most frequently in retirement research is the timing of spouses' retirements in relation to each other. The most negative impact of retirement seems to be associated with husbands' retirement prior to their wives'. Couples following this pathway tend to report lower marital satisfaction and higher marital conflict than couples in which spouses retire jointly or in which wives' retirement precedes their husbands' (Davey & Szinovacz, in press; Lee & Shehan, 1989; Moen, 2001; Myers and Booth, 1996; Szinovacz, 1996; Wan, 1985), especially if the couple abides by traditional gender role attitudes (Szinovacz & Schaffer, 2000). Several factors account for the detrimental effects of this retirement pathway. It contradicts prevailing gender role norms casting the husband as main provider, it often results from adverse circumstances that prevent couples from preferred joint retirement and may be beyond their control (O'Rand, Henretta, & Krecker, 1992), and it precludes husbands' full reorientation to the marital relationship since the wife is still engaged in occupational activities (Szinovacz, 1980).

The realization of retirement plans often depends on family circumstances (Freericks & Stehr, 1990). Illness of spouses and care for close relatives spoils postretirement plans and reduces retirement satisfaction (Clemens, 1993; Dorfman, Heckert, Hill, & Kohout, 1988; Kolland, 1988; Myers & Booth, 1996; Vinick & Ekerdt, 1991), especially for women (Szinovacz, 1989; Szinovacz & Davey, 2002). On the other hand, some retired men seem to derive self-esteem from care for ill wives (Szinovacz, 1992b). Retirement adjustment is also hampered when negative family events such as widowhood or illness or death of relatives occur in close proximity to the retirement transition (Clemens, 1993; Szinovacz & Washo, 1992; Wan, 1985). These findings support the role accumulation thesis. They demonstrate that retirement is particularly stressful if it occurs in close proximity to other life events, unless these events are identity-enhancing as seems to be the case for husbands who care for ill wives.

These empirical examples demonstrate but a few of the complex interconnections that ultimately influence retirement adaptation processes. It is important to keep in mind that the contextual features, as well as the trajectories and pathways reflected in postretirement well-being, are intricately linked to societal retirement systems and retirement transition processes. In societies that lack institutionalized old age security programs postretirement well-being will most likely be shaped by parents' economic dependence on and relationships with their children, a factor of minor importance in societies with established pension systems. On the other hand, health permeates retirees' life style and is consequently likely to affect well-being across societies. There can also be little doubt that retirement transition processes affect the retirement experience. Not only are some contextual factors that account for retirement decisions directly related to postretirement well-being (e.g., involuntary retirement due to job closures or illness), but both retirement decision processes and postretirement experiences evolve from lifelong trajectories and pathways in the realms of work, family, and leisure. It is only when we trace these trajectories and pathways over individuals' life course and within the parameters set by societal structures that we will approach a fuller understanding of the retirement experience.

Directions for Future Research

Retirement transitions constitute dynamic and complex processes that are embedded in societal and organizational structures and tied to past and current experiences in individuals' lives. One challenge to retirement research is to address and untangle these dynamics and complexities. Another challenge derives from the ever-changing nature of retirement processes, especially those associated with altered retirement policies and cohort flow.

This chapter was based on life-span perspectives of retirement that emphasize contexts and pathways of retirement transitions. It showed that recent research has started to address some of the contexts and pathways that influence retirement transition processes and experiences, but it also revealed important gaps in the literature. In view of the anticipated upheaval in retirement processes when the baby boom cohorts approach retirement, some of these gaps are particularly problematic. Although there is considerable research on actual and needed changes in policies to guarantee the viability of old age security as well as on the specific microeconomic factors impinging on retirement decisions, studies linking these two research areas remain scarce. Yet changes in policies can only succeed if they are tied to developments in other domains (e.g., enhanced willingness on the part of employers to hire or keep older workers). Current research reveals not only important tensions between policy aims and employer objectives but also demonstrates that some current policies effectively discourage the implementation of innovative firm pension plans and retirement options (U.S. General Accounting Office, 2001). Linking these two research domains could yield insights on how employers would respond to specific proposed policies and what policy changes would be necessary to encourage policy-consistent alterations in firms' employment and pension programs.

There also is a need for research on how and why selected policies influence (or fail to influence) workers' retirement decisions. Van Dalen and Henkens (2002) report, for instance, that penalties for early retirement tend to reduce workers' inclination to retire early, whereas bonuses are likely to have little effect on keeping older workers in the labor force. We know that retirement decisions are complex and reflect not only financial considerations but lifelong experiences in numerous realms. Research addressing the relative importance of these influence factors under diverging policy regimes would greatly enhance our ability to estimate the potential impact of future policy changes on retirement behaviors.

Old age security policies tend to be driven by budget considerations, yet they ultimately have an impact on the lives of individuals. Some of the expected negative consequences of current policy changes in the U.S. (e.g., on minorities' and women's old age financial security) have been outlined above, but other outcomes need to be considered as well. We may ask, for instance, to what extent policies facilitate or hinder joint retirement of spouses which appears to be favored by many couples, or whether a delay in the regular retirement age seriously interferes with older individuals' engagement in other productive activities (such as care of grandchildren or volunteering). Such interference may not only undermine individuals' morale, but it could also be costly to society as unpaid work by retirees needs to be replaced with paid services or encourages reductions in employment among younger age groups (e.g., mothers). To answer such questions, research needs to address in much more detail linkages among diverse life transitions, including retirement, and causal connections between retirement and other productive activities.

Social change offers special challenges for researchers. The decline in traditional career trajectories, technological advancements that encourage work from home, as well as policies geared toward enhanced incorporation of older workers in the labor force render boundaries between work and other life spheres less definite and more variable over the life span. These developments may alter the very character of retirement as institution and require a reorientation in retirement research. To better understand retirement processes and experiences, we will need to divert our attention from the increasingly indefinite retirement transition itself and explore linkages between trajectories and pathways in multiple life domains over time.

ACKNOWLEDGMENT

This chapter was supported by NIA grant R01 AG13180-04, Maximiliane E. Szinovacz, principal investigator.

REFERENCES

Adelmann, P. K., Antonucci, T. C., & Jackson, J. S. (1993). Retired or homemaker: How older women define their roles. *Journal of Women and Aging, 5,* 67–78.

Amann, A. (1989). Pensionierung: Hoffnung auf ein paar schöne Jahre? In L. Rosenmayr & F. Kolland (Eds.), *Arbeit—Freizeit—Lebenszeit. Neue Übergänge im Lebenszyklus. opladen Westdeutscher Verlag.*

Atchley, R. C. (1976). *The sociology of retirement.* New York: John Wiley.

Atchley, R. C. (1989). A continuity theory of normal aging. *The Gerontologist, 29,* 183–190.

Atchley, R. C. (1992). Retirement and marital satisfaction. In M. Szinovacz, D. Ekerdt, & B. H. Vinick (Eds.), *Families and retirement* (pp.145–158). Newbury Park, California: Sage.

Atchley, R. C. (1999). Continuity theory, self, and social structure. In C. D. Ryff & V. W. Marshall (Eds.), *The self and society in aging processes* (pp. 94–122). New York: Springer Publishing.

Bäcker, G., & Stolz-Wittig, B. (1997). *Betriebliche Maßnahmen zur Unterstützung pflegender Arbeit-nehmerinnen und Arbeitnehmer.* Stuttgart: Kohlhammer.

Beehr, T. A. (1986). The process of retirement: A review and recommendations for future investigation. *Personnel Psychology, 39,* 31–55.

Beehr, T. A., & Nielson, N. L. (1995). Description of job characteristics and retirement activities during the transition to retirement. *Journal of Organizational Behavior, 16,* 681–690.

Belgrave, L. L. (1988). The effects of race differences in work history, work attitudes, economic resources, and health on women's retirement. *Research on Aging, 10,* 383–388.

Bengtson, V. L., & Allen, K. R. (1993). The life course perspective applied to families over time. In P. G. Boss, W. J. Doherty, R. LaRossa, W. R. Schumm, & S. K. Steinmetz (Eds.), *Sourcebook of family theories and methods* (pp. 469–498). New York: Plenum.

Berger, P. L., & Kellner, H. (1964). Marriage and the construction of reality. *Diogenes, 46,* 1–23.

Blau, D. M. (1998). Labor force dynamics of older married couples. *Journal of Labor Economics, 16,* 595–629.

Blöndal, S., & Scarpetta, S. (1998). The retirement decision in OECD countries. *Economic Department Working Papers,* No. 202. Paris: OECD.

Bossé, R., & Ekerdt, D. J. (1981). Change in self-perception of leisure activities with retirement. *The Gerontologist, 21,* 650–654.

Bossé, R., Aldwin, C. M., Levenson, M. R., & Ekerdt, D. J. (1987). Mental health differences among retirees and workers: Findings from the Normative Aging Study. *Psychology and Aging, 2,* 383–389.

Bossé, R., Aldwin, C. M., Levenson, M. R, & Workman-Daniels, K. (1991). How stressful is retirement? Findings from the Normative Aging Study. *Journal of Gerontology: Psychological Sciences, 46,* P9–P14.

Bossé, R., Aldwin, C. M., Levenson, M. R., Workman-Daniels, K., & Ekerdt, D. J. (1990). Differences in social support among retirees and workers: Findings from the Normative Aging Study. *Psychology of Aging, 5,* 41–47.

Bossé, R., Aldwin, C. M., Levenson, M. R., Spiro, A., & Mroczek, D. K. (1993). Change in social support after retirement: Longitudinal findings from the Normative Aging Study. *Journal of Gerontology: Psychological Sciences, 48,* P210–P217.

Bosworth, B., & Burtless, G. (1998). Population aging and economic performance. In B. Bosworth & G. Burtless (Eds.), *Aging societies: The global dimension* (pp.1–110). Washington, D. C.: Brookings Institution Press.

Buchmüller, R. (1996). Ehepaare vor dem Ruhestand. In R. Buchmüller, S. Dobler, T. Kiefer, F. Magulies, P. Mayring, M. Melching, & H.D. Scheider (Eds.), *Vor dem Ruhestand* (pp. 241–256). Freiburg: Universitätsverlag.

Burke, P. J. (1996). Social identities and psychosocial stress. In H. B. Kaplan (Ed.), *Psychosocial stress: Perspectives on structure, theory, life-course, and methods* (pp. 141–174). San Diego, California: Academic Press.

Burke, P. J. (1991). Identity processes and social stress. *American Sociological Review, 56,* 836–849.

Burr, W. R. (1973). *Theory construction and the sociology of the family.* New York: John Wiley.

Calasanti, T. M. (1988). Participation in a dual economy and adjustment to retirement. *International Journal of Aging and Human Development, 26,* 13–27.

Calasanti, T. M. (1996a). Gender and life satisfaction in retirement: An assessment of the male model. *Journal of Gerontology, 51B,* S18–S29.

Calasanti, T. M. (1996b). Incorporating diversity: Meaning, levels of research, and implications for theory. *The Gerontologist, 36,* 147–156.

Carp, F. M. (1997). Retirement and women. In J. Coyle (Ed.), *Handbook on Women and Aging* (pp.112–128). Westport, Connecticut: Greenwood Press.

Clemens, W. (1993). Verrentung und Ruhestandsanpassung von erwerbstätigen Frauen. *Zeitschrift für Gerontologie, 26,* 344–348.

Costa, D. L. (1998). *The evolution of retirement: An American economic history, 1880–1990.* Chicago: The University of Chicago Press.

Crowley, J. E. (1985). Longitudinal effects of retirement on men's psychological and physical well-being. In H. S. Parnes, J. E. Crowley, J. E. Haurin, R. J. Less, L. J. Morgan, W. R. Mott, F. L. & G. Nestel (Eds.), *Retirement among American men* (pp. 147–173). Lexington, Massachusetts: Lexington Books.

Davey, A., & Szinovacz, M. E. (in press). Dimensions of marital quality and retirement. *Journal of Family Issues.*

Dekker, P. (1993). Image, self-image and participation of the elderly: An international comparison. In J. M. Timmermans (Ed.), *Report on the elderly, 1993* (pp. 103–115).

Diehl, M. (1999). Self-development in adulthood and aging: The role of critical life events. In C. D. Ryff & V. M. Marshall (Eds.), *The self and society in aging processes* (pp. 150–186). New York: Springer Publishing.

Disney, R. (1996). *Can we afford to grow older?* Cambridge, Massachusetts: MIT Press.

Dorfman, L. T., & Hill, E. A. (1986). Rural housewives and retirement: Joint decision-making matters. *Family Relations, 35,* 507–514.

Dorfman, L. T., Heckert, D. A., Hill, E. A., & Kohout, F. J. (1988). Retirement satisfaction in rural husbands and wives. *Rural Sociology, 55,* 25–39.

Dorfman, L. T., Kohout, F. J., & Heckert, D. A. (1985). Retirement satisfaction in the rural elderly. *Research on Aging, 7,* 577–599.

Ekerdt, D. J. (1986). The busy ethic: Moral continuity between work and retirement. *The Gerontologist, 26,* 239–244.

Ekerdt, D. J. (1987). Why the notion persists that retirement harms health. *The Gerontologist, 27,* 454–457.

Ekerdt, D. J., & DeViney, S. (1990). On defining persons as retired. *Journal of Aging Studies, 4,* 211–229.

Ekerdt, D. J., Bossé, R., & Levkoff, S. (1985). An empirical test of phases of retirement: Findings from the Normative Aging Study. *Journal of Gerontology, 40,* 95–101.

Ekerdt, D. J., DeViney, S., & Kosloski, K. (1996). Profiling plans for retirement. *Journal of Gerontology: Social Sciences, 51B,* S140–149.

Ekerdt, D. J., Vinick, B. H., & Bossé, R. (1989). Orderly endings: Do men know when they will retire? *Journal of Gerontology: Social Sciences, 44,* S28–S35.

Ekerdt, D. J., & Vinick, B. H. (1993). *The husband underfoot: Explaining resilient ideas about retirement's effect on marriage.* Paper presented at the Meeting of the Gerontological Society of America, New Orleans, Louisiana.

Elder, G. H., & Johnson, M. K. (2003). The life course and aging: Challenges, lessons, and new directions. In R. A. Settersten, Jr. (Ed.), *Invitation to the life course: Toward new understandings of later life* (pp. 49–81). Amityville, New York: Baywood Publishing Company.

Flippen, C., & Tienda, M. (2002). Raising retirement age weakens retirement safety net. In *Public Policy & Aging Research Brief* (pp. 2–3). Washington, D. C.: Gerontological Society of America.

Francis, D. (1990). The significance of work friends in later life. *Journal of Aging Studies, 4,* 405–424.

Freedman, M. (1999). *Prime time: How baby boomers will revolutionize retirement and transform America.* New York: Public Affairs.

Freericks, R., & Stehr, I. (1990). *Wann, wenn nicht jetzt?* Bielefeld: Institut für Freizeit-wissen-schaften und Kulturarbeit.

Gall, T. L., Evans, D. R., & Howard J. (1997). The retirement adjustment process: Changes in the well-being of male retirees across time. *Journal of Gerontology: Psychological Sciences, 52B,* P110–P117.

Gendell, M. (1998, August). Trends in retirement age in four countries, 1965–1995. *Monthly Labor Review, 20–30.*

Gonnot, J. P. (1995). Demographic changes and the pension problem: Evidence from twelve countries. In J. P. Gonnot, N. Keilman, & C. Prinz (1995). *Social security, households, and family dynamics in aging societies* (pp. 47–110). Dordrecht: Kluwer Academic Publishers.

Gonyea, J. G. (2002). Investing for retirement: Low-income workers' dilemma. In *Public Policy & Aging Research Brief* (pp. 4–5). Washington, D. C. : Gerontological Society of America.

Graebner, W. (1980). *A history of retirement: The meaning and function of retirement in America, 1885–1978.* New Haven, Connecticut: Yale University Press.

Gramlich, E. M. (1997). How does social security affect the economy. In E. R. Kingson & J. H. Schulz (Eds.), *Social security in the 21st century* (pp.147–155). New York: Oxford University Press.

Gruber, J., & Wise, D. (1999). *Social security programs and retirement around the world.* Chicago: University of Chicago Press.

Guillemard, A., & Van Gunsteren, H. (1991). Pathways and their prospects: A comparative interpretation of the meaning of early exit. In M. Kohli, M. Rein, A. Guillemard, & H. Van Gunsteren (Eds.), *Time for retirement: Comparative studies of early exit from the labor force* (pp. 362–387). New York: Cambridge University Press.

Hagestad, G. O. (1990). Social perspectives on the life course. In R. H. Binstock & L. K. George (Eds.), *Handbook of aging and the social sciences* (pp.151–168). San Diego, California: Academic Press.

Hanks, R. S. (1990). The impact of early retirement incentives on retirees and their families. *Journal of Family Issues, 4,* 424–437.

Harber, C., & Gratton, B. (1994). *Old age and the search for security: An American social history.* Bloomington: Indiana University Press.

Hardy, M. A., & Hazelrigg, L. (in press). Readjusting retirement policy in the U. S.: Risking flexibility. *Generations.*

Hardy, M. A., Hazelrigg, L., & Quadagno, J. (1996). *Ending a career in the auto industry: 30 and out.* New York: Plenum Press.

Hardy, M. A., & Quadagno, J. (1995). Satisfaction with early retirement: Making choices in the auto industry. *Journal of Gerontology: Social Sciences, 50B,* S217–S228.

Haug, M. R., Belgrave, L. L., & Jones, S. (1992). Partners' health and retirement adaptation of women and their husbands. *Journal of Women and Aging, 4,* 5–29.

Hayward, M. D., Friedman, S., & Chen, H. (1996). Race inequities in men's retirement. *Journal of Gerontology: Social Sciences, 51B,* S1–S10.

Hayward, M. D., Friedman, S., & Chen, H. (1998). Career trajectories and older men's retirement. *Journal of Gerontology: Social Sciences, 53B,* S91–S103.

Heckhausan, J., & Schulz, R. (1995). A life-span theory of control. *Psychological Review, 102*(2), 284–304.

Held, T. (1982). Rural retirement arrangements in seventeenth-to-nineteenth-century Austria: A cross-community analysis. *Journal of Family History, 7,* 227–254.

Henretta, J. C. (2001). Work and retirement. In R. H. Binstock & L. K. George (Eds.), *Handbook of aging and the social sciences* (pp. 255–271). New York: Academic Press.

Henretta, J. C., O'Rand, A. M., & Chan, C. G. (1993). Gender differences in employment after spouse's retirement. *Research on Aging, 15,* 148–169.

Herzog, A. R., & Markus, H. R. (1999). The self-concept in life span and aging research. In Bengtson, V. L., & Schaie K. W. (Eds.), *Handbook of theories of aging* (pp. 227–252). New York: Springer Publishing.

Herzog, A. R., Franks, M. M., Markus, H. R., & Holberg, D. (1998). Activities and well-being in older age: Effects of self-concept and educational attainment. *Psychology and Aging, 13,* 179–185.

Herzog, A. R., House, J. S., & Morgan, J. N. (1991). Relation of work and retirement to health and well-being in older age. *Psychology and Aging, 6,* 202–211.

Herzog, A. R., Kahn, R. L., Morgan, J. N., Jackson, J. S., & Antonucci, T. C. (1989). Age differences in productive activities. *The Journals of Gerontology, 44,* S129–S138.

Hess, B. B., Markson, E. W., & Stein, P. J. (1993). *Sociology.* 4th Edition. New York: MacMillan.

Hieden-Sommer, H. (1993). Pensionsreform im Namen der Gleichheit? *Österreichische Zeitschrift für Politikwissenschaft, 23,* 177–193.

Hieden-Sommer, H. (1994). Männer Leistung—Frauen Liebe. Gespaltene Gesellschaft, gespaltenes Menschenbild, gespaltene Frauen. *Österreichische Zeitschrift für Politikwissenschaft, 22,* 327–341.

Holden, K. C. (1997). Social security and the economic security of women: Is it fair? In E. R. Kingson & J. H. Schulz (Eds.), *Social security in the 21st century* (pp.91–104). New York: Oxford University Press.

Honig, M. (1996). Retirement expectations: Differences by race, ethnicity, and gender. *The Gerontologist, 36*, 373–382.

Hurd, M. D. (1990). The joint retirement decision of husbands and wives. In D. A. Wise (Ed.), *Issues in the economics of aging* (pp. 231–258). Chicago: The University of Chicago Press.

International Labour Office. (1999). *Yearbook of labour statistics*. Geneva: ILO.

Judy, R.W., & D'Amico, C. (1997). *Workforce 2020. Work and workers in the 21ˢᵗ century*. Indianapolis: Hudson Institute.

Juster, F. T., & Suzman, R. (1995). An overview of health and retirement study. *The Journal of Human Resources, 30*, S7–S56.

Keating, N. C., & Cole, P. (1980). What do I do with him 24 hours a day? Changes in the housewife role after retirement. *The Gerontologist, 20*, 84–89.

Kelly, J. R., & Westcott, G. (1991). Ordinary retirement: Commonalities and continuity. *International Journal of Aging and Human Development, 32*, 81–89.

Kessler, R. C., Price, R. H., & Wortman, C. B. (1985). Social factors in psychopathology: Stress, social support, and coping processes. *Annual Review of Psychology, 36*, 531–572.

Kim, S., & Feldman, D. C. (1998). Healthy, wealthy, or wise: Predicting actual acceptances of early retirement incentives at three points in time. *Personnel Psychology, 51*, 623–642.

Kim, J. E., & Moen, P. (2002). Retirement transitions, gender, and psychological well-being: A life-course, ecological model. *Journal of Gerontology: Psychological Sciences, 57B*, P212–P222.

Kimmel, D. C., Price, K. F., & Walker, J. W. (1978). Retirement choice and retirement satisfaction. *Journal of Gerontology, 33*, 575–585.

Kingson, E. R., Hirshorn, B. A., & Cornman, J. M. (1986). *Ties that bind: The interdependence of generations*. Washington, D. C.: Seven Locks Press.

Knipscheer, C. P. M. (1988). Temporal embeddedness and aging within the multigenerational family: The case of grandparenting. In J.E. Birren and V.L. Bengtson (Eds.), *Emergent theories of aging* (pp. 426–446). New York: Springer Publishing.

Kohli, M. (1986). The world we forgot: A historical review of the life course. In V. W. Marshall (Ed.), *Later life* (pp. 271–304). Beverly Hills, California: Sage.

Kohli, M. (1994). Work and retirement: A comparative perspective. In M. W. Riley, R. L. Kahn, & A. Foner (Eds.), *Age and structural lag* (pp. 80–106). New York: John Wiley.

Kohli, M., Rein, M., Guillemard, A., & Van Gunsteren, H. (1991). *Time for retirement: Comparative studies of early exit from the labor force*. New York: Cambridge University Press.

Kolland, F. (1988). Nach dem Arbeitsleben Konzentration auf die Familie? In L. Rosenmayr & F. Kolland (Eds.), *Arbeit—Freizeit—Lebenszeit. Neue Übergänge im Lebenszyklus* (pp. 75–94). opladen Westdeutscher Verlag.

Kosloski, K., Ginsburg, G., & Backman, C. W. (1984). Retirement as a process of active role transition. In V. L. Allen & E. Van de Vliert, (Eds.), *Role transitions: Explorations and explanations* (pp. 331–341). New York: Plenum Press.

Kremer, Y. (1985). Parenthood and marital role performance among retired workers: Comparison between pre- and post-retirement period. *Aging and Society, 5,* 449–460.

Laslett, P. (1977). *Family life and illicit love in earlier generations.* Cambridge: Cambridge University Press.

Laws, G. (1996). A shot of economic adrenalin: Reconstructing the elderly in the retiree-based economic development literature. *Journal of Aging Studies, 10,* 171–188.

Lee, G. R., & Shehan, C. L. (1989). Retirement and marital satisfaction. *Journal of Gerontology: Social Sciences, 44,* S226–S230.

Leonesio, M. V. (1996). The economics of retirement: A nontechnical guide. *Social Security Bulletin, 59,* 29–50.

Longino, C. F. (2001). Geographical distribution and migration. In R. H. Binstock & L. K. George (Eds.), *Handbook of aging and the social sciences* (pp. 106–124). New York: Academic Press.

Marshall, V. W., Clarke, P. J., & Ballantyne, P. J. (2001). Instability in the retirement transition: Effects on health and well-being in a Canadian study. *Research on Aging, 23,* 379–409.

Matthews, A. M., & Brown, K. (1987). Retirement as a critical life event. The differential experiences of women and men. *Research on Aging, 9,* 548–571.

McIntosh, B. R., & Danigelis, N. I. (1995). Race, gender, and the relevance of productive activity for elders' affect. *Journal of Gerontology: Social Sciences, 50B,* S229–239.

Midanik, L. T., Soghikian, K., Ransom, L. J., & Tekawa, I. S. (1995). The effect of retirement on mental health and health behavior: The Kaiser Permanente retirement study. *Journal of Gerontology: Social Sciences, 50B,* S59–S62.

Mirowsky, J., & Ross C. E. (1989). *Social causes of psychological distress.* New York: Aldine De Gruyter.

Moen, P., Kim, J. E., & Hofmeister, H. (2001). Couples' work/retirement transitions, gender, and marital quality. *Social Psychology Quarterly, 64,* 55–71.

Mollica, K. A., & DeWitt, R. (2000). When others retire early: What about me? *Academy of Management Journal, 43,* 1068–1075.

Mutran, E. J., & Reitzes, D. C. (1981). Retirement, identity and well-being: Realignment of role relationships. *Journal of Gerontology, 36,* 733–740.

Myers, S. M., & Booth, A. (1996). Men's retirement and marital quality. *Journal of Family Issues, 17,* 336–358.

National Economic Council Interagency Work Group on Social Security (1998). Women and retirement security. Available at http://www.ssa.gov/history/reports/women.html

Ngan, R., Chiu, S., & Wong, W. (1999). Economic security and insecurity of Chinese older people in Hong Kong: A case of treble jeopardy. *Hallym International Journal of Aging, 1,* 35–45.

Niederfranke, A. (1989). Bewältigung der vorzeitigen Berufsaufgabe bei Männern. *Zeitschrift für Gerontologie, 22,* 143–150.

Niederfranke, A. (1991). Lebensentwürfe von Frauen beim Übergang in den Ruhestand. In C. Gather, U. Gerhard, K. Prinz, & M. Veil (Eds.), *Frauen-Alterrsicherung* (pp. 279–291). Berlin: Sigma.

O'Brien, G. E. (1981). Leisure attributes and retirement satisfaction. *Journal of Aging Psychology, 66,* 371–384.

O'Rand, A. M. (1988). Convergence, institutionalization, and bifurcation: Gender and the pension acquisition process. *Annual Review of Gerontology, 8,* 132–155.

O'Rand, A. M., & Henretta, J. C. (1999). *Age and inequality: Diverse pathways through later life.* Colorado: Westview Press.

O'Rand, A. M., Henretta, J. C., & Krecker, M. L. (1992). Family pathways to retirement. In M. Szinovacz, D. J. Ekerdt, & B. H. Vinick (Eds.), *Families and retirement* (pp. 81–98). Newbury Park, California: Sage.

Palmore, E. B., Burchett, B. M., Fillenbaum, G. G., George, L. K., & Wallman, L. M. (1985). *Retirement: Causes and consequences.* New York: Springer Publishing.

Pampel, F. C. (1998). *Aging, social inequality, and public policy.* Thousand Oaks, California: Pine Forge Press.

Pearlin, L. I., Lieberman, M. A., Menaghan, E. G., & Mullan, J. T. (1981). The stress process. *Journal of Health and Social Behavior, 22,* 337–356.

Peretti, P. O., & Wilson, C. (1975). Voluntary and involuntary retirement of aged males and their effect on emotional satisfaction, usefulness, self-image, emotional stability, and interpersonal relationships. *International Journal of Aging and Human Development, 6,* 131–136.

Pienta, A. M. (1999). Early childbearing patterns and women's labor force behavior in later life. *Journal of Women & Aging, 11,* 69–83.

Prinz, C. (1995). Changing family structure and an emancipatory pension policy: The case of Austria. In J. Gonnot, N. Keilman, & C. Prinz (Eds.), *Social security, household, and family dynamics in ageing societies* (pp. 149–179). New York: Kluwer.

Prinz, C., & Marin, B. (1999). Pensionsreformen. Nachhaltiger Sozialumbau am Beispiel Österreichs. Frankfurt: Campus.

Quandagno, J. S., & McClellan, S. (1989). The other functions of retirement. *Generations, 13,* 7–10.

Quinn, J. F., & Burkhauser, R. V. (1990). Work and retirement. In R. H. Binstock & L. K. George (Eds.), *Handbook of aging and the social sciences* (pp. 308–327). San Diego, California: Academic Press.

Reeves, J. B., & Darville, R. L. (1994). Social contact patterns and satisfaction with retirement of women in dual-career earner families. *International Journal of Aging & Human Development, 39,* 163–175.

Reitzes, D. C., Mutran, E. J., & Fernandez, M. E. (1996). Preretirement influences on postretirement self-esteem. *Journal of Gerontology: Social Sciences, 51B,* S242–S249.

Reno, V. P., & Friedland, R. B. (1997). Strong support but low confidence: What explains the contradiction? In E. R. Kingson & J. H. Schulz (Eds.), *Social security in the 21st century* (pp.178–194). New York: Oxford University Press.

Richardson, V., & Kilty, K. M. (1991). Adjustment to retirement: Continuity vs. discontinuity. *International Journal of Aging and Human Development, 33,* 151–169.

Richardson, V., & Kilty, K. M. (1995). Gender differences in mental health before and after retirement: A longitudinal analysis. *Journal of Women and Aging, 7,* 19–36.

Riley, M. W., & Riley, J. W. (1994). Structural lag: Past and future. In M. W. Riley, R. L. Kahn, & A. Foner (Eds.), *Age and structural lag: Society's failure to provide opportunities in work, family, and leisure* (pp. 15–36). New York: John Wiley.

Rix, S. E. (1999). The politics of old age in the United States. In A. Walker & G. Naegele (Eds.), *The politics of old age in Europe* (pp. 178–196). Philadelphia: Open University Press.

Robbins, S. B., Lee, R. M., & Wan, T. T. H. (1994). Goal continuity as a mediator of early retirement adjustment: Testing a multidimensional model. *Journal of Counseling Psychology, 41,* 18–26.

Rosenkoeter, M. M., & Garris, J. M. (1998). Psychosocial changes following retirement. *Journal of Advanced Nursing, 27,* 966–976.

Rosenman, L., & Winocur, S. (1990). Australian women and income security for old age: A cohort study. *Journal of Cross-Cultural Gerontology, 5,* 277–291.

Rosow, I. (1974). *Socialization to old age.* Berkeley: University of California Press.

Ross, C. E., & Drentea, P. (1998). Consequences of retirement activities for distress and the sense of personal control. *Journal of Health and Social Behavior, 39,* 317–334.

Ross, C. E., & Wu, C. (1995). The links between education and health. *American Sociological Review, 60,* 719–745.

Savishinsky, J. S. (2000). *Breaking the watch: The meanings of retirement in America.* Ithaca, New York: Cornell University Press.

Schäuble, G. (1989). *Die schönsten Jahre des Lebens?* Stuttgart: Enke.

Scharlach, A. E., Lowe, B. F., & Schneider, E. L., (1991). *Elder care and the work force. Blueprint for action.* Lexington, Massachusetts: Lexington Books.

Schmähl, W. (1993). The 1992 reform of public pensions in Germany: Main elements and some effects. *Journal of European Social Policy, 3,* 39–51.

Schulz, R., & Heckhausen, J. (1997). Emotion and control: A life-span perspective. *Annual Review of Gerontology and Geriatrics, 17,* 185–205.

Seccombe, K., & Lee, G. R. (1986). Gender differences in retirement satisfaction and its antecedents. *Research on Aging, 8,* 426–440.

Seeman, M., & Lewis, S. (1995). Powerlessness, health and mortality: A longitudinal study of older men and mature women. *Social Science and Medicine, 41,* 517–525.

Settersten, R. A. (2003). Invitation to the life course: The promise. In R. A. Settersten, Jr. (Ed.), *Invitation to the life course: Toward new understandings of later life* (pp. 1–12). Amityville, New York: Baywood Publishing Company.

Settersten, R. A., & Hagestad, G. O. (1996). What's the latest? II. Cultural age deadlines for educational and work transition. *The Gerontologist, 36,* 602–613.

Sherman, S. R. (1989, December). Public attitudes toward social security. *Social Security Bulletin,* 2–6.

Slevin, K. F., & Wingrove, C. R. (1995). Women in retirement: A review and critique of empirical research since 1976. *Sociological Inquiry, 65,* 1–20.

Smeeding, T. M. (1999). Social Security reform: Improving benefit adequacy and economic security for women. *Policy Brief 16,* Center for Policy Research, Syracuse University.

Social Security Administration (1999). Social security programs throughout the world. In the Social Security Administration government statistics, available at http://www.ssa.gov/statistics/ssptw/index.html

Social Security Administration (2001). *Fast facts and figures about Social Security.* Washington, D. C.: Author.

Social Security Administration (2002). History page: In the Social Security Administration government statistics, available at http://www.ssa.gov/statistics/ssptw/index.html

Szinovacz, M. (1980). Female retirement: Effects on spousal roles and marital adjustment. *Journal of Family Issues, 1,* 423–440.

Szinovacz, M. (1989). Decision making on retirement timing. In D. Brinberg & J. Jaccard (Eds.), *Dyadic decision making* (pp. 286–310). New York: Springer Publishing.

Szinovacz, M. (1991). Women and retirement. In B. B. Hess & E. W. Markson (Eds.), *Growing old in America* (4th ed.), (pp. 293–304). New Brunswick, New Jersey: Transaction Books.

Szinovacz, M. (1992a). Social activities and retirement adaptation: Gender and family variations. In M. Szinovacz, D. J. Ekerdt, & B. H. Vinick (Eds.) *Families and retirement* (pp. 236–253). Newbury Park, California: Sage.

Szinovacz, M. (1992b). Is housework good for retirees? *Family Relations, 41,* 230–238.

Szinovacz, M, (1996). Couple's employment/retirement patterns and marital quality. *Research on Aging, 18,* 243–268.

Szinovacz, M. (2002). Couple retirement patterns and retirement age: A comparison of Austria and the United States. *International Journal of Sociology, 32,* 30–54.

Szinovacz, M. (in press). Retirement. *International Encyclopedia of Marriage and the Family.* New York: Macmillan.

Szinovacz, M., & Davey, A. (2001). Retirement effects on parent-adult child contacts. *The Gerontologist, 41,* 191–200.

Szinovacz, M., & Davey, S. (2002). Retirement and spouse's illness: Effects on depressive symptoms and retirement satisfaction. Unpublished manuscript.

Szinovacz, M., & DeViney, S. (1999). The retiree identity: Gender and race differences. *Journal of Gerontology: Social Sciences, 54B,* S207–218.

Szinovacz, M., & DeViney, S. (2000) Marital characteristics and retirement decisions. *Research on Aging, 22,* 470–489, 2000.

Szinovacz, M., & Ekerdt, D. J. (1995). Families and retirement. In R. Blieszner & V. H. Bedford (Eds.), *Handbook on aging and the family* (pp. 243–268). Westport, Connecticut: Greenwood Press.

Szinovacz, M., & Schaffer, A. M. (2000). Effects of retirement on marital conflict management. *Journal of Family Issues, 21,* 367–389.

Szinovacz, M., & Washo, C. (1992). Gender differences in exposure to life events and adaptation to retirement. *Journal of Gerontology, 47,* S191–S196.

Szinovacz, M., DeViney, S., & Davey, A. (2001). Influences of family obligations and relationships on retirement: Variations by gender, race, and marital status. *Journal of Gerontology: Social Sciences, 56B,* S20–S27.

Thoits, P. A. (1991). On merging identity theory and stress research. *Social Psychology Quarterly, 54,* 101–112.

Thomson, D. (1989). The intergenerational contract: Under pressure from population aging. In J. Eekelaar & D. Pearl (Eds.), *An aging world: Dilemmas and challenges for law and social policy* (pp. 369–388). Oxford: Clarendon Press.

Tornstam, L. (1989). Gero-transcendence: A reformulation of the disengagement theory. *Aging, 1,* 55–63.

Treas, J., & Spence, M. (1989). Intergenerational economic obligations in the welfare state. In J.A. Mancini (Ed.), *Aging parents and adult children* (pp. 181–195). Lexington, Massachusetts: Lexington Books.

Turner, J. H. (1978). *The structure of sociological theory.* Homewood, Illinois: Dorsey.

Turner, R. J., & Lloyd, D. A. (1995). Lifetime traumas and mental health: The significance of cumulative adversity. *Journal of Health and Social Behavior, 36,* 360–376.

U.S. Bureau of the Census (1999). Poverty in the United States (Table 1). Published August 2, 2001, available at http://www.census.gov/hhes/www/prevcps.html

U.S. General Accounting Office (2001). *Older workers: Demographic trends pose challenges for employers and workers.* Report to the ranking minority member, Subcommittee on Employer-Employee Relations, Committee on Education and the Workforce, House of Representatives. Washington, D. C.: Author.

Van Dalen, H. P., & Henkens, K. (2002). Early retirement reform: Can it work? Will it work? *Ageing and Society, 22,* 209–231.

Van Tilburg, T. (1992). Support networks before and after retirement. *Journal of Social and Personal Relationships, 9,* 433–445.

Vinick. B. H., & Ekerdt, D. J. (1991). Retirement: What happens to husband-wife relationships? *Journal of Geriatric Psychiatry, 24,* 23–40.

Vinick, B. H., & Ekerdt, D. J. (1992). Couples view retirement activities: Expectation versus experience. In M. Szinovacz, D. J. Ekerdt, & B. H. Vinick (Eds.), *Families and retirement* (pp. 129–144). Newbury Park, California: Sage.

Walker, A. (1999). The future of pensions and retirement in Europe: Towards a productive aging. *Hallym International Journal of Aging, 1,* 3–15.

Wan, T. T. H. (1985). *Well-being of the elderly.* Lexington, Massachusetts: Lexington Books.

Wheaton, B. (1990). Life transitions, role histories, and mental health. *American Sociological Review, 55,* 209–223.

Wheaton, B. (1996). The domains and boundaries of stress concepts. In H. B. Kaplan (Ed.), *Psychosocial stress* (pp. 29–70). San Diego, California: Academic Press.

Williamson, J. B., & Pampel, F. C. (1993). *Old-age security in comparative perspective.* New York: Oxford University Press.

Williamson, J. B., Watts-Roy, D. M., & Kingson, E. R. (1999). *The generational equity debate.* New York: Columbia University Press.

Wolfbein, S. L. (1949). The length of working life. *Population Studies, 3*(3), 286–294.

Woodbury, R. (2001). The motivations for business retirement policies. In S. Ogura, T. Tachibanaki, & D. A. Wise (Eds.), *Aging issues in the United States and Japan* (pp. 306–333). Chicago: University of Chicago Press.

3

Retirement Planning and Preparation

Mary Anne Taylor and Dennis Doverspike

The importance of retirement planning on postretirement adjustment cannot be overstated. Planning and feeling prepared for the changes accompanying retirement are related to a host of affective and behavioral adjustment indices. The goal of this chapter is to review the role of planning in adjustment. We envision this review of the relationship between planning and adjustment as a multilevel process, moving from a very general level of analysis to a more specific level of analysis (see Figure 3.1). For those interested in understanding the global relationship between planning and adjustment, the first level may prove most useful. The second level is more specific and entails a discussion of the different predictors of retirement adjustment and their relevance to retirement planning. This second level includes a more detailed examination of the financial, health, and social variables that impact adjustment. Information at this level would assist those who wish to understand those factors that have been proven to predict adjustment across a number of retirees. Finally, the third level focuses on retiree characteristics and incorporates a discussion of the diversity of retirees and how this diversity leads to different retirement planning needs. This third level incorporates a discussion of retiree characteristics relevant to adjustment, and may provide basic information for researchers or counselors who wish to tailor their interventions to a specific retiree group.

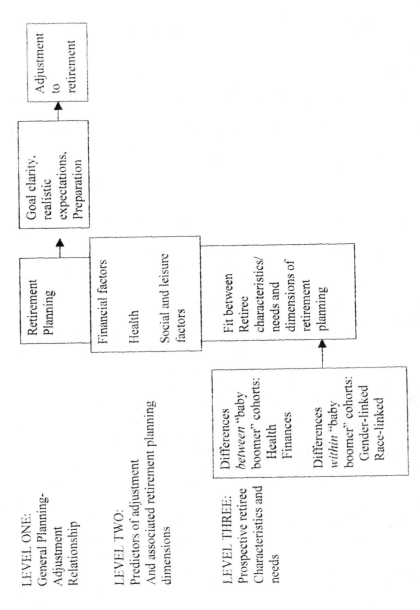

Figure 3.1 Levels of analysis in the retirement planning/retirement adjustment relationship.

Relationship

This overview of retirement planning begins at the most general level. We will initiate our discussion with an overview of the relationship between retirement planning and subsequent adjustment. The research we will present demonstrates that planning has consequences for the economic, psychological, and social satisfaction of the retiree and provides the justification for a more intensive investigation of the planning-adjustment relationship. Following our general discussion, we introduce research that probes deeper into the planning-adjustment relationship. Temporal and causal aspects of this relationship are briefly reviewed as part of this first, general analysis of planning and adjustment.

Understanding the temporal aspect of the association between planning and adjustment is an important goal and has implications for research and practice. The dimensions of retirement planning and the associated variables that impact adjustment may change from early to later retirement. We view the nature of the planning-adjustment relationship as fluid, with the variables that determine retirement satisfaction shifting over time. Retirement adjustment is itself dynamic, and we present research that suggests that retirement planning may have its greatest impact on adjustment early in the retirement process. As a second consideration within our general analysis of the planning-adjustment relationship, we also explore the causal relationship between these two variables. Understanding *why* planning impacts retirement adjustment and satisfaction may help one design more effective planning interventions and may also deepen our understanding of the retirement experience. Thus, our treatment of the planning-adjustment relationship incorporates a consideration of the changing nature of this relationship and the causal underpinnings of this association.

This general analysis of the planning-adjustment relationship sets the stage for a more in-depth investigation of the factors that impact adjustment. In our second level of analysis, we move to a more detailed treatment of the variables that shape postretirement satisfaction and the implications of these factors for retirement planning. Consistent with early models of retirement adjustment, we believe that these variables define relatively independent dimensions (Beehr, 1986). In our discussion, we define these as financial, health, and social dimensions. Our rationale for this definition is that research on adjustment as well as investigations of retirement planning often incorporates variables within these three categories and supports their centrality in postretirement satisfaction. Thus, it is possible to review research on the impact of finances, health, and social factors on adjustment while simultaneously discussing the implications of these variables for the design of retirement planning seminars.

The dimensions of financial well-being and health are traditionally incorporated into applied and basic research on retirement planning and postretirement satisfaction and adjustment. However, research on the importance of the third dimension, social factors, is an emerging area of retirement planning and merits more attention from both researchers and practitioners. We regard all three dimensions as important factors in planning and subsequent adjustment.

This progression from a first-level, general overview of the planning-adjustment relationship to a second-level, more detailed discussion of financial, health, and social predictors of postretirement satisfaction may provide a sound foundation for understanding how planning and adjustment are linked. This information alone would be sufficient to identify variables that are, in general, related to adjustment. However, many practitioners and researchers may have a need to tailor their research or their interventions to a specific group of retirees. To achieve this goal, one needs to incorporate a consideration of retiree characteristics. This is explored in the third level of analysis.

Therefore, after developing the model of planning and adjustment and discussing the specific factors which impact adjustment, we move to the third level discussion of retiree characteristics. This entails an examination of the great variability among retirees and prospective retirees and the relevance of these differences for understanding adjustment and designing retirement planning programs. Within this third level of analysis, an overview of the characteristics of "baby boomers" will be presented, since this sizable portion of the workforce is approaching retirement age. The characteristics that are most relevant to retirement planning and postretirement satisfaction are emphasized. Next, the role of gender and racial diversity in designing retirement planning is outlined. As will be seen, prospective retirees comprise a very heterogeneous segment of the workforce. Meeting the needs of this group of retirees will pose many challenges for researchers and practitioners.

We end the chapter with a discussion of the relevance of the planning-adjustment research for academicians and practitioners. Basically, we suggest that a contingency approach to research design and retirement planning may lead to the greatest understanding of the planning-adjustment relationship and the greatest benefits for prospective retirees. The financial, health, and social dimensions of retirement planning are more critical to some retiree groups than others. There are important differences within retiree groups that may moderate the relationship between planning and adjustment. This progression from a general analysis of planning and adjustment to a detailed examination of financial, health, and social considerations and retiree characteristics may provide a useful summary of the factors that may be central in determining postretirement satisfaction.

RATIONALE FOR UNDERSTANDING RETIREMENT PLANNING: A REVIEW OF RESEARCH FINDINGS

In even the most general level of analyzing the planning-adjustment relationship, it is clear that retirement planning appears to serve a number of psychological functions for individuals and affects their retirement decisions. Planning and feeling prepared for retirement are associated with lower anxiety and depression (Fretz, Kluge, Ossana, Jones, & Merikangas, 1989). Planning has a significant, positive relationship with attitudes toward retirement for both retirees and for those approaching retirement (Mutran, Reitzes, & Fernandez, 1997). Thus, it appears that planning impacts affective or attitudinal correlates of adjustment.

In addition to its influence on attitudinal variables, planning is directly related to postretirement adjustment as well as workforce exit. Participation in early retirement planning predicts more positive levels of postretirement adjustment across a variety of occupational settings (Feldman, 1994; Mutran, Reitzes, & Fernadez, 1997; Spiegel & Shultz, 2001). Furthermore, those who have actually prepared for retirement and feel ready to make the transition are more likely to exit the workforce at an earlier age (Reitzes, Mutran, & Fernandez, 1998; Taylor & Shore, 1995).

While a history of research supports the centrality of retirement planning in postretirement satisfaction, a deeper understanding of this relationship is needed to enhance our applied and research efforts with respect to planning. Researchers and practitioners interested in facilitating adjustment through planning should consider both temporal changes in the planning-adjustment relationship as well as the causal link between planning and postretirement satisfaction. First, research strongly suggests that adjustment is ongoing and dynamic. Early adjustment to retirement may be predicted by different planning-relevant factors than later adjustment. Based on existing knowledge, planning appears to have the greatest impact early in retirement. Next, the underlying reasons for the significant relationship between planning and adjustment should be addressed. If the reasons driving the positive relationship between the two factors is understood, more effective planning seminars can be designed, and our understanding of the psychological benefits of planning can be enhanced. In the next segment, we explore these temporal and causal aspects of the planning-adjustment relationship.

THE RETIREMENT PLANNING-RETIREMENT ADJUSTMENT RELATIONSHIP

The first challenge facing researchers and practitioners is that retirement adjustment is dynamic and ongoing. This complicates the assessment of the relationship between these two factors. Which planning approach is most successful in facilitating adjustment depends in part on when one measures postretirement adjustment. According to retirement research, the changes encountered in retirement are greatest early in the process (Talaga & Beehr, 1989). This finding is consistent with the suggestion that retirement researchers should view the process as an ongoing transition (Ekerdt, Bossé, & Levkoff, 1985; Gall, Evans, & Howard, 1997). Early retirement experience (less than 6 months since retirement) may be quite different from later adjustment (around 1 year after retirement). As the nature of the retirement experience changes, and the demands on the retiree shift over time, different factors may predict adjustment.

A related methodological issue is that the very nature of retirement adjustment shifts over time. Immediately after retirement, retirement satisfaction and life satisfaction are significantly correlated. Over time, these two measures diverge, and life satisfaction is less related to and less determined by retirement satisfaction. Clearly, retirement adjustment is closely linked to life satisfaction soon after retirement and becomes less salient and relevant with the passage of time. This suggests that the predictive power of the variables related to retirement adjustment may also change over time, and may change depending on the type of adjustment measure used in research. The shifting nature of the planning-adjustment relationship and the changing nature of retirement adjustment over time has implications for research. Understanding the planning-adjustment relationship should entail a consideration of the type of adjustment measure used (general life satisfaction versus retirement satisfaction) as well as when the adjustment scale was administered (Floyd et al., 1992).

The second challenge facing retirement researchers is to increase our understanding of the causal link between planning and adjustment, or the "why" and "how" behind this relationship. Although research in this area is limited, we propose that retirement planning may influence adjustment by allowing prospective retirees to develop realistic expectations of retirement and by encouraging retirees to set goals for their financial, health-oriented, and social well-being.

It seems likely that planning eases the transition into retirement because it allows the employee to form realistic expectations about the social and financial aspects of retirement (Taylor-Carter, Cook, & Weinberg, 1997). In turn, these reality-based expectations are associated with postretirement adjustment (Grant, 1991; Kamouri & Cavenaugh, 1986; Kim & Moen, 2001; Wan & Odell, 1983). Retirement expectations seem to play an important role in determining when an employee leaves an organization as well as postretirement satisfaction. Those employees who feel that retirement will be a positive experience are more likely to be interested in early retirement and are also more satisfied after retirement (MacLean, 1982; Parnes & Sommers, 1994).

Recent research suggests that having *met* expectations is particularly crucial; unrealistically positive beliefs about the financial or social nature of retirement can lower postretirement satisfaction (Taylor, Shultz, Morrison, Spiegel, & Greene, 2002). Thus, providing information that leads participants to form realistic retirement expectations should be an intrinsic goal of retirement planning programs.

A second possible explanation of the causal link between planning and adjustment is that retirement planning may facilitate goal setting.

While this area of research is not well developed, presentation of information on retirement may allow one to clarify goals for financial, health-oriented, and social well being after leaving the workforce. Research suggests that clear financial goals allow one to initiate more specific planning activities. Clarity of financial goals leads to self-initiated, specific financial planning activities for retirement (Stawski & Hershey, 2001).

Thus, realistic expectations and retirement goal setting may mediate the positive effects of planning on adjustment. This relationship can be framed in terms of retirement self-efficacy. Planning may increase retirees' belief that they can effectively manage the changes accompanying retirement (self-efficacy). It appears that the factors that make an employee feel comfortable making the retirement decision may also enhance postretirement adjustment (Fletcher & Hansson, 1991; Taylor-Carter, Cook & Weinberg, 1997; Wan & Odell, 1983). More research is needed in this area to test the proposed mediators of the planning-adjustment relationship.

Understanding the role that retirement expectations and retirement goal setting play in postretirement satisfaction can help counselors design programs that reduce the ambiguity involved in the retirement process. Ideally, individuals would participate in long-term planning to ensure that expectations are realistic and that goals are set to meet these expectations. Unfortunately, many individuals do not engage in long-term planning, and those most in need of financial and social planning may actually avoid this process (Kim & Moen, 2001; Long, 1987; Turner, Bailey, & Scott, 1994). This suggests that organizations interested in providing the most positive retirement experience for their employees may have to take a very proactive approach to retirement planning in order to make it easily accessible to all groups and to encourage employees to attend.

Not surprisingly, there is reason to believe that the causal relationship between planning and adjustment may shift over time. Planning effects are likely to emerge as significant predictors when used to predict satisfaction soon after retirement, since violated expectations and the consequences of poor planning are likely to be most salient soon after leaving the workforce. Over time, the retiree may learn to readjust his/her initial expectations or take actions that may reconcile the differences between the reality of retirement and his/her expectations (Taylor, Shultz, Morrison, Spiegel, & Greene, 2002).

Despite the methodological issues involved in studying the shifting nature of the planning-adjustment relationship, understanding the factors that determine adjustment and using this knowledge to design retirement planning programs is an achievable goal. More longitudinal research is needed to help identify the planning predictors most relevant to early and later retirement and to identify mediators of the planning-adjustment relationship over time.

Clearly, providing retirement planning for employees is important in facilitating later adjustment. The second major level of analysis in understanding the planning-adjustment relationship and in designing effective planning seminars involves identification of the components of planning most related to adjustment. The components of retirement planning can encompass a number of areas. Programs should incorporate a discussion of different dimensions of the retirement experience, including financial, social, and leisure oriented activities (Hayslip, Beyerlein, & Nichols, 1997). However, research suggests that financial planning dominates current retirement planning programs in many companies (Watson Wyatt, 1996). Providing additional information on the health-related and social aspects of retirement may help retirees anticipate and plan for change, leading to a more positive retirement experience. Such preretirement counseling may allow a worker to more accurately forecast the actual retirement experience and focus their attempts to prepare for the change (Feldman, 1994).

In the second level of analysis that follows, a consideration of the variables that impact adjustment and their relationship to adjustment will be reviewed. These may help retirement researchers and practitioners design more effective planning programs. Planning can encompass a number of different factors linked to postretirement satisfaction, from the relatively concrete variables such as financial and health-oriented factors to the more abstract variables associated with social planning for retirement. In the next segment, these predictors of postretirement satisfaction and the implications for retirement planning will be explored. The traditional predictors of health and financial status will be explored first, followed by a discussion of the importance of social support and social networks on adjustment. Throughout this discussion, the linkage between these factors and the actual content of planning seminars is emphasized.

Predictors of Adjustment and Implications for Planning

HEALTH AND FINANCES

An appreciation of the factors that should be emphasized in planning can be gained by reviewing data on the most significant correlates of retirement adjustment. In this second level of our analysis, we turn to health and finances. Some of the most consistent predictors of retirement age and adjustment are simple health and income factors. In fact, health and income often surface as the strongest forecasters of retirement age and subsequent well-being (Beehr, 1986; Brown, Fukunaga, Umemoto, & Wicker, 1996; Dorfman, 1992; Feldman, 1994; Shultz, Morton, & Weckerle, 1998).

Health is related to a host of dependent measures directly related to adjustment. This factor predicts whether people choose to stay in the workforce, their attitudes toward retirement, and postretirement satisfaction (Feldman, 1994; Taylor & Shore, 1995). Those in better health show higher levels of adjustment and satisfaction with retirement, and are more likely to accept part-time work. Research in this area is so consistent that a measure of health is typically included in most studies of retirement adjustment and planning.

Typical measures of health are short self-report questions simply asking retirees to assess their level of overall physical well-being. While these measures seem sufficient when health is treated as a control variable rather than a major variable of interest, a full appreciation of the role of health in adjustment demands a more detailed analysis of this construct. A rare example of this type of analysis can be found in work conducted by Shultz (1999). This researcher focused on measures of health as suggested by Feldman (1994). Specifically, Feldman suggests that health problems can be viewed as consisting of three different levels. These range from the most debilitating level, *major physical illness* such as heart disease, to a second and usually less serious level of *functional impairments* such as poor vision, to a third category of relatively mild *psychosomatic illnesses*. Health-related factors most strongly related to retirement are hypothesized to be those within the major physical illness category and the functional impairments category, since these have the most impact on many different work-related activities. Indeed, Shultz found that three chronic and relatively major health problems (arthritis, hypertension, and foot problems) effectively differentiated between voluntary and involuntary retirees.

This suggests that overall measures of health may be overly inclusive, and may not provide a clear understanding of the health-adjustment relationship. Shultz' work on the impact of major, chronic health conditions on voluntary versus involuntary retirement suggests that more specific measures of health status can help us understand the specific physical factors that predict adjustment. One could easily extend his work on the relationship of health to voluntary/involuntary retirement to the investigation of the impact of specific health impairments to retirement satisfaction. It is somewhat ironic that health is a very strong, consistent predictor of adjustment, yet the specific health factors underlying this relationship have not been addressed in research.

Based on available research, health appears to have direct and indirect influences on subsequent adjustment. First, health has a direct relationship to satisfaction. Those in better health feel better, are able to engage in more activities, and are happier. Health also has indirect effects on satisfaction, since it allows one access to many resources such as social support networks that, in turn, contribute to adjustment. Some researchers suggest that poor health may interrupt leisure and other social activities related to adjustment (Shultz, Morton, & Weckerle, 1998). Given the pervasive influence of health, retirement planning should incorporate a frank discussion of the importance of physical well-being on subsequent adjustment. These discussions may be particularly important in long-term planning. Maintaining physical health should be viewed as a long-term investment for those interested in retirement preparation.

Financial well-being is a second area that is critical in understanding retirement behavior. This predictor is associated with both affective and behavioral measures of interest to retirement researchers. Believing that one will have adequate postretirement income is positively related to retirement adjustment and inversely related to planned retirement age (Beehr, 1986; Beehr, Glazer, Nielson, & Farmer, 2000;

Mutran, Reitzes, & Fernandez, 1997; Taylor & Shore, 1995). Planning financially for retirement is an important determinant of adjustment and of the ability to leave the workforce when one wishes. As noted by Feldman (1994), more positive levels of finances are associated with a lower probability of continued employment. Those who wish to retire early are generally more satisfied with their finances and more likely to feel as if they can reduce their work hours (Weckerle & Shultz, 1996).

Additional evidence suggests that financial status is associated with affect toward retirement. Those with the highest incomes (over $75,000) are much more favorable toward retirement and have put more thought into the decision than have those with lower incomes (under $25,000) (Feldman, 1994). Those in low-income groups view retirement unfavorably.

Given the criticality of financial stability in adjustment, it is fortunate that a discussion of financial considerations is incorporated in most planning seminars. However, an area of concern for researchers is the long-standing finding that those who are in lower paying and lower skilled jobs are less likely to plan for retirement and are less likely to have access to retirement planning seminars (Beck, 1984; Dobson & Morrow, 1984; Kasshau, 1974). This is troubling, given that planning for retirement seems particularly important for financially disadvantaged groups. Long term planning may help one navigate the financial changes that accompany retirement and may foster more positive beliefs about retirement (Anderson & Weber, 1993).

This failure to financially prepare poses some concern for retirement researchers who wish to enhance the retirement experience. While we may not be able to increase the number of firms who offer planning, it seems reasonable that we can help educate individuals on the topic of the importance of planning. Informal planning, outside of the organization, may help facilitate the retirement transition of lower income groups, and may be more accessible to lower-income groups than formal programs. For example, companies could make information packets on retirement accessible to workers, along with a counselor's phone number. Research suggests that even those individuals who plan their own retirement without the benefit of formal planning seminars experience more positive levels of retirement satisfaction (Anderson & Weber, 1993). This informal planning may consist of advice from friends, family members, or professionals outside the work setting. While research contrasting formal and informal planning is limited, informal planning may be more useful in making psychological and social preparations for the retirement transition.

The design and dissemination of financial planning seminars targeted to low-income groups poses an important challenge for researchers and practitioners. While the critical importance of financial support and positive levels of health in adjustment is clear, other factors also feed into retirement adjustment and therefore should be incorporated in planning seminars. A pervasive influence on postretirement satisfaction and adjustment includes social networks and social support. In the next segment, each of these factors will be explored as significant considerations in retirement planning. These areas are not part of conventional planning programs. As will be seen, research bears out the importance of social factors and support in both early and later retirement adjustment.

Social and Leisure Considerations

Within our second level of analysis, we also believe that a consideration of social factors is important in understanding retirement adjustment and in designing retirement planning programs. Clearly, an important influence on satisfaction after retirement is social support. In the literature, one can identify two different dimensions of support. The first line of research identifies distinct *sources* of support, such as family, friends, and those met during leisure activities. The second line of research places less emphasis on the particular source of support and instead emphasizes the *type* of social support given. Within this second perspective, one can identify informational, emotional, and tangible types of supportive interactions (Krause 1997a, 1997b). Both perspectives are valuable if one wishes to incorporate a consideration of social factors in retirement planning.

The first operationalization of support emphasizes the *source* of supportive interactions and suggests that social support can stem from exchanges with family members or friends, and also can occur as one engages in leisure activities. These interactions can be supportive or stressful in nature, so it is important to realize that the mere presence of a social network does not necessarily mean that a retiree will receive positive outcomes from these interchanges. Stressful social interactions include negative exchanges with others as well as "costs" in terms of the demands made on the retiree by others (Krause, 1995). Thus, social interactions have costs as well as benefits (Hansson, DeKoekkoek, Neece, & Patterson, 1997). For counselors who wish to examine the amount of support retirees have in their lives, this should be taken into account. Findings regarding costs of social interactions may explain why social support does not always have the typical positive buffering effect on stress (Fernandez, Mutran, & Reitez, 1998).

On the positive side, supportive interactions with friends and family have been associated with greater life satisfaction among retirees (Hong & Duff, 1997; Levitt, Antonucci, Clark, Rotten, & Finley, 1985) and enhanced feelings of personal control in later life (Krause, 1997a). Generally, social support is viewed as a buffer that decreases the impact of potentially stressful events such as retirement on our general well-being (Cutrona, Russell, & Rose, 1986; Krause, 1987a; 1987b). Conversely, those who believe they will be bored, isolated, and miss work-related friendships report later intended retirement dates (Adams & Beehr, 1998). Clearly, social support is a central factor in postretirement affect and adjustment.

It would be overly simplistic to suggest that one could simply measure support, make recommendations for enhancing support, and predict retirement adjustment over a sustained period of time. The relationship of one's social network to adjustment may shift as one looks at postretirement adjustment as years pass since retirement. For instance, retirement is correlated with a decline in marital satisfaction soon after workforce exit, but this negative effect is largely mitigated when marital satisfaction is examined two years after retirement (Moen, Kim, & Hofmeister, 2001). As noted earlier, this emphasizes the point that adjustment is dynamic and the role of different types of retirement planning on adjustment will not necessarily be stable over time. Regardless of this complexity, it is generally the case that social networks provide outlets for leisure and also provide an important source of psychological support for individuals.

A second operationalization of social support views it in terms of the *type of interaction* that occurs, regardless of source. Interactions can take different forms (Krause, 1997a;1997b). Social support may take the form of receiving concrete, necessary resources such as transportation (tangible support) or receiving information needed to solve problems (informational support). A third form of social support involves receiving affection from others (emotional support).

In a recent study, informational support from others was found to be most important for early adjustment, while emotional and tangible support were not as relevant early in the process (Taylor, Goldberg, & Shore, 2002). This suggests that researchers should realize that more than one type of social support measure should be used in studying the relationship between support and adjustment. In addition, this multidimensional view of social support can help counselors understanding how to diagnose and advise workers with respect to social support needs before and after retirement (Krause, 1997a; 1997b).

For researchers, the multidimensional nature of social support holds implications for measurement. Using a global or summary measure of social support may mask important differences in the predictive power of specific dimensions of the construct. A multidimensional approach to the examination of social interactions can allow both counselors and researchers to give more detailed advice to retirees and to counselors.

Despite the importance of social networks and social interactions in adjustment, little attention is paid to social support variables in typical retirement planning seminars. However, a comprehensive plan for entering this phase of life should address the social network of retirees and the nature of their social needs. As noted, a lack of social support is associated with lowered retirement adjustment; retirees who obtain most of their social interactions at work may have a particularly difficult transition to retirement. Recent reviews of the literature suggest that the most often cited disadvantage of retirement is the lack of interaction with coworkers, with 72% of respondents citing this as an issue (Moen, Fields, Quick, & Hofmeister, 2000).

While the research reviewed supports the criticality of social contacts in retirement adjustment, many do not plan for the social changes that accompany retirement. A common finding is that individuals plan for the financial changes associated with retirement to a much greater degree than they make plans regarding postretirement hobbies and interests (Moen, Erickson, Agarwal, Fields, & Todd, 2000). Given the relevance of leisure to satisfaction throughout the life span, the work-leisure balance in an individual's life may be a significant predictor of postretirement adjustment (Sterns & Gray, 1999). Sterns and Gray emphasize an individualized approach to leisure counseling for retirees, since the type and amount of leisure activity associated with satisfaction varies enormously across individuals.

For those who have a restricted social network or a network lacking in support, planning should incorporate strategies for enhancing this dimension of life. Social support can be enhanced and planned for by examining potential leisure activities as a means for social interaction (Burrus-Bammel & Bammel, 1985; Mobily, Lemke, & Gisen, 1991). Leisure interests and social contacts are significant predictors of postretirement adjustment, and those who look forward to pursuing leisure interests in retirement are happier after leaving the workforce (Floyd et al., 1992; George & Maddox, 1977). Identifying leisure interests and helping retirees locate social outlets consistent with their interests could provide important benefits for retirees.

The reported findings on the importance of informational support also lead to recommendations for planning. Fortunately, informational support is most congruent with the nature of most planning seminars. Most are designed for the dissemination of basic information, particularly on how to deal with financial issues. In order to provide a comprehensive planning seminar, one must first identify the issues facing retirees. Retirement planning specialists may wish to conduct exit interviews with those who have left work in order to identify common questions of retirees, and then address these issues in retirement planning seminars. This basic "how-to" type of informational social support may seem very basic but is critical in initial adjustment after leaving the workforce.

Thus far, the research suggests that a consideration of health, financial, and social needs is necessary for designing effective retirement planning interventions. The other major consideration in planning is the characteristics of the targeted group. Retirees are not homogeneous, and an understanding of their differences can help us design planning seminars that target the needs of the retiree audience.

In the next segment, the characteristics of the upcoming group of retirees, the baby boomers, will be examined. In the initial part of this segment, differences in two cohorts of boomers are discussed. Next, gender and racial diversity within the baby boomers is investigated. Knowledge of the requirements and needs of different groups of retirees can lead to more effective plans for retirement. This third level of analysis focuses on those characteristics of the baby boomers that are most relevant to the design of retirement planning seminars and to our understanding of the retirement experiences of different groups.

Characteristics of Upcoming Retirees

BABY BOOMER CHARACTERISTICS

The baby boomer generation presents retirement researchers with many new questions and issues. This group of individuals represents the largest single sustained population increase in U.S. history, consisting of 83 million individuals (American Association of Retired Persons, 1999). Baby boomers span nearly two decades, from 1946 to 1964 and are not as homogeneous as popular media often suggests. The group actually consists of two cohorts. The younger cohort, 54% of all baby boomers, lies between 38 to 46 years old in 2002; the remainder are 47 to 56. By the end of the year 2005, the first of the boomers will reach age 60 (Poulos & Nightingale, 1997).

The entire group of baby boomers is distinct from previous cohorts in many ways. These differences encompass demographic factors as well as psychological factors; they are distinct from their predecessors in terms of the way they view retirement. The unique retirement attitudes along with the sheer numbers in the baby boomer group have important consequences for understanding the retirement experience and helping individuals plan for the transition.

First, characteristics of the two cohorts that form the "baby boom" will be examined. An emphasis will be placed on health and financial factors, since these are central in retirement adjustment and planning. Research in this area will demonstrate that within-group differences in boomers are larger than one might expect. In terms of ethnicity, gender, race, financial comfort, education, and health, these individuals are quite diverse. The focus will be on how these differences among retirees change the study of retirement planning and adjustment for both researchers and practitioners.

Boomers can be defined as falling within two cohorts: leading-edge or early boomers were born from 1946–1955. Trailing edge or later boomers were born from 1956–1964. As we will see, there are important differences within these cohorts. First, the income, education, and health of the boomers will be discussed, followed by a discussion of the gender, ethnic, and racial diversity of this group.

HEALTH AND FINANCES OF BABY BOOMERS

Health is a significant factor in adjustment, and the importance of this factor should be emphasized in long-term planning for retirement. Older individuals have more positive levels than in previous generations. Over 75% of those 55–64 years old have no disabilities. Other reports indicate that 75% in the 55–64 year old range, and 82% of those in the 45–54 year old range, describe their health as either "excellent" or "good" (Kausler and Kausler, 1996). As will be seen, this positive level of physical fitness is not true across the board; significant racial differences emerge when one examines this variable.

Financial status within both baby boom generations also creates a positive first impression. Inflation-adjusted incomes for both groups exceed that of their parents' generation. In 1989, the older cohort's income was approximately 53% higher in real terms than their parents' generation and the younger cohort's income was approximately 35% higher than the earlier generation at the same age (Poulos & Nightingale, 1997). Thus, studies usually suggest that boomers are generally better off financially than their parents (American Association of Retired Persons, 1999). Similarly, education, correlated with income, is higher in the boomer group than previous groups, making the baby boomer generation the most educated in history.

This overall picture is somewhat deceptive. There are important differences within these boomer groups. There is an increase in single parent homes in the boomer groups, and these individuals do not share the same economic advantages as those two-income earning families in the same cohort. Similarly, less educated individuals earn disproportionately lower incomes than other boomers. Despite the increase in education as a whole, 11–13% of boomers lack high school degrees (Poulos & Nightingale, 1997).

Looking at segments of the boomer population rather than looking at overall mean earnings may provide a more accurate picture of financial status. Roughly the top fifth of boomers earn more than $75,000, have retirement savings, will have adequate pensions, own their homes, and have adequate health insurance. The middle-income earners, about 55% of baby boomers, make from $25,000–75,000 dollars and have more moderate levels of savings, pensions, and health insurance. Those who fall in the bottom 25% are more likely to be characterized as single-earner families, lack pensions, have intermittent work histories, have little savings, and rent their homes.

Thus, the overall picture of boomers as wealthy is misleading. Wage stagnation in the 1970s influenced salaries of younger boomers. Real median income of family householders age 45–54 increased 43% in the 1950s and again in the 1960s. This dropped drastically to 6% in the 1970s (Siegel, 1993). Those younger boomers without high school degrees have real incomes 12% lower than the previous generation (Poulos & Nightingale, 1997).

Furthermore, boomers in the older cohort had accumulated more wealth than younger boomers at comparable ages (American Association of Retired Persons, 1999). This substantial group of low-income individuals in the younger cohort will increase poverty rates in the United States. There will be 2.2. million more poor individuals over age 45 in 2005 than in 1995, and these will be relatively unskilled workers. Furthermore, data suggest that people are not saving enough funds for retirement. Recent estimates suggest that the typical boomer is saving only a third of the amount needed to retire at 65 and maintain their current standard of living (Watson Wyatt, 1996; 1999). However, only about 23% of boomers believe they will have to "struggle to make ends meet" in retirement (American Association of Retired Persons, 1999).

Attitudes toward saving are also diverse within the boomer group. A recent AARP poll suggests boomers' retirement attitudes are more influenced by income than any other variable (American Association of Retired Persons, 1999). Those with more positive income levels hold more positive views of retirement.

Consistent with research cited earlier in this chapter, those who are less financially secure are less likely to engage in retirement planning. Failure of this group to plan has been attributed to weaknesses in planning programs. Some feel that the planning seminars do not reach workers at a date early enough to allow them to change their financial future, or that they are not explicit enough in their financial planning advice. Other problems characterize the boomer: financial obligations may keep workers from setting aside retirement savings, or they may simply be choosing to ignore the advice (Watson Wyatt, 1996).

In either case, it is clear that there is a significant need for retirement planning that incorporates long-term financial investments, and this should be targeted toward the younger group of baby boomers. As noted earlier, organizations will have to be aggressive in providing retirement planning in this area if they wish to care for their employees. Those most in need of planning may avoid it. It is disturbing to note that many retirees feel they should have planned more for their retirement in advance. Of those who did not feel prepared, poor financial preparation was mentioned most often (Moen, Erickson, Agarwal, Fields, & Todd, 2000).

In the next segment, diversity considerations other than age of the baby boomer will be considered. As will be seen, the racial and gender diversity of the workforce has shifted fairly dramatically. This poses new questions and new challenges for retirement planning.

GENDER AND RACIAL CONSIDERATIONS WITHIN THE BOOMER GROUPS

The first major demographic shift in the workforce is the striking growth of women in the labor force. Prior to the baby boom generation, most women worked because they were unmarried or poor (Dailey, 1998). In 1940, only 24% of all women worked. In 1990, participation of women reached an all time high, with 57.5% of all women working. If one focuses only on the baby boomer generations, labor participation rates are even higher. For early boomers, in the first cohort, the labor force participation rate was 76.5%, similar to the 73.6% rate for the younger cohort. In contrast, the labor force participation rate for men was 94.3% in 1990 (Dailey, 1998).

This increased growth of female workers should be qualified, since this pattern has not been the same for women of all races and ethnicities. Historically, labor rates have been higher for Black women than White women. For example, in 1970, 70% of all married Black women worked, as contrasted with 49% of White women. As women in the baby boom entered the workforce in larger numbers, this difference between labor force participation among Black women and White women decreased. Both groups of women have approximately equal labor force participation rates today (approximately 75% of both groups work) (Dailey, 1998).

Hispanic women have also increased their workforce participation rates. They accounted for nearly 13% of the increase in women in the workforce in the period from 1981–1990. However, baby boomer participation rates for Hispanic women lagged somewhat behind that of Black and White women (around 63.3%). This is often attributed to lower educational attainment of Hispanic women. This may impede the attempts of Hispanic women to gain employment (Dailey, 1998).

This increase in women's labor force participation has important consequences for our models of retirement and our understanding of how to help women prepare for retirement. As noted by researchers, we know little about women's retirement as compared to men. George, Fillenbaum, and Palmore (1984) stated nearly 20 years ago that retirement models based on men may not be appropriate for understanding women's retirement. Later research suggests that separate models may be appropriate. Research suggests that the specific predictors of retirement behaviors may interact with gender, and the very nature of retirement may differ as a function of gender.

Examples of the interaction between gender and predictors of retirement behaviors are accumulating in the literature. The number of dependents living in the home may be positively associated with male participation in the workforce but negatively associated with female participation (Talaga & Beehr, 1995). The relationship between spouse's health and retirement also differed as a function of sex; men were more likely to continue working when the spouse was in poor health and women were more likely to retire. Additional research shows that financial security may be lower for women, particularly those who have had interruptions in their career, those with lower education, and those who have more children. Those women who are more educated and in a higher paying job are more likely to receive a pension and to be financially secure (Dailey, 1998; Hansson, DeKoekkoek, Neece, & Patterson, 1997).

At a broader level, it is clear that the employment and retirement process may differ as a function of gender. For instance, men's identification with the term "retiree" seems to be linked with traditional employment indices, while women's identification with the "retiree" role is not so closely tied to work-related criteria (Szinovacz & DeViney, 1999). Similarly, Hansson and his colleagues suggest that gender role differences and differences in work and caretaker demands between women and men deserve more attention than they have been given in retirement research (Hansson, DeKoekkoek, Neece, & Patterson, 1997). They also found differences in the beliefs held by men and women regarding when one should attain an educational degree and when one should retire. Calasanti (1996) added that the occupational experiences of men and women might be significantly different in the two groups. Thus, the meaning of work, retirement, and career progression may be quite different for men and women (Moen, 1996).

The findings above lead to specific recommendations for the study of retirement planning for women. Clearly, retirement models based solely on a male sample may overestimate the financial security of women in general. More importantly, there may be qualitative differences in the predictors of adjustment for men and women. For those interested in designing retirement planning programs, economic planning may be particularly important for women. Research suggests that men begin planning for retirement earlier than women and that men generally plan more financially and discuss retirement more than women (Moen, Erickson, Agarwal, Fields, & Todd, 2000).

Significant differences between African Americans and Caucasians on a number of adjustment-relevant variables also characterizes the baby boomer group. A major consideration for retirement researchers is whether the data on retirement, typically gathered from white males, can be generalized to the African-American population. Research would suggest that this is not the case; the two groups are not equivalent. A particularly disturbing finding is that there are much higher disability rates among Black men than White men. Reviews of research on disability rates for Whites and Blacks have supplemented this work; disability rates indeed tend to be elevated for Blacks (Brown, Fukunaga, Umemoto, & Wicker, 1996). This is not surprising, given their overrepresentation in physically demanding jobs and the fact that disability rates are higher in these types of jobs (Hayward, Friedman, & Chen, 1996). While research on the psychological consequences of this disability rate is limited, some studies suggest that the presence of even a moderate disability can have implications for African Americans self-identification as a retiree, their labor force participation rate, and the portion of their life spent working (Hayward, Friedman, & Chen, 1996; Szinovacz & DeViney, 1999).

Related research suggests that self-reported health of older Black men is more negative than for White males, and permanent work force withdrawal occurs at an earlier age (Hayward, Friedman, & Chen, 1996; National Academy on an Aging Society, 2000). As an illustration of these differences, the percentage of young retirees (age 51–59) indicating that their health was "fair" to "poor" was 51% of White males and 65% of Black males. For White women, only 35% reported fair to poor health. In contrast, 67% of Black women reported fair to poor health. Clearly, there is a pressing need for research that investigates the impact of these disturbingly high levels of poor health and high disability rates on subsequent adjustment.

In addition, African American men do not have the same level of education as whites; their educational attainment, on average, is lower. As previously noted, they are overrepresented in physically demanding jobs. These occupational characteristics, high physical demands and the low compensation that typically accompanies these jobs, may combine to lead to a significantly more negative retirement experience for this racial and gender group (Hayward, Friedman, & Chen, 1996). Again, long-term financial and health-oriented planning may be critical for those African Americans who fall within this description.

Given the importance of health, the finding of such high disability rates among African Americans is troubling. Again, it is not the single influence of poor health but the combined influence of this factor along with concentration in jobs which tend to be physically demanding, pay less, and offer relatively few benefits that is particularly significant (National Academy on an Aging Society, 2000). Poor health and low financial status are two central factors in postretirement satisfaction, with those who are under financial strain or in poor health showing poorer adjustment (Krause, 1987a; Krause & Baker, 1992; Beehr, 1986). Frankly, little information exists on retirement behavior of African Americans and more data needs to be gathered to understand why the difference in health exists and what preventive measures may be successful in enhancing the health of this group. Clearly health and poor finances are central issues for some African Americans, and long-term counseling and planning is needed.

From a methodological standpoint, the research models based on White men may or may not be applicable to the behavior of Black men. We simply do not know at this point. However, it is clear that data based on White men, which suggests that boomers have positive levels of health and relatively positive levels of finances, may paint a very inaccurate picture of the health of African-Americans.

In summary, the health and financial status of boomers looks quite impressive at first glance. Simply considering the average levels of these variables, however, leads one to underestimate the wide variability within this group. The fact that there are a significant proportion of the boomers that do not have favorable levels of finances and lack job skills will present a growing challenge to retirement researchers who try to design tailored planning seminars in order to improve retirement conditions for individuals. From a methodological standpoint, we need more models of retirement based on a more diverse sample of individuals. These models would provide a more accurate reflection of the workforce and would also take into account the fact that not all gender and racial groups may have identical retirement experiences

DISCUSSION: IMPLICATIONS FOR RETIREMENT PLANNING

What conclusions can we draw from the information reviewed in this chapter on the increased diversity in the workforce and the factors that shape retirement adjustment? The literature reveals a rather complicated picture of retirement. In response to these issues, several researchers have addressed the issue of emerging needs for retirement planning. Two major themes emerge in this research.

First, we should avoid our tendency to treat older workers as a homogeneous, undifferentiated group. The demographic research reviewed suggests that new retirees are a very diverse group. In many ways, the diversity of the two baby boomer cohorts is greater than any previous workforce group. Retirement advisors suggest that this calls for a more individualzed approach to retirement planning (Hall & Mirvis, 1995). As noted by Sterns and Miklos (1995), retirement plans are not strongly tied to age, and may vary greatly as a function of other characteristics. The research reviewed in this paper attests to that fact.

A contingency approach to retirement planning and research seems appropriate. Rather than assuming that the financial, health, and social aspects are equally important for all groups, these dimensions of planning may interact with retiree characteristics in determining the effectiveness of retirement planning programs as a means to enhance later adjustment. If possible, practitioners would be well-advised to assess the characteristics of the group targeted by the planning interventions in order to provide the most helpful and relevant information for the group. In addition, research is needed to further document the significance of gender, racial, and ethnic differences in retirement adjustment. As noted, different demographic groups may have rather unique retirement experiences and may have different planning needs.

A second major theme is the importance of continuous learning and life-long career planning (Cahill & Salomone, 1987; Hall & Mirvis, 1995). Although retirement researchers have called for long-term planning for some time, it may be the case that organizations are more interested in making this type of investment now that a labor shortage is forecast and the skilled labor force is predicted to decrease. Changing one's standing on financial, health, and social variables requires a substantial time commitment in many cases. While social needs can be addressed by shorter term interventions such as leisure counseling, health and finances require long-term investments on the part of employees. Long-term planning can address the needs of many of the baby boomers, and should be tailored to meet the needs of the diversity of the boomer group.

For practitioners and researchers, perhaps the bottom line is that retirement planning should encompass a consideration of the nature of the factors central in adjustment as well as the characteristics of the targeted group. A "one size fits all" approach to planning will be inadequate. Our models of planning have extended from the critical core of financial and health-oriented issues to encompass social factors in adjustment. As the concept of retirement has evolved, the predictors associated with retirement adjustment have shifted as well.

Shultz discusses other modern changes in the nature of retirement in chapter 9 of this text. These shifts in the options open to older workers cover a range of part-time and bridge employment options as well as full retirement. These changes in the offerings open to retirees should be reflected in retirement planning. Measuring the very concept of "retirement" is more complicated than in the past. It is no longer a dichotomous measure of "retired" or "not retired." An excellent overview of the types of retirement options available and the implications of these options for measuring the construct of "retirement planning" is offered by Ekerdt, DeViney, and Kosloski (1996).

It is clear that the relationship between planning and adjustment is more complex than once believed. Adjustment shifts over time, and planning consists of several relatively independent dimensions, some of which contain distinct subfacets. These issues pose measurement and implementation challenges for practitioners and researchers alike. However, an appreciation of the complexity of this relationship holds the promise of a deeper and richer understanding of the nature of retirement adjustment and how we can facilitate the process.

REFERENCES

Adams, G., & Beehr, T. A. (1998). Turnover and retirement: A comparison of their similarities and differences. *Personnel Psychology, 51,* 643–655.

American Association of Retired Persons. (1999). Baby boomers envision their retirement: An AARP segmentation analysis. Available at: http://research.aarp.org/econ/boomer_seg_1.html

Anderson, C. E., & Weber, J. A. (1993). Preretirement planning and perceptions of satisfaction among retirees. *Educational Gerontology, 19,* 397–406.

Beck, S. H. (1984). Retirement preparation programs: Differential in opportunity and use. *Journal of Gerontology, 39,* 596–602.

Beehr, T. A. (1986). The process of retirement: A review and recommendations for future investigation. *Personnel Psychology, 39,* 31–55.

Beehr, T. A., Glazer, S., Nielson, N. L., & Farmer, S. J. (2000). Work and nonwork predictors of employees' retirement ages. *Journal of Vocational Behavior, 57,* 206–225.

Brown, M. T., Fukunaga, C., Umemoto, D., & Wicker, L. (1996). Annual review: 1990–1996: Social class, work and retirement behavior. *Journal of Vocational Behavior, 49,* 159–189.

Burrus-Bammel, L. L., & Bammel, B. (1985). Leisure and recreation. In J. Birren & K. W. Shaie (Eds.) *Handbook of the psychology of aging* (pp. 848–863). New York: Van Nostrand Reinhold.

Cahill, M., & Salomone, P. R. (1987, March). Career counseling for work life extension: Integrating the older worker into the labor force. *The Career Development Quarterly,* 188–196.

Calasanti, T. M. (1996). Gender and life satisfaction in retirement: An assessment of the male model. *Journal of Gerontology: Social Sciences, 51B* , S18–S29.

Cutrona, C., Russell, D., & Rose, J. (1986). Social support and adaptation to stress by the elderly. *Journal of Psychology and Aging, 1,* 47–54.

Dailey, N. (1998). *When Baby Boom Women Retire.* Westport, Connecticut: Praeger.

Dobson, C., & Morrow, P. C. (1984). Effects of career orientation on retirement attitudes and retirement planning. *Journal of Vocational Behavior, 24,* 73–82.

Dorfman, L. T. (1992). Academics and the transition to retirement. *Educational Gerontology, 18,* 343–363.

Ekerdt, D. J., Bossé, R., & Levkoff, S. (1985). An empirical test for phases of retirement: Findings from the Normative Aging Study. *Journal of Gerontology, 40,* 95–101.

Ekerdt, D. J., DeViney, S., & Kosloski, K. (1996). Profiling plans for retirement. *Journal of Gerontology: Social Sciences, 51B,* S140–S149.

Feldman, D. C. (1994). The decision to retire early: A review and conceptualization. *Academy of Management Review, 19,* 2, 285–311.

Fernandez, M. E., Mutran, E. J., & Reitzes, D. C. (1998). Moderating the effects of stress on depressive symptoms. *Research on Aging, 20,* 163–182.

Fletcher, W. L., & Hansson, R. O. (1991). Assessing the social components of retirement anxiety. *Psychology and Aging, 6,* 76–85.

Floyd, F. J., Haynes, S. N., Doll, E. R., Winemiller, D., Lemsky, C., Bergy, T., Werle, M., & Heilman, N. (1992). Assessing retirement satisfaction and perceptions of retirement experiences. *Psychology and Aging, 7,* 609–621.

Fretz, B. R., Kluge, N. A., Ossana, S. M., Jones, S. M., & Merikangas, M. W. (1989). Intervention targets for reducing preretirement anxiety and depression. *Journal of Counseling Psychology, 36,* 301–307.

Gall, T. L., Evans, D. R., & Howard, J. (1997). The retirement adjustment process: Changes in the well-being of male retirees across time. *Journal of Gerontology, 52B,* 110–117.

George, L. K., Fillenbaum, G. G., & Palmore, E. (1984). Sex differences in the antecedents and consequences of retirement. *Journal of Gerontology, 39,* 364–371.

George, L. K., & Maddox, G. L. (1977). Subjective adaptation to loss of the work role: A longitudinal study. *Journal of Gerontology, 32,* 456–462.

Grant, P. B. (1991, March). The "Open Window"-Special early retirement plans in transition. *Employee Benefit Journal,* 10–16.

Hall, D. T., & Mirvis, P. H. (1995). The new career contract: Developing the whole person at midlife and beyond. *Journal of Vocational Behavior, 47,* 269–289.

Hansson, R. O., DeKoekkoek, P. D., Neece, W. M., & Patterson, D. W. (1997). Successful aging at work: Annual review, 1992–1996: The older worker and transitions to retirement. *Journal of Vocational Behavior, 51,* 202–233

Hayslip, B., Beyerlein, M., & Nichols, J. A. (1997). Assessing anxiety about retirement: The case of academicians. *International Journal of Aging and Human Development, 44,* 15–36.

Hayward, M. D., Friedman, S., & Chen, H. (1996). Race inequities in men's retirement. *Journal of Gerontology, 51B,* S1–S10.

Hong, L. K., & Duff, R. W. (1997). Relative importance of spouses, children and friends in the life satisfaction of retirement community residents. *Journal of Clinical Geropsychology, 3,* 275–282.

Kamouri, A. L., & Cavenaugh, J. C. (1986). The impact of preretirement education programmes on workers' preretirement socialization. *Journal of Occupational Behaviour, 7,* 245–256.

Kasshau, P. L. (1974). Reevaluating the need for retirement preparation programs. *Industrial Gerontology, Winter,* 42–55.

Kausler, D. H., & Kausler, B. C. (1996). *The graying of America: An encyclopedia of aging, health, mind and behavior.* Urbana: University of Illinois Press.

Kim, J. E., & Moen, P. (2001). Moving into retirement: Preparation and transitions in late midlife. In M. E. Lachman (Ed.), *Handbook of midlife development.* New York: John Wiley.

Krause, N. (1995). Negative interaction and satisfaction with social support among older adults. *Journal of Gerontology: Psychological Sciences, 50B,* P59–P73.

Krause, N. (1987a). Life stress, social support, and self-esteem in an elderly population. *Psychology and Aging, 2,* 349–356.

Krause, N. (1987b). Chronic financial strain, social support, and depressive symptoms among older adults. *Psychology and Aging, 2,* 185–192.

Krause, N., & Baker, E. (1992). Financial strain, economic values, and somatic symptoms in later life. *Psychology and Aging, 7,* 4–14.

Krause, N. (1997a). Social support and feelings of control in later life. In G. R. Pierce, B. Lakey, I. G. Sarason, & B. R. Sarason (Eds.). *Sourcebook of social support and personality* (pp. 335–353). New York: Plenum Press.

Krause, N. (1997b). Received support, anticipated support, social class and mortality. *Research on Aging, 19,* 387–422.

Levitt, M. J., Antonucci, T. C., Clark, M. C., Rotten, J., & Finley, G. E. (1985). Social support and well-being: Preliminary indicators based on two samples of the elderly. *International Journal of Aging and Human Development, 21,* 61–77.

Long, J. (1987). Continuity as a basis for change: Leisure and male retirement. *Leisure Studies, 6,* 55–70.

MacLean, M. J. (1982). Differences between adjustment to and enjoyment of retirement. *Canadian Journal on Aging, 2,* 3–8.

Mobily, K. E., Lemke, J. H., & Gisen, G. J. (1991). The idea of leisure repertoire. *The Journal of Applied Gerontology, 10,* 208–223.

Moen, P. (1996). A life-course perspective on retirement, gender, and well-being. *Journal of Occupational Health Psychology, 1,* 131–144.

Moen, P., Erickson, W. A., Agarwal, M., Fields, V., & Todd, L. (2000). *The Cornell Retirement and Well-Being Study: Final Report.* Cornell: Brofenbrenner Life Course Center.

Moen, P., Fields, V., Quick, H. E., & Hofmeister, H. (2000). A life-course approach to retirement and social integration. In K. Pillemer, P. Moen, E. Wethington, & N. Glasgow (Eds.), *Social integration in the second half of life.* Baltimore: Johns Hopkins University Press.

Moen, P., Kim, J. E., & Hofmeister, H. (2001). Couples' work/retirement transitions, gender, and marital quality. *Social Psychology Quarterly, 64,* 1, 55–71.

Mutran, E. J., Reitzes, D. C., & Fernandez, M. E. (1997). Factors that influence attitudes toward retirement. *Research on Aging, 19,* 251–273.

National Academy on an Aging Society (2000, December). *Do young retirees and older workers differ by race?* Washington, D. C.: Author.

Parnes, H. S., & Sommers, D. G. (1994). Shunning retirement: Work experience of men in their seventies and early eighties. *Journal of Gerontology: Social Sciences, 49,* S117–S124.

Poulos, S., & Nightingale, D. S. (1997). *The aging baby boom: Implications for employment and training programs.* U.S. Dept. of Labor, Employment and Training Administration, Contract No. F-5532–5–00–80–30.

Reitzes, D. C., Mutran, E. J., & Fernandez, M. E. (1998). The decision to retire early: A career perspective. *Social Science Quarterly, 79,* 607–619.

Shultz, K. S. (1999, April). *The influence of health and voluntariness on retirement decisions.* Presented at the 14th annual conference of the Society for Industrial and Organizational Psychology, Atlanta, Georgia.

Shultz, K. S., Morton, K. R., & Weckerle, J. R. (1998). The influence of push and pull factors on voluntary and involuntary early retirees' retirement decision and adjustment. *Journal of Vocational Behavior, 53,* 45–57.

Siegel, J. A. (1993). *A generation of change: A profile of America's older population.* New York: Sage.

Spiegel, P. E., & Shultz, K. (2001, April). *Military retirement adjustment: Do planning and transferable skills help?* Presented at the 109th annual conference of the American Psychological Association, San Francisco, California.

Stawski, R. S., & Hershey, D. A. (2001, November). *Goal clarity as an indicator of financial planning for retirement.* Presented at the annual meeting of the Gerontological Society of America, Chicago, Illinois.

Sterns, H. L., & Miklos, S. M. (1995). The aging worker in a changing environment: Organizational and individual issues. *Journal of Vocational Behavior, 47,* 248–268.

Sterns, H., & Gray, J. H. (1999). Work, leisure & retirement. In J. C. Cavenaugh & S. K. Whitbourne (Eds.), *Gerontology: An interdisciplinary perspective (pp. 355–390).* New York: Oxford University Press

Szinovacz, M. E., & DeViney, S. (1999). The retiree identity: Gender and race differences. *Journals of Gerontology: Social Sciences, 54B,* S207–S218.

Talaga, J. A., & Beehr, T. A. (1989). Retirement: A psychological perspective. In C. L. Cooper & I.T. Robertson (Eds.), *International review of industrial and organizational psychology* (pp. 185–211). Chichester, England: Wiley.

Talaga, J. A., & Beehr, T. A. (1995). Are there gender differences in predicting retirement decisions? *Journal of Applied Psychology, 80*(1) 16–28.

Taylor, M. A., Goldberg, C., & Shore, L. (2002). *The role of social support and retirement expectations on post-retirement adjustment.* Manuscript submitted for publication.

Taylor, M. A., Shultz, K., Morrison, R. , Spiegel, P., & Greene, J. (2002). *Occupational attachment, retirement expectations, and post-retirement adjustment of naval officers.* Manuscript submitted for publication.

Taylor, M. A., & Shore, L. F. (1995). Predictors of planned retirement age: An application of Beehr's model. *Psychology and Aging, 10*(1) 76–83.

Taylor-Carter, M. A., Cook, K., & Weinberg, C. (1997). Planning and expectations of the retirement experience. *Educational Gerontology, 23,* 273–288.

Turner, M. J., Bailey, W. C., & Scott, J. P. (1994). Factors influencing attitude toward retirement and retirement planning among midlife university employees. *Journal of Applied Gerontology, 13,* 143–156.

Wan, T. H., & Odell, B. G. (1983). Major role losses and social participation of older males. *Research on Agi 1g, 5,* 173–196.

Watson Wyatt. (1999). *Phased retirement: Reshaping the end of work.* Available at: www.watsonwyatt.com/homepage/us/res/phasretintro-tm.htm

Watson Wyatt (1996). *Baby boomer retirement planning: Whose responsibility?* Washington, D.C.: Author.

Weckerle, J. R., & Shultz, K. S. (1996, April). *Influences on the bridge employment decision among older workers.* Presented at the Society for Industrial and Organizational Psychology, San Diego, California.

4

Endgame: The Design and Implementation of Early Retirement Incentive Programs

Daniel C. Feldman

Early retirement incentives are financial inducements—lump sum payments, increases to pension benefits, extensions of fringe benefits, and/or commitments for continued part-time employment—that organizations offer older workers to get them to retire in the near future. For a variety of reasons, organizations are increasingly turning to early retirement incentives (ERI) as a means of rebalancing their workforce.

In some cases, the pressure to offer early retirement incentives comes from declining profitability or slower rates of growth within the firm. As a short-term strategy for reducing labor costs, many firms decide to offer older workers early retirement incentives instead (Beehr, Glazer, Nielson, & Farmer, 2000; Leana & Feldman, 1992). Similarly, when faced with mergers, acquisitions, or downsizing, firms often turn to ERI as a means of decreasing the number of employees who would otherwise have to be laid off. In other cases, early retirement incentives are used to avoid litigation costs associated with lawsuits for wrongful discharge. Rather than firing older workers for cause and dealing with potential lawsuits over age discrimination, some organizations choose to offer them early retirement incentives instead (Hanson, DeKoekkoek, Neece, & Patterson, 1997; Kim & Feldman, 2000, 1998).

While early retirement incentives are more commonly associated with negative economic conditions, they can also be used as a positive force in reshaping a firm's strategic direction. As companies enter new ventures and divest themselves of declining or peripheral businesses, ERI may be a useful means of rebalancing the portfolio of employee skills. Instead of investing heavily in retraining, organizations may find it more cost-efficient to offer older employees early retirement incentives and use the wages saved to hire new employees with the right skills. In other cases, organizations might find ERI an effective strategy for creating a new, or different, corporate culture. Rather than attempting to change the attitudes and beliefs of long-time employees, firms may conclude that voluntary separations of older workers would be more instrumental in increasing morale and changing the company's core values (Adams, 1999).

Whatever their initial motivations, though, all companies offering early retirement incentives have to balance three overarching goals: (1) getting the *right number* of older workers to take ERI; (2) getting the *right older workers* to take ERI; and (3) obtaining older workers' commitments to retire early at the *right cost* to the organization. That is, organizations implementing early retirement incentive programs want to ensure that they get the desired number of older workers to take their offers, that the older workers they most want to leave accept those offers, that the older workers they most want to retain decline those offers, and that the costs of offering ERI do not outweigh their potential benefits.

In most organizational settings, there are tradeoffs involved in reaching these three goals (Feldman & Kim, 2000, 1998). For instance, to get enough older workers to retire, organizations may have to offer generous early retirement incentives that create unacceptable long-term pension liabilities. Conversely, if an organization offers incentives that are sufficiently generous to get poor performers to leave it may inadvertently create incentives for better performers to leave, too ("they made me an offer I couldn't refuse").

The present chapter is divided into five sections. The first two sections deal with defined benefit and defined contribution retirement plans, respectively. For each major type of retirement plan, we discuss how organizations decide upon the scope of eligibility requirements, the size of one-time, lump-sum payments, and the size of increases to pension benefits. In the third section, we consider auxiliary financial incentives, besides lump-sum payments and pension benefits, which can be used to induce older workers to retire (e. g., cost of living adjustments and extended availability of continued fringe benefits). The fourth section addresses nonfinancial factors that inhibit (or reinforce) the acceptance of ERI, including demographic status, family status, age, health, and outside interests. Here, our emphasis will be on how organizations can better predict, if not control, group-level and individual-level rates of ERI acceptances. In the fifth and final section, we consider directions for future research and management practice in the area of early retirement incentive programs.

Early Retirement Incentives in Defined Benefit Pension Plans

NATURE OF DEFINED BENEFIT PENSION PLANS

In organizations that utilize defined benefit pension plans, employees who retire are guaranteed an annual pension, generally calculated on the basis of salary and years of service (Doerpinghaus & Feldman, 2001). Usually, employees have to be vested (that is, have worked for the same company) for five years to be eligible for pension benefits. Illustrative of defined benefit calculation formulae is the following organizational policy: Annual Pension Benefit = Average of Three Highest Years of Salary X 2% X Years of Service.

For example, a worker whose wages during his/her three paid highest years of employment averaged $100,000, and who worked for 30 years for the company, would receive an annual pension of $60,000. An employee who retired at age 65 and/or with 30 years of service would typically be considered to have received "full" pension benefits.

In many defined benefit pension plans, there are also penalties associated with "early retirement" (Doerpinghaus & Feldman, 2001). That is, if employees retire before they have accrued 30 years of service or before they reach 65 years of age, organizations with defined benefit pension plans usually penalize their pension benefits. For example, it is quite common for retirees' pension benefits to be decreased by 3%–5% for every year under age 65 or below 30 years of service they retire. Thus, using the same pension formula as above, consider a case where a worker retires at age 60 with 25 years of service and the annual penalty associated with early retirement is 4%. His/her pension benefits would be reduced by 20% (5 X 4%); the employee's annual pension benefit, then, would be $48,000 instead of $60,000.

EARLY RETIREMENT INCENTIVES AND PERFORMANCE LEVELS OF EMPLOYEES

For a variety of legal and social policy reasons, early retirement incentives are almost always offered to *groups* of potential retirees rather than on a case-by-case basis. Because organizations need to avoid both the appearance and the reality of age-biased performance evaluations, ERI are generally offered on the basis of some objective criteria, such as years of service, hierarchical level, functional area, or divisional membership (Grant, 1991; Lopez, 1993).

As a result of the legal environment of defined benefit pension plans, it is very difficult for organizations to get poor performers to leave and good performers to stay. All workers in a given category have to be offered ERI packages on the same terms. To make an ERI attractive enough to get some of the poorer performers (and, presumably, the poorer paid employees) to leave, organizations may have to offer very lucrative incentives. Unfortunately, those same incentives—when calculated on base salary—may be strong incentives for the better performers (and, presumably, the higher paid employees) to leave as well.

It appears, then, that the closest organizations with defined benefit plans can get to managing work force reductions strategically is by linking eligibility to functional area, divisional area, or hierarchical level. For instance, an organization can offer older employees in the chemicals division ERI, but not the employees in the consumer products division, if it wants to exit or shift resources out of its chemical production business.

There has been very little empirical research on whether the best or weakest employees are most likely to leave when offered early retirement incentives. The voluntary turnover literature would suggest that the best performers would be most likely to accept ERI because, as high performers, they would have earned higher salaries, accrued more savings, and have greater opportunities for employment (Arnold & Feldman, 1982). However, in their study of university professors being offered ERI, Kim and Feldman (1998) found that it is actually the poorer performers who are most likely to accept early retirement incentives. Using archival measures of productivity (for example, numbers of articles, books, and citations), the authors found that poor performers were more likely to accept ERI because they have less hope of getting significant pay increases if they remain on the job and lower expectations of deriving any further intrinsic satisfaction from their work. Thus, while the use of ERI always entails the risk of losing some of the best older workers, organizations might reasonably expect to lose a *disproportionate number* of poor performers relative to good performers.

Although this possibility has not yet been empirically tested, it is also plausible that the relationship between performance and acceptance of ERI is curvilinear. That is, the poorest performers may be more likely to take ERI because of declining future rewards, while the best performers may also be more likely to take ERI because they have greater opportunities for employment elsewhere. Early retirement incentives may, in fact, be least successful in getting average performers to leave. Clearly, this question warrants much more careful attention in future research on early retirement programs.

LUMP SUM PAYMENTS

Organizations sometimes offer older workers lump-sum payments as inducements to accept early retirement. Most commonly, these lump-sum payments are based on some percentage of salary (often in the 5%—10% range) or on number of years of service with the company (e. g., 13 weeks' pay for 26 years of service). While lump-sum payments are occasionally given as the sole incentive for early retirement, in defined benefit pension plans they are almost always given in addition to some type of increase in long-term pension benefits as well.

Research on the effectiveness in getting older workers to retire early has been sparse and is very difficult to conduct in a methodologically rigorous way. As noted above, rarely are lump sum payments used as the sole incentive to retire, so it is very difficult to untangle the effects of lump-sum payments from the effects of concurrent increases in pension benefits. Moreover, it is impossible to examine the effects of different-sized payments in real organizational settings because lump-sum retirement incentives are one-time events and are distributed on the same basis to all affected workers. To date there has not been experimental research on the main effects of lump-sum payments of different sizes on acceptance of ERI or on their interactions with different kinds of pension benefit increases.

The historical reason for offering lump-sum payments is to give older workers sufficient capital to reduce debt (e. g., pay off mortgages or car loans) and to cover transition costs out of the workforce (e. g., defray costs of house sales or geographical moves). On the margin, these lump-sum payments may serve as inducements for older workers to retire. However, both financial and behavioral research on the acceptance of ERI suggests that individuals are most heavily swayed by perceptions of future streams of earnings when making retirement decisions (Gordon & Blinder, 1980; Gustman & Steinmeier, 1991; Ruhm, 1989). Except in cases where older workers are receiving very high payouts (e. g., golden parachutes) or are heavily in debt, it is hard to see how lump-sum payments would materially affect older workers' retirement decisions. Whether the practice of giving modest lump-sum payments continues to be cost-efficient as an ERI is really open to question.

CHANGING THE BASIS OF CALCULATING PENSION BENEFITS

The major tool that organizations with defined pension benefit plans have to induce older workers to retire is increasing the size of long-term pension benefits (Blinder, Gordon, & Wise, 1980). To do so, firms usually alter the ways in which pension benefits are calculated to increase potential retirees' future streams of earnings. Below, we consider some of the potential advantages and disadvantages of various organizational tactics to achieve this goal.

Years of Service. One way organizations can increase incentives to retire early is to add years of service in calculating pension benefits. For example, companies may calculate pension benefits *as if* older workers had five more years of service; a 25–year veteran would receive pension benefits as if he or she had 30 years of service. This strategy has two potential advantages: (1) it visibly increases the future stream of earnings; and (2) it increases the likelihood that marginal employees who are just "putting in years" to retire at full benefits will accept the offer. While the first advantage has been demonstrated empirically, the second has not (Doerpinghaus & Feldman, 2001). However, given the importance of increasing the proportion of poorer performers who accept ERI, this question warrants careful attention by both researchers and HR practitioners.

Rather than increasing years of service, other organizations have decreased penalties for older workers who are leaving before attaining eligibility for full pension benefits. That is, rather than recalculating pensions as if older employees had worked more years, organizations simply don't impose penalties for early departure. This strategy also increases future streams of earnings but does so more subtly and less visibly. No empirical research has directly addressed whether increasing years of service or decreasing penalties is more effective in generating ERI acceptances, particularly while holding constant the total real value of the incentive offered.

Chronological Age. In some organizations with defined benefit pension plans (many in the public sector), employees are allowed to retire with full benefits when they reach *either* 30 years of service *or* age 65. Analogous to the discussion above, then, organizations can create incentives for older workers to retire by adding some number of years (typically 3–5) to their chronological age in calculating pension benefits. Research suggests that this strategy is also effective as an early retirement incentive (Kim & Feldman, 2000, 1998). Here, too, it is possible to eliminate penalties for retiring before age 65 rather than adding years of chronological age to the pension benefit calculation.

An important practical problem faced by senior management is deciding whether they should tinker with age, years of service, or both factors in designing ERI. It is difficult to answer this question directly because chronological age and years of service are strongly and positively related to each other. That is, workers with long years of service tend to be older than those with few years of service. Moreover, the effects of age and years of service on retirement behavior in defined benefit pension plans are not perfectly linear. Once employees have achieved the maximum level of years of service credit, they are more likely to retire whether they have reached age 65 or not. Conversely, once employees have reached the maximum level of credit for chronological age, they are more likely to retire whether they have accrued 30 years of service or not (Doerpinghaus & Feldman, 2001).

Salary Component. By and large, most organizations use a figure of close to 2% in calculating pension benefits; rarely does one see programs that pay less than 1. 75% per year of service or more than 2. 25% per year of service. Part of that reason is historical. At a time when most people retired at age 65 and counted on Social Security as an important source of income, workers could retire comfortably on 60% or so of their salary. With a decrease in taxable income and the addition of tax-free Social Security and Medicare benefits, older workers could basically retire at the same level of after-tax income (Burtless & Moffitt, 1985; Clark & McDermed, 1986).

However, another reason for the 2% figure is its frequent utility in balancing employees' and organizations' financial needs. With the exception of very highly paid employees, the vast majority of older workers cannot afford to retire on only 45% of their salary (what employees would receive in pension benefits if they worked 30 years and got only 1. 5% of their salary per year of service). On the other hand, if companies offer 2. 5% of salary per year of service, it might be economically irrational for employees to continue working after 25 years of service. For instance, with the latter type of pension formula, 46–year-old employees with 25 years of service could retire with 62. 5% of their salary and still have 20 years to earn income elsewhere.

Eligibility for ERI. Surprisingly little research has been done on the effectiveness of early retirement incentives that have *multiple criteria* for eligibility. Most commonly, early retirement incentives are offered to employees who are *either* at least age 55 *or* have had at least 25 years of service. However, it might be judicious for organizations to offer ERI to employees who are *both* at least age 55 *and* have at least 25 years of service. The downside of this strategy, of course, is that fewer older workers will be eligible to accept ERI. However, the upside of this strategy is its potential savings for long-term pension liabilities and its disincentives for talented middle-aged employees to leave (like the 46–year-olds with 25 years of service discussed above).

Organizations might also want to consider base salary as a potential criterion for eligibility in designing early retirement incentive plans. Depending on the organization's strategic needs and long-term pension liabilities, it might want to limit its ERI offers to employees above or below certain salary cutoffs. Allowing only lower-paid employees to be eligible for ERI may be effective at decreasing the number of lower-skilled employees in the firm and put less strain on the firm's long-term pension debt. On the other hand, allowing only higher-paid employees to be eligible for ERI may be effective at substantially decreasing the current payroll and the current number of managers in the firm, but the costs of these employee separations are shifted downstream as significant future pension liabilities (Fronstin, 1999).

Early Retirement Incentives in Defined Contribution Pension Plans

NATURE OF DEFINED CONTRIBUTION PENSION PLANS

In defined contribution retirement plans, the financial commitment of the organization to employees is depositing a prescribed percentage of annual salary into each worker's tax-deferred pension fund and delegating control for the management of those funds to individual employees themselves. For example, under a defined contribution plan, a company might deposit 5% of annual salary into Employee A's pension fund. From that point on, Employee A is responsible for saving or investing those pension funds wisely. The range of annual pension contributions is generally between 5% and 15% of salary, depending upon the skill-level of employees, standards in the industry, or norms in the occupation (Doerpinghaus & Feldman, 2001).

Some employees will make good investment and saving decisions and will generate extensive capital; other employees will make poorer financial decisions and will generate less capital. For better or worse, though, an older employee's ability to afford early retirement is under his or her own control rather than the organization's control. Moreover, the organization's liability for pension funding ends with the deposit of money into individual employees' pension funds. The organization is not responsible for implementing or administering any kind of company-run pension plan. The ability of any one individual to retire, then, is as reliant upon his or her own investment prowess as on the retirement incentives he or she receives.

For a variety of reasons, the amount of research on early retirement incentive plans in defined contribution pension plans has been much more limited than in defined benefit plans. Compared with defined benefit plans, defined contribution plans are newer in origin and have not been as widely used. With the introduction of IRAs and other types of retirement savings accounts in the 1960s and 1970s, such plans have now become much more popular. However, there are relatively few people age 60 today who have been solely reliant on defined contribution plans throughout their careers.

DEFINED CONTRIBUTION PLANS AND EMPLOYEE PERFORMANCE

To date, there are no compelling data on whether better or worse performers are more likely to retire early under defined contribution plans. In general, we would predict that better performers would be more likely to accept ERI than poorer performers. Current salaries and future streams of earnings are major determinants of employees' willingness to retire early. Consequently, assuming salaries are at least modestly related to performance levels, we would expect that better performers would accumulate more assets in their pension funds and could better afford to leave the workforce at an early age and/or with fewer years of service.

However, it is also possible that some lower-paid employees might invest more wisely, thereby generating larger sums of money with which to retire than their better-paid colleagues. "The Millionaire Next Door" is often a blue-collar worker who simply lived frugally and purchased mutual funds on a monthly basis. Thus, while it is more likely that better (and higher-paid) performers will accept ERI, the link here is more tenuous.

Lump-Sum Payments

While lump-sum payments may not be the central component of ERI in defined benefit plans, they are pivotal to ERI in defined contribution plans. In defined contribution plans, the amount of the pension benefit will be the result of the employee's own investment decisions. Consequently, one major financial inducement a defined-contribution organization has to entice older workers to retire is adding a significant lump-sum payment to the employee's retirement account (either given at one point in time or distributed over a 1–3 year period).

In some cases, these payments will be in the form of cash (often as a percentage or multiple of annual salary); in other cases, these payments will be made in the form of stock ownership, annuities, or deferred stock options. In all these cases, though, the aim is the same: to give older workers sufficient assets to generate a stream of income great enough to sustain them in early retirement (Godofsky, 1988).

An important issue for future research here is the willingness of workers in defined contribution plans to absorb the risks associated with early retirement incentives. In defined benefit plans, the organization absorbs almost all the risk associated with early retirement. It is the organization that is responsible for generating a set amount of money for each employee each month and it is the organization that is responsible for keeping the pension plan adequately funded over time. In contrast, in defined contribution plans, the employee absorbs almost all the risk. If an older employee retires assuming he/she will experience a 10% annual rate of growth on investments—and then the economy hits a lengthy recession—it is the employee who absorbs the costs of these unexpected financial reverses. Given that the comfort level for risk appears to decline with age, older workers in defined contribution plans may be less likely to accept ERI because of greater uncertainty about their future streams of income.

Chronological Age and Years of Service

As noted above, organizations with defined contribution plans do not calculate benefit contributions on the basis of chronological age or years of service. However, a different issue arises in the context of defined contribution plans, namely, how important are age and years of service in employees' decisions to accept ERI?

Our hypothesis would be that, in defined contribution plans, age would be a greater determinant of accepting ERI than years of service. In these plans, too, age and years of service will be positively correlated. However, retiring under defined contribution plans entails much more risk for individual employees. Perceptions of inflationary trends, interest rates, stock market growth, changes in tax policy, and viability of the Social Security system all factor into assessments of how much money is truly needed to retire (Blinder, Gordon, & Wise, 1980). The oldest workers, simply because they have fewer years to live and consequently are less vulnerable to wide gyrations in macro-economic forces, may be more able to make stable estimates of the real value of early retirement incentives with confidence. In contrast, a 50–year-old with 30 years of service faces a greater amount of uncertainty in estimating the amount of money needed to retire early; therefore, he or she may err on the side of conservatism and reject ERI offers (Hanoch & Honig, 1983; Kahn, 1988; Mitchell & Fields, 1984).

Another possibility that organizations could consider is increasing the percentage of salary contributions they make into older workers' pension funds, based on either age or years of service. For example, organizations could increase the likelihood of older workers retiring by increasing the percentage of salary contributed from 1. 9 to 2. 2% for all workers over age 55 or 25 years of service. To date, there is no empirical evidence on the effectiveness of such a strategy.

ELIGIBILITY FOR EARLY RETIREMENT INCENTIVES

It is much more difficult for organizations with defined contribution plans to predict or control how many employees will accept ERI offers. Organizations often have little data about the real value of assets accumulated in individuals' own retirement accounts and, with the exception of lump-sum payments, have little power to manipulate the amount of annual pension benefits older workers would receive (Feldman, 1994). The closest organizations can come here is to estimate—using employees' current salaries and conservative rates of market returns on prior pension fund contributions—the size of older workers' current pension assets. Then, organizations can offer lump-sum payments that would allow older workers to generate, in total, roughly 60% of their current salaries in future streams of income.

Nonetheless, as is the case with defined benefit plans, firms with defined contribution plans can target eligibility for ERI strategically at different categories of workers: by functional area, by hierarchical level, by salary level, by division membership, and so forth. In general, though, we would expect *rates of acceptance* of ERI in defined contribution plans to be lower than those in defined benefit plans— even at the same level of estimated future earnings—because of the increased level of risk and the increased level of uncertainty to which individual employees are exposed.

Auxiliary Financial Components of ERI Programs

Clearly, lump-sum payments and increases in pension benefits are the major incentives that organizations use to encourage early retirement. However, there are several additional financial considerations that firms need to consider in designing ERI as well. Below, we address the five most important of these considerations: (1) estimating the rates of acceptance of ERI; (2) determining the frequency of ERI offers; (3) assessing the costs of the "free rider" problem; (4) offering bridge employment; and (5) including cost-of-living adjustments and fringe benefits in ERI incentive packages.

ESTIMATING RATES OF ERI ACCEPTANCE

One of the most challenging tasks facing corporations is estimating the aggregate rates of acceptance of ERI offers in a specific firm. There is some national evidence on the aggregate rates of acceptance of ERI offers; those data suggest that the typical rate of acceptance ranges from 25% to 39%. Moreover, because increasing numbers of older workers want to retire at an earlier age (generally, between ages 55 and 59), the rate of acceptance of ERI appears to be inching up over time (Chen, 2001; Rose & Larimore, 2001).

What the ERI acceptance rate will be for any given firm depends to a large extent on the generosity of the incentives themselves as well as on macroeconomic factors such as inflation rates, rates of interest on conservative investments like bonds, unemployment rates, stock market appreciation, and so forth. Rates of acceptance will be higher under low inflation rates, low unemployment rates, and high stock market appreciation (as in the 1990s). In contrast, rates of acceptance are lower under conditions of high inflation and high unemployment, because potential retirees face erosion of real income over time and fewer opportunities to supplement that income with alternative employment.

Much less research has been conducted on the specific effects of various retirement incentives on early retirement behavior (i. e., how much increase in acceptance of ERI is created by every percentage increase in pension benefits). Moreover, because of large differences across industries, evidence from one firm is not easily generalizable to others. A study by Kim and Feldman (1998) tried to assess the marginal effects for different predictors of acceptance of early retirement incentives; a marginal effect is the change in the dependent variable (accepting retirement) for every unit change in a predictor variable. In that study, for instance, the authors found that a monthly increase in pension benefit of $1,000 increased the ERI acceptance rate by 4. 9%. At a minimum, organizations can use their own historical data on retirement behavior (average rates of retirement by age group, salary level, hierarchical level, and functional area) to estimate changes in retirement rates in response to changes in retirement benefits.

Another question for future research to address is the impact of "voluntariness" of early retirement incentives (DeWitt, Trevino, & Mollica, 1998). Most of the research on early retirement incentives has been conducted in organizations where the alternative to not accepting ERI was continued employment. That is, while organizations might have been offering ERI to decrease the size of work force and asking for volunteers, older workers were not under threat of layoffs if they did not accept the ERI package. However, in other organizations, many older employees realize that if they do not accept an ERI their alternative outcome may be no work *and* no generous severance package. Certainly, rates of acceptance will be higher with impending layoffs, but how much the threat of layoff increases propensity to accept ERI is not yet known (Feldman & Kim, 1998).

DETERMINING THE FREQUENCY OF ERI OFFERS

Because estimating the number of early retirement incentive acceptances is such a difficult task, organizations are often forced to make multiple ERI offers over a period of years to get the right number of people to retire. The frequency of previous early retirement incentives, individuals' rejections of previous ERI offers, and employees' perceptions of the likelihood of future ERI offers all play a role in determining who will leave—and at what price—in subsequent situations.

There are not many studies on this topic, but those that have been done suggest that the greater the perceived likelihood of future early retirement incentives, the less likely older workers will be to accept the current ERI. Employees who are ambivalent about early retirement have a convenient way of justifying to themselves why they should put off the difficult decision, while employees for whom early retirement is only marginally affordable may hold out for additional retirement incentives at a later date. In general, then, the more frequently early retirement incentives are offered, the more generous each future ERI will have to be to induce acceptance (Feldman, 1994).

Archival data on declines of previous ERI offers may also be able to be used to estimate the likelihood of individuals' acceptance of subsequent ERI offers. Again, there is not a great deal of research on this topic. Nonetheless, the research that has been conducted in this area suggests two countervailing trends. First, there does not appear to be much impact from having declined *one* previous ERI on rates of acceptance of the next ERI. Second, individuals who have declined *two* previous ERI are more likely to accept the third offer. In Kim and Feldman's (1998) study, older workers who had declined two previous offers were 7% more likely to accept the third incentive. One plausible explanation for these results is that employees who have declined two previous offers may not want to "push their luck" by turning down a third ERI while hoping for a fourth.

THE "FREE RIDER" PROBLEM

Organizations often overestimate the effects of their early retirement incentives (and underestimate their costs) by failing to consider the "free rider" problem. That is, in any given year, a certain percentage of older workers will retire whether they are given any additional incentives or not; hence, they will be doubly rewarded for a behavior they would have engaged in anyway.

Consider a very simple example: in a typical year, 100 employees in Firm A retire at the "normal" age (ages 60–65). The organization then introduces an ERI that would give all eligible employees who retire within the next twelve months a lump-sum payment of $20,000. At the end of that year, 200 of the firm's employees retire. The incentive, though, did not really generate 200 retirements, but rather 100; half of the retirees would have probably retired anyway, even without the ERI. Thus, the organization actually paid 100 employees a $20,000 bonus for doing what they would have done without incentives—and at a cost of $2,000,000. While organizations can never avoid free rider costs, ignoring them leads to overestimates of the effects of a specific ERI and underestimates of its costs.

OPPORTUNITIES FOR BRIDGE EMPLOYMENT

By the term "bridge employment" we mean jobs which older workers take after leaving career-long positions but before exiting the workforce altogether (Doeringer, 1990; Feldman, 1994). In large part, bridge employment has been studied as a means for older workers to adjust more successfully to retirement. The evidence is quite strong that bridge employment does facilitate adjustment to retirement by providing older workers with some structure to their time, supplemental income, and opportunities to develop new routines and interests before leaving work behind for good (Beehr & Nielson, 1995; Isaksson & Johansson, 2000; Weckerle & Shultz, 1999).

However, bridge employment can be considered as another type of ERI itself (Kim & Feldman, 2000, 1998). Guaranteed opportunities to continue working part-time or temporarily after retirement may reduce older workers' anxieties about finances and their reluctance to quit work "cold turkey" without going through some period of decompression. In a series of studies on bridge employment, Kim and Feldman (2000, 1998) found that bridge employment opportunities are effective in increasing acceptances of early retirement incentives.

Indeed, employees who were offered opportunities to work on a part-time basis after retirement were 9% more likely to accept ERI than their counterparts who were not planning on taking bridge employment. By increasing both financial and psychological well-being, then, bridge employment may tip the balance in getting older workers to accept these incentives.

EXTENDED EMPLOYEE BENEFITS

The perceived financial feasibility of accepting early retirement incentives will also be dependent upon the extent and generosity of retirees' fringe benefits packages. Of chief concern here are cost-of-living adjustments (COLA) to pension benefits and continued employer contributions to health insurance costs (Cutler, 2001; Higgins, 2001; Leonard, 2001).

Early retirement raises anxieties about financial security because people living on fixed incomes are particularly vulnerable to downdrafts in the equity and bond markets. These concerns are particularly heightened today by the rising age of eligibility for "full" Social Security benefits, increased taxes on Social Security benefits, and the uncertain future of the Social Security system itself. If organizations want to increase the likelihood that older workers will accept early retirement incentives, those ERI offers should also include guarantees of reasonable cost-of-living adjustments to pension benefits. When older workers fear that their income will be seriously eroded by inflation, they are much less likely to retire at an earlier age.

Retirees and other individuals living on fixed incomes are also especially vulnerable to sudden price increases in major goods and services. Of particular concern today are the rapid increases in the costs of health care, prescription drugs, and health insurance premiums. Fortunately, employees are legally guaranteed the right to remain in an organization's health insurance group for over a year after they retire; however, they are not guaranteed the right to continued organizational contributions to their health insurance premiums. As the costs of health care escalate, extended employee benefits in this area are likely to become an increasingly important factor in the acceptance of ERI packages (Cutler, 2001; LaRock, 1999).

Nonfinancial Considerations in ERI Programs

As important as financial considerations are in older workers' decisions to accept early retirement offers, these decisions are influenced by a variety of nonfinancial issues as well. Some of these factors (e. g., the availability of retirement counseling) are under the organization's control. Other factors (e. g., family status and health status) are not under the organization's control, but nonetheless have a significant impact on employees' willingness to accept ERI. Below, we consider how organizations can use non-financial considerations in implementing ERI programs more effectively and in making more accurate forecasts of employees' acceptances of early retirement incentive offers.

PRERETIREMENT COUNSELING

There is a growing body of literature that suggests preretirement counseling facilitates adjustment to retirement and, to a lesser extent, increases the likelihood of early retirement as well (Higgins, 2001; Rosen & Jerdee, 1989; Taplin, 1989). While the reasons underlying the potential effectiveness of preretirement counseling are often left implicit, two rationales appear to be the most convincing theoretically. First, by giving older workers accurate and specific information about pension benefits and other financial matters (e. g., tax and estate planning or availability of part-time employment), retirement counseling reduces employees' anxieties about financial security. Second, by providing older workers comprehensive advice before retirement itself, counseling programs give employees time to get used to the idea of retirement and to start making appropriate changes in their lifestyles (e. g., taking up new hobbies) in advance (Feldman, 1994).

While the general effectiveness of preretirement counseling has been adequately demonstrated, it is still not clear which specific elements of preretirement counseling are most critical in getting employees to accept ERI. In some studies, simply the availability of counseling is used as the predictor variable; in other studies, attendance at preretirement counseling is used as the predictor. In some studies, preretirement counseling is assessed in terms of length; in others, it is assessed in terms of perceived quality or helpfulness. In addition, because the content of preretirement counseling programs varies significantly from firm to firm (e. g., some focus only on financial matters and some include lifestyle issues as well), it is difficult to know exactly which components of counseling programs are most critical in boosting acceptance of ERI (Feldman & Kim, 2000). This issue is worthy of future attention from academics and practitioners alike, particularly in defined contribution pension plans where older workers' financial uncertainties may be greater.

AGE DISCRIMINATION

There is also some evidence that suggests age discrimination, both overt and covert in nature, is related to older workers' willingness to accept early retirement incentives. Despite legislation that protects older workers from the worst abuses of age discrimination, older workers are often subjected to considerable informal pressure to retire. In environments like these, the rates of acceptance of ERI are likely to be higher as well (Feldman, 1994).

Cleveland and Shore (1992) make an interesting observation about how age is perceived in organizations. They distinguish between chronological age, subjective age (self-perceptions of being old), and relative age (age relative to the mean age of group members). The findings of Cleveland and Shore suggest that *chronological age,* in and of itself, may not be the best predictor of acceptance of ERI; instead, *relative age* may be the more important factor. That is, when individuals are substantially older than the mean age of their peers, pressure on them to accept ERI might be greater.

In the context of ERI offers, considerations of *"normative age"* may also play an important role. That is, in different organizational settings, there may be expectations about when it is time for older workers to retire from their jobs; these normative expectations are often based on when previous occupants of positions have retired in the past (Lawrence, 1988). Thus, older workers may receive more pressure to accept ERI when they have exceeded the age at which their predecessors have typically retired.

In short, then, age discrimination increases external pressures to retire and increases older workers' self-doubts about the wisdom of continuing to work as well. Overall, the encroaching feeling of exclusion motivates older workers to "get out while the getting's good. "

Employee Health and Disability Claims

In general, the weight of the research evidence suggests that poor physical health contributes to early retirement decisions. Major illnesses (e. g., heart disease) make it more difficult for older workers to continue to perform effectively on the job; severe functional impairments (e. g., onset of deafness or severe arthritis) may make it almost impossible to do so. Thus, when early retirees are offered continued health insurance coverage, employees in poor health are much more likely to accept ERI (Colsher, Dorfman, & Wallace, 1988; Hayward, Grady, Hardy, & Sommers, 1989). In contrast, when retirees will lose their health care benefits, older workers with major health problems may be less likely to accept ERI out of fear of enormous, nonreimbursable medical expenses (Anderson & Burkhauser, 1985).

Doerpinghaus and Feldman (2001) have examined whether employees who file disability claims (and have them turned down) are more or less likely to retire early. Their results suggest that filing unsubstantiated disability claims is a strong signal of job dissatisfaction; as such, these claims signal older workers' willingness to retire early whenever possible. However, given that employees who file disability claims may reasonably be expected to have some health problems (even if not as severe as they allege in their disability claims), their higher acceptance rate of ERI may be due to both lower job satisfaction *and* poorer health.

Demographic Status of the Workforce

The main relevance of demographic composition of the workforce in the present context is its impact on willingness to accept ERI offers. Besides age, the demographic variables most frequently studied in relation to early retirement are marital status, family status, and gender.

The weight of the evidence suggests that *marital status* and *family status* do, in fact, impact the likelihood of accepting ERI (Daniels & Daniels, 1991; Feldman, 1994). Specifically, married workers are more likely to accept ERI and to retire earlier than single employees. Married workers (especially those in two-career couples) are more likely than single workers to have accumulated greater capital over time and to have achieved financial security. Moreover, married workers are more likely than single workers to have steady companionship when they retire (Daniels & Daniels, 1991; Goudy, Powers, & Keith, 1975).

However, there are three notable exceptions to the above discussion. Married workers tend to time their retirements so that they retire around the same time as their spouses. Therefore, in cases where older workers' spouses are still employed and will not be around to provide companionship, the rates of acceptance of ERI are likely to be lower (Erdner & Guy, 1990). Furthermore, in cases where potential retirees still have dependent children to support (either because their children are still in college or because they started second families later in life), rates of acceptance of ERI are also likely to be lower (Kim & Feldman, 2000). Third, in organizations and jobs where salaries (and hence pension benefits) are relatively low, single people may be more likely to accept ERI than married workers (Doerpinghaus & Feldman, 2001). Under these circumstances, single employees may be better able to afford retirement because they have fewer financial demands on their resources than their married colleagues (particularly those who are the sole wage earners in their families).

To date, the research on *gender* differences in willingness to accept ERI is inconclusive (Moen, 1996; Talaga & Beehr, 1995). In cases where women start working later in life and/or have more temporary exits from the workforce, they tend to be less enthusiastic about accepting ERI because they have accumulated less income and are more excited about continuing their careers. Richardson and Kilty (1991) refer to this phenomenon as "career disorderliness" and suggest it is associated with women's greater reluctance to retire early. However, in cases where women are married to older and wealthier men, they appear to be more willing to retire early because they want to provide their husbands with companionship and have greater financial resources to leave the work force (Kim & Feldman, 2000, 1998). In general, then, it is very difficult to untangle the effects of gender from those of marital status, family status, family income, and age differential from spouse.

OPPORTUNITIES FOR OUTSIDE EMPLOYMENT

In the discussion of bridge employment above, we highlighted the importance of bridge employment both as an inducement to early retirement and as a means of satisfactory adjustment to retirement. While that discussion focused on organizational offers of bridge employment as components of ERI, half of all bridge jobs, in fact, involve changes in occupation and/or industry (Doeringer, 1990; Feldman, 1994; Ruhm, 1989).

In order to understand older workers' willingness to accept ERI, then, we also need to understand the availability of bridge employment external to the firm. Labor economists have noted that there are major differences in what they call "opportunity structures in career paths" (Doeringer, 1990; Ruhm, 1989, 1990). That is, different career paths offer differential opportunities for continued part-time employment and/or opportunities to find satisfactory bridge employment in retirement. An older worker can readily be a management consultant without an organizational employer and can perform that activity with as great, or as low, a frequency as he or she wants. In contrast, it is very difficult to be a part-time neurosurgeon working for a variety of employers; moreover, to pay for office space and cover large malpractice premiums, neurosurgeons cannot just operate one or two mornings a week. Thus, the more restrictive the opportunity structures in career paths, the less likely older workers will be to accept ERI because of the difficulties associated with finding bridge employment outside their present employer. Similarly, the less portable older workers' skills, the less likely they will accept ERI because of the difficulties associated with finding bridge employment outside their present vocation.

Interestingly, several theoretical articles have argued that bridge employment with the same long-time employer should lead to greater satisfaction with retirement because of greater continuity of tasks, work environments, and coworkers (Atchley, 1989; Feldman, 1994). However, a recent study by Kim and Feldman (2000) suggests this positive relationship may not necessarily hold across all work situations. Retirees who are unhappy with their pay, the lack of respect they receive from coworkers and superiors, and the work itself are actually more satisfied with bridge jobs outside their long-time careers and organizations. Indeed, their willingness to accept a company's early retirement incentive is often fuelled by their desire to escape from dispiriting jobs and deteriorating work situations altogether (Feldman & Kim, 2000). Thus, job attitudes—as well as opportunity structures—play a major role in older workers' willingness to accept early retirement incentives.

Directions for Future Research and Management Practice

In this final section, we address directions for future work on the topic of early retirement incentives. First, we examine avenues for future theory building and improvement in research methodology; then, we consider potential implications for management practice.

DIRECTIONS FOR FUTURE RESEARCH

Financial Considerations. Enhancements to pension benefits and the distribution of lump-sum payments have historically dominated the research on early retirement incentives, and for good reason: without sufficient income, older workers simply will not retire early. This line of research has largely focused on how early retirement incentives offered by the firm impact older workers' future stream of earnings after exiting the workforce. However, other monetary considerations play major roles in individuals' willingness to retire as well. For married couples, the spouse's income (and/or pension) is an important source of income. In addition, many employees today have IRAs or other types of tax-deferred annuities besides organizational pension benefits. Although it is very difficult to get data on personal wealth, some older workers also have accumulated savings and inheritances that they can use in retirement. We also know very little about the success of employees' investments in defined contribution plans relative to the income yielded in traditional defined benefit plans.

Until we get a better handle on family income, family wealth, nonorganizationally provided benefits, and self-managed investments, our ability to predict responses to ERI will remain quite modest. As it stands now, researchers are sort of playing draw poker with their research subjects: from looking at two cards face up (organizational salary and pension), researchers are trying to infer from their subjects' "bets" (retirement decisions) what the four cards facing down (spouse's income, other investments, savings, and inheritances) must have been.

Similarly, the economic context of early retirement incentives also needs to be more carefully examined. Various studies of ERI have been done under significantly different macroeconomic conditions of inflation, unemployment, and stock market growth. It is hard to generalize across studies without a better understanding of the economic conditions under which ERI were offered. At the minimum, such data should be reported in future studies of the effectiveness of early retirement incentives so that subsequent meta-analyses can assess their overall effects.

Latent Functions of Work. The financial perspective on retirement suggests that jobs are taken primarily to fulfill what sociologists call the "manifest" function of work, that is, to provide income; when financial needs are met, desire to work is reduced. However, as the preceding discussion suggests, organizational researchers and gerontologists are increasingly focusing attention on the "latent" functions of work (Jahoda, 1982; Kuhnert, 1989). While employment indeed provides income, it also serves several other important (but less obvious) functions for workers, i.e., providing a structure for individuals' time, opportunities for social interaction, and symbols of status in the community.

Although previous research has extensively examined how older workers *adjust to lack of activity,* there has been much less attention paid to how older workers *plan for continued activity* after retirement. Bridge employment is one means to help older workers adjust to this sense of "rolelessness"—but it is not the only one (Kilty & Behling, 1985). Researchers have also examined whether involvement in church activities, volunteer work, and hobbies facilitate adjustment to retirement, but in general those results have been quite modest or inconclusive. Other researchers suggest it is not the type or extent of alternative activity that impedes acceptance of ERI, but rather individuals' uncertainty of their plans for retirement (Feldman, 1994; Hornstein & Wapner, 1985).

As research on early retirement incentives goes forward, greater attention needs to be given to the latent functions of work and how older employees plan to use their time in retirement. Ideally, such research would help determine whether comprehensive preretirement counseling (that is, programs that include both financial and lifestyle planning) have any marginal effectiveness over conventional "benefits counseling" taking place in most organizations today.

Family Considerations in Retirement Planning. Most of the previous research on acceptance of ERI has focused on the individual employee and his of her opportunities and constraints on retiring. With the majority of employees today having working spouses, the process of retirement decision making becomes noticeably more complex (Moen, 1996; Talaga & Beehr, 1995). For example, while employees who are older are generally more likely to accept ERI, workers with considerably younger spouses and dependent children are less likely to do so because of greater financial burdens (Kim & Feldman, 1998). Likewise, while older workers in poor health are more likely to accept early retirement incentives, many older workers in good health accept ERI because they have to provide care for spouses or parents who are in poor health (Doerpinghaus & Feldman, 2001).

As important as individual-level factors are in understanding the willingness to retire early or to accept ERI, family-level considerations warrant much more detailed attention, too. Surprisingly, previous research on family status has not yielded strong and consistent findings. However, the shape and composition of American families are changing so rapidly that it is hard to account for all the variations in what the term "family" currently means. Fewer than half the children in this country grow up with both biological parents in the same household. Instead, there are a variety of alternative family relationships in place: second marriages, step-parenting, grandparents raising grandchildren, shared custody arrangements, same-sex partners with adopted children, and so forth. Moreover, parents' financial obligations often extend beyond those implied by the construct of "minor children living at home. " Young adults are graduating from college at later and later ages, and many still live at home well into their 20s; other families have grandparents or other members of their extended families living with them; some older workers are still paying child support to their ex-spouses. Much more detailed and thoughtful attention is needed to understand how different patterns of family composition—and the financial responsibilities they entail—facilitate or impede acceptance of ERI.

Early Retirement vs. Early Retirement Incentives. Another important direction for future research is untangling the research findings on early retirement decisions from those on early retirement incentives. The research on "early retirement" has typically examined the factors that lead older employees to retire before the age of "full" retirement benefits (e. g., before becoming eligible for Social Security benefits or before becoming eligible for maximum organizational pension benefits). In comparison, the research on "early retirement incentives" has examined how employees respond at any one point in time to a specific ERI offer from an organization. Early retirement may or may not take place accompanied by ERI, but ERI usually implies retirement before the individual becomes eligible for full retirement benefits.

As this paper suggests, there are obvious links between these two streams of literature and each line of research helps to inform the other. Nonetheless, important differences exist between the decision to retire early and the decision to accept ERI. First, ERI offers are often made with little advance notice, with no more than two months' time to decide, and implemented on the organization's time frame. Second, ERI offers are often made at times of declining organizational fortunes when the alternative to accepting ERI may be layoffs and prolonged unemployment (DeWitt, Trevino, & Mollica, 1998). Thus, the contexts of the decision to retire early and the decision to accept ERI are often quite different and some caution needs to be taken in generalizing from one research domain to the other.

DIRECTIONS FOR MANAGEMENT PRACTICE

Estimating Acceptance Rates of ERI. Perhaps the most challenging task facing HR professionals responsible for designing and implementing early retirement incentives is accurately estimating how many people will accept ERI, which people will accept ERI, and how generous the ERI needs to be to get the right number of people—and the right people—to accept. As we have suggested in this paper, these kinds of predictions are very difficult to make because of the number of factors outside the organizations' knowledge and the lack of systematic data on other organizations' ERI programs.

Nonetheless, by using archival data creatively, organizations may be able to get closer to the mark in their estimates. For instance, in defined benefit plans, organizations can develop prediction equations on individuals' likelihood of accepting ERI based on five sets of factors: (1) historical trends in retirement by chronological age, years of service, gender, and marital status; (2) the difference between "normal" pension benefits and the compensation being offered in the ERI; (3) the value of fringe benefits and bridge employment being offered to potential retirees; (4) changes in net after-tax income if ERI is accepted; and (5) macroeconomic indices like the inflation rate, the unemployment rate, and stock market appreciation.

While those prediction equations will necessarily be imperfect, they can still help organizations make better estimates than pure guesswork. The importance of getting the right estimate the first time cannot be understated: once early retirement incentives become part of the organization's culture, it takes increasingly generous offers to yield the same rate of acceptance of ERI. For this reason, too, well-designed preretirement counseling should be included as an integral part of ERI programs.

Designing the ERI Package and Eligibility Requirements. Another major task facing HR professionals is deciding which specific inducements should be included in the ERI package. While comprehensive empirical evidence is not available on this point, the bulk of related research suggests that lump-sum payments are relatively unimportant in workers' willingness to retire early, while extended health insurance benefits, cost-of-living adjustments, and opportunities to engage in bridge employment may play larger roles than organizations realize. In short, some of the money currently spent on lump-sum payments at the front end of ERI packages might be better utilized to increase streams of earning on the back end.

Setting the parameters on eligibility for ERI is equally challenging. In defined benefit plans, traditionally organizations have offered ERI packages to older workers who are at least age 55 *or* have at least 25 years of service (or some close approximations to those numbers). The downside risk for organizations in these situations is that large numbers of relatively young employees with high years of service will accept ERI, thereby depriving the firm of talented employees in their early 50s. Organizations with defined benefit plans also risk encumbering themselves with substantial long-term pension liabilities. To guard against this risk, organizations might consider multiple hurdles for ERI eligibility; for example, employees are only eligible if they are at least age 57 *and* have at least 27 years of service. While such a strategy might decrease the number of acceptances, it also decreases the average cost associated with those acceptances.

Perceptions of Injustice. Recent research in the area of voluntary work force reductions suggests that organizations should be concerned with perceptions of injustice in how early retirement incentive programs are implemented (DeWitt, Trevino, & Mollica, 1998). In some cases, employees perceive that the ERI are not *distributively* just. That is, workers feel that the amount of money offered to some groups of employees is lucrative above and beyond what past contributions to the firm warrant. In other cases, employees perceive that the voluntary separation package is not *procedurally* just. In these circumstances, workers feel that the criteria for eligibility are not fair, that the explanations provided for the workforce reduction program are unclear or inconsistent, or that some employees are under enormous pressure to "voluntarily" exit (Greenberg, 1990).

In a recent court case in the Ninth Circuit U. S. Court of Appeals (Bins v. Exxon, No. 98–55662), an interesting issue of procedural justice was tested. The plaintiff alleged that the employer had an affirmative duty to disclose information about a proposed early retirement incentive plan to potential employees as soon as information on the ERI was available (Employee Benefit Plan Review, 1999). Obviously sensitive to concerns about procedural justice in the implementation of ERI, the court ruled:

> An employer seriously considering a proposal to offer more generous retirement or severance benefits knows that such information is material to participants who are making plans to retire. A fiduciary's fundamental duty is to protect the interests of all participants and beneficiaries, and a blanket disclosure rule appropriately requires the employer to provide information about a potential change in benefits to all employees who might be affected . . .

Extrapolated to the context of early retirement incentives, this research suggests that ERI may impact not only the behaviors and attitudes of older workers, but also the behaviors and attitudes of employees who remain behind. When remaining employees perceive that managers are being given exorbitant packages to exit, that ERI packages are inequitably distributed, or that eligibility parameters are unreasonably constrained, their own commitment to the firm suffers and their intentions to leave the firm increase. The costs associated with ERI, then, are not limited to the retirees themselves. Without some procedural safeguards, those costs can color younger employees' perceptions of how older workers in the firm are treated in general and how fairly they themselves can expect to be treated in the future.

Retirees as Contingent Employees. Finally, the present article suggests that organizations should more fully consider the potential untapped resources which older workers and early retirees represent. At a time when many organizations are trying to cut core workforces and increase the use of contingent employees, early retirees are a better-trained and more readily available alternative than many other staffing options.

Indeed, the increased availability of telecommuting technology, home offices, and flextime can be put to better use in helping early retirees wind down their careers. If the ultimate goal of bridge employment is to facilitate the transition from full-time work to full-time retirement, allowing older workers to spend increasing amounts of time at home seems to be a rational strategy during this transition period. It allows older workers a chance to gradually unwind from hectic jobs while still performing valued work activities, such as training, mentoring, and coaching their successors (Shultz, Morton, & Weckerle, 1998).

Perhaps, most critically, treating older workers respectfully and designing thoughtful early retirement options for them signals to both old and young employees that the organization has humane core values. As the management of work force size becomes increasingly dependent upon the management of older workers, discovering why and when employees decide to accept early retirement incentives has important implications for academics and practitioners alike (Feldman, 1994).

REFERENCES

Adams, G. A. (1999). Career-related variables and planned retirement age: An extension of Beehr's model. *Journal of Vocational Behavior, 55,* 221–235.

Anderson, K. H., & Burkhauser, R. V. (1985). The retirement-health nexus: A new measure for an old puzzle. *Journal of Human Resources, 20,* 315–330.

Arnold, H. J., & Feldman, D. C. (1982). A multivariate analysis of the determinants of job turnover. *Journal of Applied Psychology, 67,* 350–360.

Atchley, R. (1989). A continuity theory of aging. *Gerontologist, 29,* 183–190.

Beehr, T. A., Glazer, S., Nielson, N. L., & Farmer, S. J. (2000). Work and nonwork predictors of employees' retirement ages. *Journal of Vocational Behavior, 57,* 206–225.

Beehr, T. A., & Nielson, N. L. (1995). Descriptions of job characteristics and retirement activities during transition to retirement. *Journal of Organizational Behavior, 16,* 681–690.

Blinder, A., Gordon, R., & Wise, D. (1980). Reconsidering the disincentive effects of Social Security. *National Tax Journal, 33,* 431–422.

Burtless, G., & Moffit, R. (1985). The joint choice of retirement age and postretirement hours of work. *Journal of Labor Economics, 3,* 209–236.

Chen, C. Y. (2001). Retirement guide 2001: Everything you always wanted to know about retirement but were afraid to ask. *Fortune, 144* (3), 109–116

Clark, R. L., & McDermed, A. A. (1986). Earnings and pension compensation: The effect of eligibility. *Quarterly Journal of Economics, 101,* 341–361.

Cleveland, J. N., & Shore, L. M. (1992). Self- and supervisory perspectives on age and work attitudes and performance. *Journal of Applied Psychology, 77,* 485–503.

Colsher, P. L., Dorfman, L. T., & Wallace, R. B. (1988). Specific health conditions and work-retirement status among the elderly. *Journal of Applied Gerontology, 7,* 485–503.

Cutler, N. E. (2001). Future pensions, current financial worries, and the human wealth span. *Journal of Financial Service Professionals, 55,* 24–27.

Daniels, C. E., & Daniels, J. D. (1991). Factors affecting the decision to accept or reject a golden handshake. *Benefits Quarterly, 7,* 33–46.

DeWitt, R., Trevino, L. K., & Mollica, K. A. (1998). The influence of eligibility on employees' reactions to voluntary workforce reductions. *Journal of Management, 24,* 593–610.

Doeringer, P. B. (1990). *Bridges to retirement.* Ithaca, NY: Cornell University ILR Press.

Doerpinghaus, H. I., & Feldman, D. C. (2001). Predicting early retirement decisions in defined benefit pension plans. *Journal of Managerial Issues, 24,* 26–35.

Employee Benefit Plan Review. (1999, November). Employer had affirmative duty to disclose information about proposed early exit plan, pp. 136–138.

Erdner, R. A., & Guy, R. F. (1990). Career identification and women's attitudes towards retirement. *International Journal of Aging and Human Development, 30,* 129–139.

Feldman, D. C. (1994). The decision to retire early: A review and reconceptualization. *Academy of Management Review, 19,* 285–311.

Feldman, D. C., & Kim, S. (2000). Bridge employment during retirement: A field study of individual and organizational experiences with post-retirement employment. *Human Resource Planning, 23,* 14–25.

Feldman, D. C., & Kim, S. (1998). Early buyout offers in the context of downsizing: Empirical data from the Korean electronics industry. *International Journal of Human Resource Management, 9,* 1008–1025.

Fronstin, P. (1999). Retirement patterns and employee benefits: Do benefits matter? *Gerontologist, 39,* 37–47.

Godofsky, D. R. (1988). Early retirement pensions: Penalty or perk? *Personnel Journal, 65,* 69–73.

Gordon, R. H., & Blinder, A. S. (1980). Market wages, reservation wages, and retirement decisions. *Journal of Public Economics, 14,* 277–308.

Goudy, W. J., Powers, E. A., & Keith, P. (1975). Work and retirement: A test of attitudinal relationships. *Journal of Gerontology, 30,* 193–198.

Grant, P. B. (1991). The "open window": Special early retirement plans in transition. *Employee Benefits Journal, 16,* 10–16.

Greenberg, J. (1990). Organizational justice: Yesterday, today, and tomorrow. *Journal of Management, 16,* 399–432.

Gustman, A. L., & Steinmeier, T. L. (1991). The effects of pensions and retirement policies on retirement in higher education. *American Economic Review, 81,* 111–115.

Hanoch, G., & Honig, M. (1983). Retirement, wages, and labor supply of the elderly. *Journal of Labor Economics, 1,* 131–151.

Hansson, R. O., DeKoekkoek, P. D., Neece, W. M., & Patterson, D. W. (1997). Successful aging at work: Annual review, 1992–1996: The older worker and transitions to retirement. *Journal of Vocational Behavior, 51,* 202–233.

Hayward, M. D., Grady, W. R., Hardy, M. A., & Sommers, D. (1989). Occupational influences on retirement, disability, and death. *Demography, 26,* 393–409.

Higgins, B. (2001). Post-retirement planning takes off in new directions. *National Underwriter, 105*(32), 4–6.

Hornstein, G. A., & Wapner, S. (1985). Modes of experiencing and adapting to retirement. *International Journal of Aging and Human Development, 21,* 291–315.

Isaksson, K., & Johansson, G. (2000). Adaptation to continued work and early retirement following downsizing: Long-term effects and gender differences. *Journal of Occupational and Organizational Psychology, 73,* 241–256.

Kahn, J. (1988). Social Security, liquidity, and early retirement. *Journal of Public Economics, 35,* 97–117.

Kilty, K. M., & Behling, J. H. (1985). Predicting the early retirement intentions and attitudes of professional workers. *Journal of Gerontology, 40,* 219–227.

Kim, S., & Feldman, D. C. (2000). Working in retirement: The antecedents and consequences of bridge employment and its consequences for quality of life in retirement. *Academy of Management Journal, 39,* 367–380.

Kim, S., & Feldman, D. C. (1998). Healthy, wealthy, or wise: Predicting actual acceptances of early retirement incentives at three points in time. *Personnel Psychology, 51,* 623–642.

LaRock, S. (1999). Early retirement: A global perspective and a view of retirement in 2009. *Employee Benefit Plan Review, 54,* 51–52.

Lawrence, B. S. (1988). New wrinkles in the theory of age: Demography, norms, and performance ratings. *Academy of Management Journal, 31,* 309–337.

Leana, C. R., & Feldman, D. C. (1992). *Coping with job loss: How individuals, organizations, and communities respond to layoffs.* New York: Macmillan/Lexington Books.

Leonard, B. (2001). Despite ebbing economy, workers plan to stay the course with retirement investments. *HR Magazine, 46,* 147–149.

Lopez, J. A. (1993). Out in the cold: Many early retirees find the good deals not so good after all. *The Wall Street Journal, October 23,* B1.

Mitchell, O. S., & Fields, G. S. (1984). The economics of retirement behavior. *Journal of Labor Economics, 2,* 84–105.

Moen, P. (1996). A life course perspective on retirement, gender, and well-being. *Journal of Occupational Health Psychology, 1,* 131–144.

Richardson, V., & Kilty, K. M. (1991). Adjustment to retirement: Continuity vs. discontinuity. *International Journal of Aging and Human Development, 21,* 291–315.

Rose, C. C., & Larimore, L. K. (2001). Social Security benefit considerations in early retirement. *Journal of Financial Planning, 6,* 116–121.

Rosen, B., & Jerdee, T. H. (1989). Retirement policies: Evidence of the need for change. *Human Resource Management, 28,* 87–103.

Ruhm, C. J. (1990). Bridge jobs and partial retirement. *Journal of Labor Economics, 8,* 482–501.

Ruhm, C. J. (1989). Why older workers stop working. *Gerontologist, 29,* 294–299.

Shultz, K. S., Morton, K. R., & Weckerle, J. R. (1998). The influence of push and pull factors on voluntary and involuntary early retirees' retirement decisions and adjustment. *Journal of Vocational Behavior, 53,* 45–57.

Talaga, J. A., & Beehr, T. A. (1995). Are there gender differences in predicting retirement? *Journal of Applied Psychology, 80,* 16–28.

Taplin, P. T. (1989). Spencer survey of preretirement counseling: Ongoing, early retirement programs described. *Employee Benefits Plan Review, 44,* 14–17.

Weckerle, J. R., & Shultz, K. S. (1999). Influences on the bridge employment decision among older USA workers. *Journal of Occupational and Organizational Psychology, 72,* 317–329.

5

Extending Work Lives: Are Current Approaches Tools or Talismans?

Martin M. Greller and Linda K. Stroh

The purpose of this essay discussion is to encourage some appropriate doubt and concern, for it is quite possible we have placed ourselves at risk through overconfidence about what we do and do not know about fostering work life continuity. Our position is that we know rather less than we think we do about what is required if we are to intervene to extend working lives. If true, this means we are woefully ill-prepared to cope with demographic issues we have long been able to anticipate.

State of the Art

There is a veritable cottage industry turning out articles and even books that bemoan the unaddressed problems of an aging population. These mostly are cautionary tales outlining the likely consequences of traditional employment and retirement practices applied to a proportionately older population (Greller & Nee, 1989; Johnston & Packer, 1987; Sunoo, 1997; Commonwealth Fund, 1993). The foreseeable results are nasty indeed: loss of skills, decreased productivity, reduced supply increasing the cost of labor (so, ironically employers will be paying relatively more and receiving relatively less), decreased contributions to Social Security in the face of increasing draws up on it, and increasing taxes on those still in the workforce to support those who have left it.

Yet, these predictions are hardly new (Atchley, 1976; Streib & Schneider, 1971; Torrey & Kingkade, 1990; Wattenberg, 1987). The phenomenon is evident. It is slow and inexorable in its approach. How is it possible to crash into the adverse effects that have been so abundantly forewarned without taking some evasive action? Consider this statement, published in 2000, "As members of the baby boom begin to retire and collect Social Security, pension, and other benefits, many changes to both the public and private retirement systems may occur, such as raising the ages of eligibility, creating more flexible pension plans, and introducing phased retirement' " (Purcell, 2000, pg. 19). It is not that there is anything wrong with Purcell's observations or expectations. The problem is that they are still being described prospectively in 2000, long after similar ideas had been floated for discussion. Indeed, this suggests retirements (and the associated labor shortages, Social Security shortfalls, and so on) will have to occur before a serious effort is made to respond. A recent report by the Government Accounting Office about the government's own concerns as an employer suggested, "To address potentially serious implications of the aging of the U.S. labor force and avoid possibly acute occupational labor shortages in the future, the relevant government agencies should work together to identify sound policies to extend the work-life of older Americans . . ." (General Accounting Office (GAO), 2001, p. 34). Again, the notion is prospective—action is needed, but it will be in the future.

The future is now. In one study (Weckerle & Shultz, 1999) of 2,771 U.S. workers over 50, 42% were considering early retirement, 11% continuing work, 29% bridge employment in the same job, and 18% bridge employment in a different job. In other words, barring some change, only 11% are thinking in terms of continuing full-time regular employment. These workers may not be able to implement their preferred career solution. Some who want a particular form of bridge employment may discover that it is not available. However, their fallback position is not necessarily continued full-time employment; they might choose retirement over full-time work. These numbers suggest that the preference for retirement is almost four times that for continued employment. Moreover, with the expectation or desire to leave one's present job (60% in this sample), is it likely that these people will maintain their work skills at a level that would be attractive to potential employers? Are they reducing their human capital (Simpson, Greller, & Stroh, 2002)?

One explanation for the seeming passivity in the face of a challenge with serious consequences is the belief that we already understand what to do. Indeed, if we do understand how to extend working lives and it is only a matter of flipping a socioeconomic switch, there may be no reason to do so prematurely. Why consume resources until the challenge is upon us? But, do we really know what to do?

Most of our literature examines why people retire. Often this is studied using people who have already retired. Direct linear predictors are sought. Frequently, we rely on retiree re-constructions of the last parts of their working lives. Most of the workplace events or interventions that we examine are ones which are associated with early retirement. So, much of what we do know is based on the factors that accelerate retirement. This implies that if we just stopped doing the things that make them retire, they would stop retiring so soon. Even if one were confident of the reasons for retirement, it does not mean they are reversible any more than known causes of physiological aging are necessarily reversible.

To better consider whether we have adequate tools for extending work life some of the more prominent programs suggested for doing so will be examined. The mental models which underlie thinking about these interventions will then be considered.

Intervention Models

There are several approaches that have been put forward as ways to extend working lives; phased retirement, training older workers, social security adjustments, and work ability. Each of these will be discussed. Phased retirement has become a relatively fashionable approach recently and is being widely mentioned in the popular business press. Training, or perhaps more accurately, retraining, older workers has always played a role in extending careers. Social Security interventions are the ones most closely linked to economic thinking and are one type of intervention that is already in play. Work ability is a European approach to addressing the forces that lead to premature career endings.

PHASED RETIREMENT

Phased retirement is really part of a broader array of flexible work arrangements (e.g., job sharing, telecommuting, mommy track) that have been used to try to retain workers (Graig & Paganelli, 2000). Such flexibility was used to help younger workers achieve a level of work—family balance that would permit them to remain in the workforce. Flexibility has been used as a tool to recruit already retired workers into part-time or contingent employment. As phased retirement essentially means working for fewer hours during the year, the logic is that it is better to work fewer hours than none at all. It defers retirement in the sense that retirement is nonparticipation in the work force (Purcell, 2000). There are a considerable number of people occupying such roles. Frequency of part-time employment among those over 50 is increasing (Weckerle & Shultz, 1999) so we know "partial retirement" is feasible.

The argument in favor of something like phased retirement is that it so obviously meets employer and employee needs (Hutchens, 2001). On the employee side, there are presumably some people who do retire who would not do so if they had the opportunity to reduce hours, limit demands, and avoid some of the more onerous elements of their current jobs (Hurd & McGarry, 1993). This is supported by the behavior of the older self-employed who tend to retire later, but gradually reduce their work commitments (Quinn, Burkhauser, & Myers, 1990).

Phased retirement is consistent with worker expectations. According to an *Employee Benefit Research Institute* report, 25% of those currently "retired" work part-time, and 67% of current workers expect that they will do so (U.S. Department of Labor, 2000). Phased retirement programs have the added advantage that they already exist. They are not just something that could be done; they are something that is being done. However, for the most part, they are designed to encourage early retirement. That is, they make retirement seem more appealing and thereby induce people who would otherwise remain in the work force full-time to start some form of retirement (albeit partial) sooner, not later. If one uses an Internet search engine to look up "phased retirement," early retirement programs for colleges and universities will clutter the screen.

If phased retirement has been much used in academic settings what is the effect? Berry, Hammons, and Denny (2001) found that early retirement was more attractive to community college faculty than phased retirement; however, phased retirement in conjunction with new employment opportunities could be attractive. Both phased and early retirement packages accelerate the departure of experienced faculty. The same effect was found with University of North Carolina system faculty (Ghent, Allen, & Clark, 2001). (See Feldman & Kim, 2000 for further discussions of early faculty retirement).

Early thinking on phased or flexible retirement envisioned it as a tool that could be used to guide the less productive and less satisfied workers out of work, while offering a range of work continuity options (Ford & Fottler, 1985). Henretta (1994) discussed three types of bridges associated with early retirement: state sponsored programs geared to remove older workers so as to create work opportunities for younger workers, company sponsored incentives for exit, and individual adaptations to labor market forces.

Certainly, it should give us pause that this tool, now lionized as the hope for retaining older workers, has been so successfully used as a mechanism for fostering *early* retirement. This does not mean that it cannot be part of a program of work life continuity. But, it might justify asking for strong proof of the utility of the approach in accomplishing an outcome the exact opposite of that which it usually achieves.

Part of the problem may be definitional. There are different descriptions of what constitutes retirement. Advocates of phased retirement tend to define "retirement" as no longer participating in paid work (Purcell, 2000). The phasing comes from the fact that one is working, but at less intensity (e.g., part-time or seasonal). One could be receiving a full pension, or not. One might be in one's original job, or not. One could even work for a different employer.

Despite the fact that surveys report more companies considering or using phased retirement (Duff, 1999), it is difficult finding companies that offer phased retirement to help their employees ease into retirement for the purpose of keeping them on the job longer (Reves, 2000). This may be because phased retirement is often a tool employers use to address very specific needs. So, when we see success stories of retention through phased retirement they may be like the example of a 44-year-old executive who is tiring of work and whose employer needs to keep him in place until a successor can be found and trained (Kirk, Downey, Duckett, & Woody, 2000). Or, we hear about programs such as that at Aerospace Corporation that allow early retirement (as early as age 55) with the opportunity to work part-time or on a consulting basis. Success in retaining services is indicated by the fact that some people continue to participate in the program into their 70s and 80s (Hirschman, 2001). Such career continuity is impressive, but we do not know what proportion of the services Aerospace Corporation wanted to retain were actually retained. Does phased retirement work as a human resource planning strategy? Did Aerospace Corporation cause people who would otherwise have retired to extend their working lives, or did they cause a large number of people to retire sooner with a small subset continuing to work part-time? Were the people retained a substantial portion of the ones the company wanted to retain? Without answers to such questions, we do not know whether phased retirement programs result in more or fewer people working, or more or fewer total working hours. Thus, we should not formulate policy that suggests we have a magic bullet for extending careers.

Certainly, in a highly targeted program there are ways to retain specific people a company cannot afford to lose. In a Watson Wyatt survey of 16 firms that reported using phased retirement as a tool for retention, typically the people involved were already eligible for retirement. So, the companies hired these people back after retirement in part-time or consulting roles (Purcell, 2000). In many cases these arrangements seem to be idiosyncratic or ad hoc arrangements rather than systemic policies. Hutchens (2001) notes that most surveys addressing phased retirement are not representative of all employers, and answers to the questions often leave us unclear as to whether the options are offered to all employees. If the patterns remain similar to those found by Barth, McNaughton, and Rizzi's (1993) research, a large number of companies may do some things that are consistent with phased retirement (i.e., 70% hired back some retirees), while not having a broad-based policy to encourage or manage such activities (20%). Most companies do not make phased retirement available to all employees, and such opportunities are more frequent in human service and educational enterprises (Watson Wyatt Worldwide, 1999).

Employers are not public services. Their purpose is not to effect social change. Employment decisions are appropriately made to further the organization's goals. If that can be achieved by hiring back a few people on an ad hoc basis, then that is entirely appropriate. What is distressing is that most available reports are like hunting stories:

people brag about the successes. We do not have any reliable information about the failures. To understand that, we would need to know something about the population originally targeted for retention. What proportion of those targeted were retained? Were there distinct characteristics describing those who did, versus those who did not, respond to the offer? What we know is that if phased retirement is offered, some people will take the company up on the offer.

We should not be too quick to assume that those who take the offer are doing so to achieve their ambition of extending a career. Recall that only 11% of those over 50 said that was their goal. The remaining 89% were thinking in terms of some sort of reduction in work (Weckerle & Shultz, 1999). Is it not likely that a phased retirement program would entice those who want to leave sooner to do so in half measure?

Much of the current discussion about phased retirement involves discussions of pension reform (U.S. Department of Labor, 2000). Often the rules of defined benefit pensions discourage continued work. Such programs promise workers pension payments based on a formula, usually the average salary over the last few years of work multiplied by a fraction which increases with years of service. These programs typically prohibit drawing benefits while still employed in a firm participating in the plan. Part-time or reduced employment would reduce final average earnings and produce a corresponding downward adjustment to one's pension. Arrangements in which the individual surrenders employee status result in no further seniority being accrued, thus capping the percent of final average salary to which the individual would be entitled. This has led to some review of the way plan documents are written and of the regulations governing them.

Others have looked at the pattern of events and surmised that the real effect of phased retirement may be to reduce the aggregate pension costs to employers and incidentally reduce the benefits received by older workers. Those targeted by phased retirement programs are typically employees in their 50s, a time when people accrue the greatest benefits in an defined benefit system—because their added years of employment and prospects of increased final average salary work multiplicatively to increase pension benefits (Walsh, 2001). This is of relatively little consequence if the sole objective is selective retention of employees already eligible for full retirement. But there are far

·broader consequences for the well-being of those induced to withdraw from the plan years before they would be eligible for full benefits. From this perspective, phased retirement may be viewed as just another way of turning veteran employees into a contingent workforce, while recapturing 'surplus' from the pension plan. (Note: "Surplus" can be recaptured from a defined benefit pension fund, because there are statutory requirements compelling an employer to fund such programs based on actuarial estimates of future obligations. If the employer reduces the expected future obligations, the funds already in the plan may exceed expected future requirements, in which case the company could suspend contributions to the plan.)

Even a less jaundiced view cannot help but notice the connection between defined benefit plans and phased retirement. In defined contribution systems (i.e., one in which the employer contributes a specific sum each year, but the benefit varies based on the investment performance of these funds) veteran employees are typically fully vested. They have beneficial ownership of the assets regardless of whether they quit, work, or retire. Under such plans the employer's major tool for retention is the nature of the work and compensation offered. There is little an employer can do to alter access to defined contribution pensions. As defined contribution plans replace defined benefit plans—a well established pattern—it is likely phased retirement programs will have to take on a new look. The resources required to motivate continued participation will not be available from reworking actuarial assumptions in a defined benefit plan. Either incentives charged against current earnings will have to be offered or changes in the nature of the work to better meet older employees' needs will have to be made.

TRAINING

While most recognize that older workers have significant firm-specific human capital, many question whether older workers keep pace with the changing nature of the workplace by obtaining ongoing training (Schaie & Schooler, 1998). Training has been a concern with regard to work life continuity because older workers have traditionally been viewed as not participating adequately in training, thus reducing their value in the market and, in turn, making redundancy more likely and re-employment more difficult to secure (Booth, 1993; Far-ber, 1996; Franzis, Gittleman, & Joyce, 1998; Rix, 1996). Indeed, retraining can play a role in increasing the job opportunities and re-ducing the time out of work for displaced older workers (Wolf, Lon-don, Casey, & Pufahl, 1995).

While there is much stereotypical thinking about training older workers (along the lines of old dogs and new tricks) the truth is that most older workers are quite capable of learning new skills. In a well controlled experiment, Charness, Kelley, Bosman, and Mottram (2001) found that while it took older workers slightly longer to learn entirely new keyboarding skills, there was little difference in final perfor-mance. Much of the differences could be explained by differences in experience. If older workers receive training, they do benefit.

So, why don't older workers receive training? Traditional eco-nomic thinking argued that it was more expensive to train older work-ers and there was an inadequate period during which to recoup the expense (Andrasani & Daymont, 1987). Yet, these results are not borne out by recent experience. Older workers are participating in adult education programs and higher education in ever increasing numbers (Institute for Higher Education Policy, 1996; Tucket & Sargant, 1996). Indeed, there is reason to believe that traditional research underesti-mated the prevalence of career development activities of older work-ers by looking primarily at on-the-job training programs (Simpson, Greller, & Stroh, 2002.)

This focuses attention on a significant point of vulnerability in older workers' training—what happens on the job. If training opportu-nities are not available for one's present job, it preordains that work life continuity will have to be outside one's current employment. Fail-ures to provide older workers training at work may be a function of supervisor behavior and embedded ageism (Committee for Economic Development (CED), 1999). However, it may also reflect the self-doubts and concerns of the older worker, some of whom are appre-hensive about their abilities to succeed through training, whether this means mastering the material or, having learned it, securing advan-tage on the job from that training (Mauer, 2001).

External training programs certainly can be beneficial for older workers, particularly if they provide clearly relevant job skills. This is probably best evidenced in computer related training, where there are consistent success stories (Lodge, 2001). The European Union is even funding computer training of people over 40 to ease skills shortage in IT related areas, not simply as a tool for encouraging employment of older workers.

SOCIAL SECURITY

One definition of work life continuity relies on whether or not pension benefits are being drawn (Purcell, 2000). While it is certainly possible to draw a pension and perform compensated work, whether one draws on benefits is a crucial question for those tasked with maintaining the solvency of the pension plan. Indeed, one of the reasons for caring about whether people continue to work and do so at a similar rate of pay is that this helps increase the resources in pension plans (including Social Security).

Of course, a social security system can preserve its assets by changing its rules and delaying the age at which people become eligible for full benefits. While this may preserve assets, unless it induces people to continue their working lives, it does not increase the pool of assets. There is also the question of whether such a change is politically feasible in a government sponsored program.

As far as using Social Security as a tool for fostering career extension, the mechanism most discussed is changing the rules of eligibility, essentially making it too costly for people to retire. To put it harshly, if they're hungry enough they will work. And, indeed, there is evidence that this is so. Uchitelle (2001) describes the pattern of increasing employment by women over 60 who are forced to continue or find employment due to economic necessity. Much of this is a by-product of divorce which has left them without pension resources. So, inadequate resources can lead to work life continuity—although the qualitative aspect of this might lead to questions about its desirability.

A form of this strategy is currently being used since the age of eligibility for full benefits under the U.S. Social Security scheme is scheduled to be rolled back starting with those people born in the early part of the baby boom. In one sense this is quite mild. Earlier retirement reduces but does not eliminate benefits. By continuing to work one enhances the monthly benefits after retirement. The adjustments also take some note of the extended life expectancy of today's retirees.

Moving back the date of full benefit eligibility may not have the expected effect. Many people now do not wait for full eligibility before retiring. Through the 1990s there has been a slight increase in the proportion of men taking Social Security benefits before age 65, rising until about 75% of men were doing so (Purcell, 2000). On the other hand, the fact that one is receiving a pension does not necessarily mean he or she has stopped working. For example, in 1999 about 20% of men ages 55–64 received some sort of pension, but of these one-third continued to work (Purcell, 2000). Note this only addresses those who have elected to receive a pension. Certainly, there are more people who are eligible to receive such benefits but elect not to, allowing them to accrue greater value while they continue to work.

We must be careful not to fall into the trap of believing that people will do precisely what they are paid to do. In the case of pension programs the incentives are usually subtle—but not always. When the health service in the United Kingdom sought to alleviate spot shortages of medical staff by offering significant bonuses, many medical staff emphatically rejected sizable incentives. So, Social Security may be able to slow disbursements by changing eligibility, but there is no guarantee it will significantly extend careers.

WORK ABILITY

"Work ability" is a new concept for many Americans, but it is a well established tool in Europe. Its origins are found with Juhani Ilmarinen and the Finnish Institute of Occupational Health (Ilmarinen, 1999). As with other institutes committed to the preservation of workplace health and well-being, Ilmarinen and his colleagues were interested in predictors that could give early warning of potential occupational health problems. This would allow well-targeted interventions to avoid work-related injuries and illnesses.

Frequently disabilities lead older workers to earlier career endings than would otherwise have been the case. If there were a way to predict who was at greatest risk of a disabling injury it might be possible to intervene and allow the individual's career to be extended. This is what the Work Ability Index does. It is used diagnostically within organizations. Possible interventions include individual health screenings, social psychological interventions, and work reassignment.

Over several decades this has provided the basis for a range of demonstrably successful programs in European companies (Ilmarinen, 1999). Such programs have kept people in the work force who might otherwise have exited due to illness or injury.

When American industrial psychologists look at the Work Ability Index they may see a mix of work satisfaction, higher order need motivation, and positive affectivity. While the advocates of the Index are not overly fond of this interpretation, it does make sense that people with positive attitudes who are motivated by work would be eager to recover from accidents so that they could return to work. This opens up a line of inquiry. Just how motivating do people find their work in late career? Most of the discussion so far seems to treat the quality of work as a constant. Could it be that people are leaving their jobs early because their work is unfulfilling?

McEvoy and Blahna (2001) note that older workers may be substantially less satisfied than cross-sectional research suggests. Their dissatisfaction is focused on a lack of respect for achievements from supervisors, a lack of autonomy to use their experience to do the job right, and a lack of opportunity for reward. These conditions, if addressed, might lead them to extend their careers.

MENTAL MODELS

One of the problems with existing approaches to work life continuity is that they rely on relatively simple, linear models—not just statistical models, but approaches to problem solving. It is very much as though we are trying to understand ballet through still photography. A photo of a dancer in mid-air certainly is dramatic and allows detailed study of muscles and position, but it also makes it appear that dancers can suspend themselves in mid-air. A more dynamic approach is needed.

ELDER WORK VERSUS WORK LIFE CONTINUITY

What is the goal of fostering work life continuity? If people over 60 were compelled to work a few hours at something unpleasant and dispiriting would we have achieved anything of merit? Yet, this would seem to be allowed by the criteria of "continued work participation" or "not drawing pension or Social Security payments". But, would it not be more appropriate to create choices that afford individuals the opportunity to do things that are meaningful and lucrative?

One taxonomy divides the types of work older people can undertake into four categories. (1) *Career continued,* meaning that the work performed follows naturally upon the work done previously in one's career. While the hours and responsibilities may be scaled back, they need not be. Because of the human capital the individual may bring to this situation, it has the greatest economical potential; (2) *Retired,* meaning no longer engaging in compensated work; (3) *Postretirement workers,* who are employed but at something quite different from the work done during the major portion of their careers. The choice to work is positive, although the reasons may have more to do with socializing, diversion, or an intrinsic interest in the work itself; (4) *The unretired* who want to retire, but economic necessity dictates they must work. For them, the work is mostly instrumental (Greller, 1989).

While there may be a better grounded taxonomy, this does sketch out the reasons that may lie behind work choices in late career. The currently popular interventions seem to be relatively insensitive to the differences portrayed in this taxonomy. Any intervention should at least consider its impact on individuals and their ability to make personally valuable career choices. Such consideration would evidence a more humane understanding of the individual, and recognition of the different motivations for work and retirement (e.g., Mor-Barak, 1995) would also be more likely to avoid failed or unintended consequences of intervention policies.

LABOR ECONOMICS

For years labor economics was the field that took the study of late career seriously. The resulting literature has left a legacy affecting the way we look at employment of older workers. A number of factors that would justify decreasing investment in older workers received an imprint of scientific validity. While it was the *beliefs* (not any objective fact) that older workers were too expensive, benefited too little from training, or had such short careers before them that resulted in employers not training or developing them (Greller & Simpson, 1999), the research tended to justify those beliefs and reinforce their use in the future.

The other influence on the way we think is embedded in the methodology (a methodology common to much of the social sciences). The effort to explain changes in the employment of older workers typically examined a number of variables and assessed the independent linear relationship of the variables with the employment outcome of interest. If a system of variables were at work, this approach would identify the most proximal variables as the best predictors and eliminate other variables even though they may determine the level of the ones identified.

ATTRIBUTIONAL ISSUES ASSOCIATED WITH LABOR POOL DEPARTURE

If statistical identification is a legacy from labor economics, the behavioral literature on the decision to retire introduces the problem of individual attribution. This is in part a function of retrospective research in which retirees (or those who rejected an early retirement offer) are asked to describe the factors that influenced them at the time. People who see their retirement as voluntary have happier retirements. Those who report being most influenced by the attractions of retirement (i.e., "pull factors") are more likely to see their retirements as voluntary (e.g., Shultz, Morton, & Weckerle, 1998). But, how much of this is a rewriting of history to allow one to move forward with a positive attitude? Two years into retirement, what purpose is there to emphasize the force that pushed one from work? Typically, there are a number of reasons that played a role in the decision to retire (Henretta, Chan, & O'Rand, 1992). And, it is not just a matter of time shading one's memory. Is there any reason to believe that people have accurate insights into the causes of their decisions? Certainly, this is not always in the case in other decision contexts. Retirees' attributions for their own retirement decisions can be subject to a wide range of influences.

SOCIAL AGING

The notion that aging and careers are substantially influenced by social factors makes sense. Transitions are times of uncertainty, and uncertainty inclines people to look towards others to reduce the ambiguity. Many of the pressures on older workers come from organizational policies, which are the result of social constructions. Day-to-day interaction with others influences the roles we assume. To the extent others' interactions with us are influenced by their perception of our age, it would be reasonable to expect age to influence roles including work roles.

Despite the reasonableness of the proposition, much of the research has looked at something other than social influence or norms. Indeed, the dominant paradigm as developed by Neugarten, Moore, and Lowe (1965) essentially establishes that there are shared beliefs about people of different ages. Lawrence carried this forward in terms of career timetables, at what age we might expect to see a person in a given organization role (Lawrence, 1988). It is not that these are unimportant, just incomplete. It is not clear when or how these expectations are communicated. While the beliefs may be widely shared, are there sanctions if one violates the norm? How is age deviance addressed? If we are to understand the role of age norms in late career, there is more that needs to be understood about the communication, enforcement, and mutual influence associated with these norms.

The way in which we think about late career and the extension of work life tends to be by discipline, driven by specific disciplinary questions. They are good questions. They speak to the issues of the various fields that touch on extending working life. But, it is not clear whether such work in isolation can generate answers. Efforts to address late career as the focal topic results in reviews of literature in fields as disparate as sociology, medicine, policy studies, psychology, human resources, and economics (e.g., Greller & Simpson, 1999; Greller & Stroh, 1995; Griffith, 1997; Mor-Barak, 2000). Those seeking to address the topic as a practical policy problem find themselves calling for action in such widely separated areas as attitude toward older workers, company practices, tax law, and social policy (e.g., CED, 1999; Department for Education and Employment, 2000; GAO, 2001; Ilmarinen, 1999).

The concern is not the number of potentially relevant variables. Multiple direct influences can be understood and used in an additive manner to address the issue. That would allow things to proceed pretty much as they have. The real reason for concern is that the variables may be related in a systemic, nonlinear way with effects appearing with different variables and having different latencies. While this is intellectually interesting, it also makes for difficulty in teasing out causes and effects. It argues for studying the variables over time with special attention to variables that may exert a mutually reinforcing effect. It also gives warning that efforts to make change, to flick that sociopolitical switch, may prove more difficult than anticipated.

Need for an Integrative Approach

What are the practical implications of all this? For one, we ought to be less confident that we know how to manage the timing of career endings for any significant portion of the work force. If asked what the nation could do to extend the average age of retirement by three years we would be hard pressed to provide much feasible advice. If we added that the task should be accomplished by affording more individual choice, we would be still harder pressed.

There are, however, some trends that may be helpful as we try to understand this process. The concept of careers, and also of career endings, is changing. While people are not any different than they have been through the centuries, their expectations are changing. That said, it is important to note the fallacy in projecting the characteristics of future cohorts based on research of prior cohorts.

Research on turnover in general suggests that it may be more useful to look at an opportunity model than a model based on dissatisfaction—people moving toward a new situation, not merely away from their current situation (Lee & Mauer, 1997). While it would be fair to say that this is inherent in the discussion of push versus pull factors associated with retirement, there has, perhaps, been a tendency to view these external factors as acting upon individuals who are primarily reactive rather than proactive.

The notion of evolving and more individualized psychological contracts (Rousseau, 1995), particularly in the framework of careers that span organizations and take account of nonwork as well as work roles (Arthur & Rousseau, 1996), opens the door to a different view of late careers. Even if this has not been descriptive of older workers in the past, to the extent boundarylessness has played a role in the careers of those who are now entering the retirement cohort, it is reasonable to expect boundarylessness to continue playing a role even as people contemplate retirement. This at least offers a grounded model in which to integrate the complex set of influences that shape the contract (or series of contracts) associated with career ending. It also emphasizes the importance of the individual in shaping the outcome and influencing the conditions of work.

The focus on the work arrangements in an extended career may address some of the issues identified with current programs. The major incentives are apt to be the quality of work conditions, supervision, and rewards available from continued employment. This is important if most of the workers are covered by defined contribution pension plans, which make it difficult to provide financial incentives rooted in pension payments. Either some sort of "signing" bonus (or "continuity" bonus) would have to be offered, or incentives for performance may replace adjustments to pensions. It also means that the issues of respecting and valuing the older worker would need to be addressed (McEvoy & Blahna, 2001). The decision to adopt new positive roles in late career may be understood as a process similar to that studied in the work—family balance literature where alternative roles are evaluated encompassing both work and personal life (Greller & Stroh, 2002, in press).

Somewhat less certain is the role to be played by systems dynamic models. These nonlinear models have been attracting some interest in the behavioral sciences in recent years, given their underlying assumption of mutual dependence and the recognition that change is constant. These nonlinear models are underused as explanations for changing behavior (Lichtenstein, 2000). We suspect these dynamic models might make significant contributions to the study of both older workers and the contributions older workers can continue to make in the workplace, society, and their families. Whether these models provide useful tools is still an open question. Certainly, nonlinear models that allow tracing the effects of multiple variables that exert influence on each other over time would seem to have much to offer the study of late career. While it is too early to assess the effects of such models, there is certainly significant potential to shape both research and the way we think about the unfolding of late career.

REFERENCES

Andrasani, P., & Daymont, T. (1987). Age changes in productivity and earnings among managers and professionals. In S. H. Sandell (Ed.), *The problem isn't age: Work and older Americans* (pp. 52—70). New York: Praeger Publishers.

Arthur, M. B., & Rousseau, D. M. (1996). The boundaryless career as a new employment principle. In M. B. Arthur & D. M. Rousseau (Eds.), *The boundaryless career* (pp. 3—20). New York: Oxford University Press.

Atchley, R. C. (1976). *The sociology of retirement.* New York: John Wiley and Sons.

Barth, M. C., McNaughton, W., & Rizzi, P. (1993). Corporations and the aging workforce. In P. H. Mirvis (Ed.), *Building the competitive workforce: Investing in human capital for corporate success* (pp. 156—200). New York: Wiley.

Berry, L. H., Hammons, J. O., & Denny, G. S. (2001). Faculty retirement turnover in community colleges: A real or imagined problem. *Community College Journal of Research and Practice, 25,* 123—136.

Booth, A. L. (1993). Private sector training and graduate earnings. *The Review of Economics and Statistics, 75,* 164—170.

Charness, N., Kelley, C. L., Bosman, A. A., & Mottram, M. (2001). Word-processing training and retraining: Effects of adult age, experience, and interface. *Psychology and Aging, 16,* 110—127.

Committee for Economic Development (CED) (1999). *New opportunities for older workers.* New York: Author.

Commonwealth Fund. (1993). The untapped resource. The final report of the Americans over 55 at work program. New York: Author.

Department For Education and Employment (2000). *Factors affecting employment.* Nottingham, England: DfEE Publications.

Duff, S. (1999). Polls: More plan sponsors tapping the phased retirement approach. *Employee Benefits News, 13*(8), 50—51.

Farber, H. (1996). The changing face of job loss in the United States, 1981–1993. *NBER Working Paper,* No. 5596. Cambridge, Massachusetts: National Bureau of Economic Research.

Feldman, D. C., & Kim, S. (2000). Bridge employment during retirement: A field study of individual and organizational experiences with post-retirement employment. *Human Resource Planning, 23,* 14–25.

Ford, R. C., & Fottler, M,. D. (1985). Flexible retirement: Slowing early retirement of productive older workers. *Human Resource Planning, 8,* 147–156.

Franzis, H., Gittleman, M., & Joyce, M. (1998). *Determinants of training: An analysis using both employee and employer characteristics.* Washington, D. C.: Bureau of Labor Statistics.

General Accounting Office (GAO) (2001). *Older workers: Demographic trends pose challenges for employers and workers,* GAO-02–85. Washington, D. C.: U.S. Government Printing Office

Ghent, L. S., Allen, S. G., & Clark, R. L. (2001). The impact of a new phased retirement option on faculty retirement decisions. *Research on Aging, 23,* 671–693.

Graig, L. A., & Paganelli, V. (2000). Phased retirement: Reshaping the end of work. *Compensation and Benefits Management, 16,* 1–9.

Greller, M. M. (1989). Making the aging workforce a strategic advantage in your organization. *Perspectives in human resources: 41ˢᵗ national conference proceedings* (pp. 5–13). Alexandria, Virginia: American Society for Personnel Administration.

Greller, M. M., & Nee, D. M. (1989). *From baby boom to baby bust: How business can meet the demographic challenge.* Reading, Massachusetts: Addison Wesley.

Greller, M. M., & Stroh, L. K. (1995). Careers in mid-life and beyond: A fallow field in need of sustenance. *Journal of Vocational Behavior, 47,* 232–247.

Greller, M. M., & Stroh, L. K. (2002, April). What's age got to do with it? A work—family balance approach to late career. In K. S. Shultz & T. J. Rothausen (Co-Chairs), *What's age got to do with it? Revising mid- and late- career research models.* Symposium conducted at the Society for Industrial and Organizational. Psychology meeting, Toronto, Ontario.

Greller, M. M., & Stroh, L. K. (in press). A work balance approach to research on late career. In M. Kumashiro (Ed.), *Aging and Work* (pp. 146–154). London: Taylor & Francis.

Greller, M. M., & Simpson, P. (1999). In search of late career: A review of contemporary social science research applicable to the understanding of late career. *Human Resource Management Review, 9,* 309–347.

Griffith, A. (1997). Aging, health, and productivity: A challenge for the new millennium. *Work and Stress, 11,* 197–214.

Henretta, J. C. (1994). Recent trends in retirement. *Reviews in Clinical Gerontology. 4,* 71–81.

Henretta, J. C., Chan, C. G., & O'Rand, A. M. (1992). Retirement reasons vs. retirement process: Examining the reasons for retirement typology. *Journal of Gerontology: Social Sciences, 47,* 51–57.

Hirschman, C. (2001). Exit strategies. *HR Magazine, 46*(12), 52—57.

Hurd, M. D., & McGarry, K. (1993). *The relationship between job characteristics and retirement,* Report # 4558. Cambridge, Massachusetts: National Bureau of Economic Research.

Hutchens, R. M. (2001, March). Employer surveys, employer policies, and future demand for older workers. *Roundtable on the Demand for Older Workers.* Washington, D. C.: Retirement Research Consortium, Brookings Institution.

Ilmarinen, J. (1999). *Ageing workers in the European Union—Status and promotion of work ability, employability and employment.* Helsinki, Finland: Finnish Institute of Occupational Health.

Institute for Higher Education Policy (1996). *Life after forty: A portrait of today's and tomorrow's post-secondary students.* Washington, D. C.: Author.

Johnston, W. B., & Packer, A. H. (1987). *Work force 2000: Work and workers for the 21ˢᵗ century.* Indianapolis: Hudson Institute.

Kirk, J. J., Downey, B., Duckett, S., & Woody, C. (2000). Name your career intervention. *Journal of Workplace Learning, 12,* 205–216.

Lawrence, B. S. (1988). New wrinkles on the theory of age: Demography, norms, and performance ratings. *Academy of Management Journal, 31,* 309–337.

Lee, T. W., & Mauer, S. D. (1997). The retention of knowledge workers with the unfolding model of voluntary turnover. *Human Resource Management Review, 7,* 247–275.

Lichtenstein, B. B. M. (2000). Emergence as a process of self-organizing: New assumptions and insights from the study of nonlinear dynamic systems. *Journal of Organizational Change Management, 13,* 526–544.

Lodge, M. (2001, Feb. 12). Green Thumb training program teaches valuable computer skills to older workers. *Information Week, 824* (Feb. 12), 116–122.

Mauer, T. J. (2001). Career relevant learning and development, worker age, and beliefs about self-efficacy for development. *Journal of Management, 27,* 123–140.

McEvoy, G. M., & Blahna, M. J. (2001). Engagement or disengagement? Older workers and the looming labor shortage. *Business Horizons, 44* (5), 46–52.

Mor-Barak, M. E. (1995). The meaning of work for older adults seeking employment: The generativity factor. *International Journal of Aging & Human Development, 41,* 325–344.

Mor-Barak, M. E. (2000). The inclusive workplace: An ecosystems approach to diversity management. *Social Work, 45,* 339–352.

Neugarten, B. L., Moore, J. W., & Lowe, J. C. (1965). Age norms, age constraints, and age socialization. *American Journal of Sociology, 70,* 710–717.

Purcell, P. J. (2000). Older workers: Employment and retirement trends. *Monthly Labor Review, 123,* 19–30.

Quinn, J. F., Burkhauser, R. V., & Meyers, D. A. (1990). *Passing the torch: The influence of economic incentives on work and retirement.* Kalamazoo, Michigan: W. E. Upjohn Institute for Employment Research.

Reves, K. (2000). Unphased retirement. *Modern Maturity, 43* (5), 101–102.

Rix, S. E. (1996). Investing in the future: What role for older worker training? In W. H. Crown (Ed.), *Handbook on employment and the elderly* (pp. 304–323). Westport, Connecticut: Greenwood Press.

Rousseau, D. M. (1995). *Psychological contracts in organizations: Understanding written and unwritten agreements.* Thousand Oaks, California: Sage Publications.

Schaie, K.W., & Schooler, C. (1998). *Impact of work on older adults.* New York: Springer Publishing.

Simpson, P., Greller, M. M., & Stroh, L. K. (2002). Variations in human capital investment by age. *Journal of Vocational Behavior, 61,* 109–138.

Shultz, K. S., Morton, K. R., & Weckerle, J. R. (1998). The influence of push and pull factors on voluntary and involuntary early retirees' retirement decisions and adjustment. *Journal of Vocational Behavior, 53,* 45–57.

Streib, G. F., & Schneider, C. J. (1971). *Retirement in American society: Impact and process.* Ithaca, New York: Cornell University Press.

Sunoo, B. P. (1997, December). Millions may retire. *Workforce, 76,* 48–50.

Torrey, B. B., & Kingkade, W. N. (1990). Population dynamics in the United States and Soviet Union. *Science, 247,* 1548–1552.

Tuckett, A., & Sargant, N. (1996). Headline findings on lifelong learning from the NIACE/Gallup Survey 1996. *Adult Learning, 7,* 219–223.

Uchitelle, L. (2001, June 26). Lacking Pensions, Older Divorced Women Remain at Work. *The New York Times,* 1A

U.S. Department of Labor (2000, November 14). Working Group Report on Phased Retirement. Available at: http://www.dol.gov/pwba/adcoun/phasedr1.htm

Walsh, M. W. (2001, April 15). No time to put your feet up as retirement comes in stages. Available at: http://www.globalaging.org/elderrights/us/notime.htm

Watson Wyatt Worldwide (1999). *Phased retirement: Reshaping the end of work.* Bethesda, Maryland: Watson Wyatt.

Wattenberg, B. J. (1987). *The birth dearth: What happens when people in free countries don't have enough babies.* New York: Pharos Books.

Weckerle, J. R., & Shultz, K. (1999). Influence of the bridge employment decisions among older USA workers. *Journal of Occupational and Organizational Psychology, 72,* 317–329.

Wolf, G., London, M., Casey, J., & Pufahl, J. (1995). Career experiences and motivation as predictors of training behaviors and outcomes for displaced engineers. *Journal of Vocational Behavior, 47,* 316–331.

6

The Economics of the Retirement Decision

Charles B. Hatcher

The aging of the world's population, perhaps the most significant demographic event in recorded history, will bring a long list of new challenges. Perhaps at the top of this list is how the economy will manage the dramatic changes in the labor market, which will undoubtedly occur as the 1945–1960 birth cohort, known as the baby boom, begins its collective exit from paid work. This mass exodus from the labor force, which will most likely occur between the years 2010–2020, will bring with it a major shift in the age and experience profile of the labor force. A second challenge will be to determine how resources will be set aside to support this cohort. Even today's society spends considerable amounts of resources, particularly health care resources, on individuals nearing the end of life. Once the baby boom reaches these older ages, difficult questions regarding the extent to which the relatively small number of working Americans can support the elderly will need to be addressed.

One major parameter that is extremely relevant to any of these discussions is commonly referred to as retirement. Understanding when and why individuals decide to exit the labor force, collect a public or private pension, or enter a nursing home, is of vital importance to understanding the constraints society faces in the next 50 years. The objective of this paper is to provide a framework for understanding the economics of the retirement decision. Thinking about retirement in this way acknowledges that retirement, at least in part, involves the allocation of scarce resources towards competing uses. The major (but not only) resource in question here is the *time* of the prospective retiree; whether or not to put one's time to use in paid work (for wages or salary, plus any fringe benefits, monetary and nonmonetary) or to use it in fruitful pursuits outside of work, commonly referred to as leisure (i.e., "free time"). In industrialized countries, paid work is most often a decision made in concert with an employer (workers need employers to hire them), so consideration must be paid to the relationship between workers and their employing organizations, and the motives of each. By exploring this relationship in detail in the first section of this chapter, we will also be exploring the early motives for why traditional retirement—a period of full-time work, followed by an often mandatory retirement date, followed by a period of no work at all—existed in the first place.

Anyone planning for their own retirement can tell you that it is not only a question of when to stop working, but also when to spend one's money resources. The way in which a prospective retiree (and his or her family) spends and saves income is inextricably linked to when he or she will retire. The second section of this chapter will consider the problem of retirement almost exclusively as a consumption decision, given one's date of retirement (i.e., holding constant what we learned in the earlier section about work decisions). By taking the employee-employer relationship out of the equation, we accomplish two goals. The first is that we make it much easier to focus on consumption by simplifying the story. The second is that we create a model much more compatible with the late twentieth-early twenty-first century labor market, one where employees have much more freedom over (and responsibility for) their impending retirements.

The third section of this chapter examines the way economists have attempted to put the two resource goals (when to work, and when to save or spend) into more comprehensive models of retirement decision making (after all, aren't these decisions made jointly?). There is a mountain of evidence suggesting that individuals, to some extent, act as rational economic beings—they act in their best interests subject to their constraints. The highlights of this evidence will be reviewed in this third section. The fourth section presents some of the questions left unanswered by the economic literature regarding how people financially plan for retirement.

Retirement as an Employer-Driven Institution

There is evidence that the productivity of the average worker in a sedentary occupation begins to decline at around the age of sixty. All workers experience a depreciation of their skills and training, and at the same time add to that skill set through on the job training (Murphy and Welch, 1990). It is, for most of us, right around the age of sixty when the former begins to overtake the latter, and our value to our employer begins to decline. The extent of this phenomenon is certainly worker-specific, and using this information to make an inference about any specific worker would be inappropriate (stereotyping). Nevertheless, this sort of decline has produced the kind of social norm that has led to the phenomenon of retirement, which has existed at least since the end of World War II. As a result, males tend to exit from the labor force at or around this age.

This general phenomenon is depicted in Figure 6.1, which illustrates the tendency for men to exit the labor force as they age in general, but especially in their early sixties. For women, this trend also exists, but in tandem with the trend towards higher rates of labor force participation for women of all ages since World War II.

I will not comment so much on the existence of social norms and their influence on individual behavior, because I believe that is ground that my colleagues have covered in other chapters of this tome. Nevertheless, the average effects of age on worker productivity might indeed cause an employer to construct age-specific employment policies that encourage or force workers to retire. Large employers, for whom supervision costs are high and individual productivity is difficult to measure, might actually find value in the kind of age stereotyping alluded to above. Lazear (1979) illustrates a model where mandatory retirement is the result of an implicit contract where workers are paid less when young in exchange for more pay when older. The effect of such a policy, where workers "post bond" by surrendering wages early in their career and getting it back later, is threefold: first, it encourages workers to stay with one firm. This can be quite

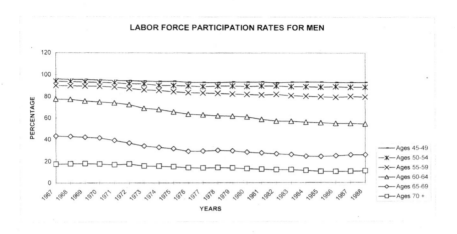

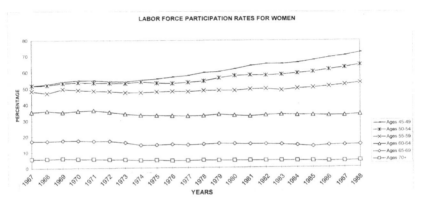

Figure 6.1 Labor force participation rates by age and gender, 1967–1998.

valuable to a firm that has worker tasks that are specific to that firm and come with high training costs. Second, this sort of policy increases the costs to a worker of shirking job responsibilities—being terminated results not only in losing one's job, but also the bond you have posted. Therefore, these types of policies are also attractive to employers that have high worker supervisory costs. Third, it means that firms are paying workers more as they age, even if their productivity is decreasing. Therefore, mandatory retirement is required to "force" the worker into retiring at R (mand). That is, the date they would

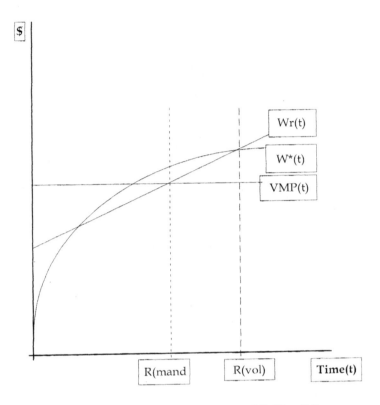

VMP(t)=Productivity, Wr(t)=value of leisure, W*(t)=Wage Policy

Figure 6.2 Lazear's (1970) model.

retire if they received merely their marginal productivity throughout their life.

Lazear's model can be illustrated with the use of graphical analysis. Imagine that a firm strikes up a contract with a worker such as the one in Figure 6.2. VMP(t) is the worker's Value of the Marginal Product, the value of the worker's productivity to her firm at time t . The worker at time zero has agreed to accept a wage stream W*(t), which pays her less than what she is worth when young, in exchange for more than she is worth when old. For her to prefer this contract to one that pays her VMP for all time periods, the following two conditions must hold:

$$\int_0^T \left(VMP(t) - W*(t)\right)R(t)\partial t > 0 \tag{1}$$

$$\int_0^T \left(W*(t) - Wr(t)\right)R(t)\partial t > 0 \tag{2}$$

where Wr(t) is the individual's opportunity cost of time at t, and R(t) is the present value of one dollar delivered at time t (future dollars must be discounted to the present to account for interest). Wr(t) is also called the worker's *reservation wage*. It is the smallest wage at which she is willing to sacrifice her leisure time by working. Equation (1) is the condition that the lifetime value of the marginal product must exceed lifetime wages for the firm to enter into the stream W*(t) (over the long term, she has to be worth at least as much to the firm, in terms of her productivity, as the firm will pay) and Equation (2) is the condition that the present value of lifetime wages exceed the present value of reservation wages for the worker to enter into W*(t) (over the long term, the pay must be worth the worker's value of her time). Presumably, the motivation for this type of contract comes from the firm, because a contract such as this yields more productivity from the worker than one that pays her period-by-period VMP (deferred compensation decreases "shirking"). For any contract to be efficient for everyone involved, it must end at R(mand), where the worker's reservation wage hits VMP; otherwise, the firm would be getting less productivity from the worker than she could get elsewhere. If the worker worked after R(mand), her time is actually more valuable to her in the form of leisure than it is to the firm in the form of productivity. However, she would stay because her *pay* is greater than the value of her leisure time. This makes such a contract inferior to one where the worker is terminated at R(mand). This was essentially Lazear's argument for why mandatory retirement existed in the first place.

Lazear contends, therefore, that it is not necessarily a worker's declining productivity that results in mandatory retirements. It is actually the nature of implicit long-term labor contracts, which result in workers who, by the nature of the contract, are paid more than they are worth at older ages. Actually, one alternative to mandatory retirement would be employers attaching pay declines or wage freezes to their "Lazear-ian" wage policy. In other words, why doesn't the firm simply engage in a wage policy like the one in Figure 6.2 *until* R(mand), followed by an offer for the worker to continue thereafter at her lower VMP? This would mean that after R(mand), the worker would not have much incentive to stay working at the particular firm, since there is no longer any sort of long-term implicit contract. The exception would be if there is a great deal of firm-specific training and skills accumulated over the career that make her VMP at the specific firm higher than her VMP anywhere else. Nevertheless, this could explain the phenomenon of "career retirement," where a worker retires from a career job and enters a lower-paying occupation after that career. It can also explain the "bridge employment" phenomenon discussed in other chapters of this book.

In the current environment, the sort of policy described above, where an employer's wage policy is to terminate employment (or offer lower wages) at a prescribed age, would undoubtedly be branded a violation of the Age Discrimination in Employment Act (ADEA), which outlaws employment practices that discriminate on the basis of age. The passing of the original version of the ADEA in 1965 subsequently led to the elimination of nearly all corporate and public mandatory retirement policies that were in effect before its existence, and has led to the implementation of a wide range of employer retirement incentives. The employer-sponsored pension, originally designed merely to provide income to a past worker in his retirement, is now often used to encourage workers to retire at specific ages (Fields & Mitchell, 1984; Hutchens, 1986; Ippolito, 1994).

Retirement as an Employee-Driven Institution

Even in the post-ADEA environment, withdrawal from the labor force in old age is still the norm, suggested by the graphs in Figure 6.1. Certainly there was at least some incentive, pre-ADEA, not only for the employer, but also for the employee, to leave his job and retire. Although there is substantial evidence for the veracity Lazear's model, the fact that employees accepted pre-ADEA age policies (and continue to exit the labor force in old age post-ADEA) is circumstantial evidence that the retirement phenomenon is at least partly a voluntary decision for many Americans. If this is the case, an individual choice model, where one compares the costs and benefits of retiring at a point in time, is the appropriate lens in which to view the retirement decision.

The voluntary retirement decision is not simply a problem of comparing the cost and benefits of spending another year at work, but also a problem of financing consumption while not working. In this way, it is very much a corollary to the life-cycle model of saving (Ando & Modigliani, 1963). According to this model, the consumer's goal is to take into account one's lifetime resources ex-ante and spend them across one's lifetime. Well-functioning capital markets would then make the particular timing of earnings irrelevant to when they were actually spent. This means that the wealth at which a person voluntarily retires should correspond to a "permanent income measure" which should be, as Ando and Modigliani reason, "based on considerations relating to the life cycle of income and consumption 'needs' of households" (Ando & Modigliani, 1963, p. 55). The phrase "permanent income" comes from similar work on "permanent income" and the relationship between income and consumption undertaken by Friedman (1957).

Ando and Modigliani were somewhat ambiguous about what they meant by permanent or "expected" income, but a thoroughly explicit example offered by Zorn and Gerner (1986) is shown here. In this example, full wealth at time t is expressed in terms of the present value of initial assets at time t and of future earnings.

$$FW_t = NW_t + \sum_{i=t}^{t+T} \left(\frac{Income_i}{(1+r)^i} \right) \tag{3}$$

where

FW_t = full wealth at time t
NW_t = net worth in time t
$Income_i$ = income in time i
r = interest rate
T = life expectancy.

Equation 3 states that one's resources at a given time include what you have now and the present value of future income entitlements. "Net worth" represents all assets and liabilities for which the individual has now. The summation to the right of net worth in Equation 3 is all future income which will occur at some time past t. The point is that what also goes into "full wealth" are future claims which are contingent upon working (which would include wages in those years, pension accruals, etc.).

Permanent income, then, would be defined as follows:

$$PI_t = FW_t \left(\frac{r}{1 - \left(\frac{1}{(1 + r)^{T+1}} \right)} \right) \tag{4}$$

where PI_t = Permanent Income at time t. The part of Equation 4 to the right of full wealth is simply an annuity factor, which calculates how much per-period income full wealth would afford, given a length of life T. In Ando and Modigliani's notation, this was simply called $\Omega(t)$. Ando & Modigliani's hypothesis was that consumption at time t did not depend upon income at time t but on permanent income at time t. If you believe the permanent income hypothesis, then you must also believe that for someone who voluntarily exits the labor force, full wealth at time t = net worth at time t (because retiring implies no "income" at any time > t). This implies that net worth at time t must equal permanent income at time t, divided by the annuity factor Ω. The retirement decision framed in this manner is one where the worker is constantly observing the income level which their net worth could afford them over their lifetime.

Figure 6.3 illustrates an individual with income Y from time t = 0, ... ,R (R is the time of retirement); and planned consumption C from t = 0, ... ,T (T is the time of death).

Although at present we take these consumption and work plans as given, note that for the plans to be feasible, interest rates have to be such that the present value of savings from 0 to R (marked as area A) must be equal to the present value of "antisavings" from time R to T (marked as area B). This example is stylized in that the life course is deterministic (T= time of death), work life is continuous and stops discretely at R, and consumption and income are constant. The present value of savings equal to the present value of antisavings/borrowing is a feasibility condition. The retirement age, R and lifetime consump-

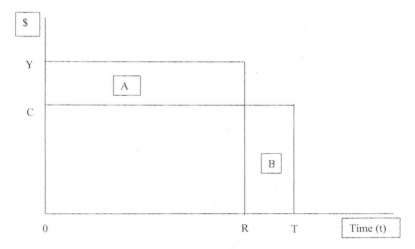

Figure 6.3 A stylized lifetime labor-consumption plan.

tion level, C are presumably solutions to a lifetime maximization problem, subject to the feasibility condition above.

Figure 6.4 shows how per-period wealth, that is, the amount of future per-period consumption that the individual's net worth can finance, accumulates over time. During the period [0,R], per-period wealth is increasing exponentially because of two factors—compound interest (your wealth earns interest) and a decreasing life expectancy (as you get older, the amount per-period that your net worth can afford you until death goes up, because there are fewer periods to finance). Since just enough was saved by point R to guarantee $C per period of consumption, and since this is exactly how much is being consumed, per-period wealth stays at C during the period [R, T]. Even in a world where T is not known with certainty, annuities can conceivably guarantee a flat wealth and consumption path over retirement.

This stylized example assumes that it is somehow better to take your leisure in "bunches," in this case, at the end of your life. One reason why it may be advantageous to work in one continuous stretch is that the decline in productivity discussed earlier may occur at a greater rate when skills are not utilized. This would mean that it would be optimal for a worker to have one continuous career, as

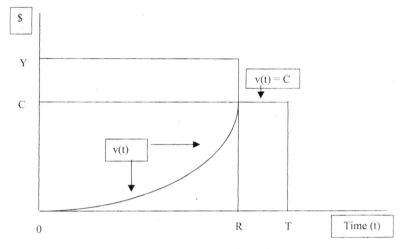

Figure 6.4 A stylized wealth-accumulation plan.

opposed to sporadic periods of work. In any event, using this frame-work implies that retirement is a consumption financing issue arising from the fact that leisure is more valuable in old age relative to younger ages.

Major assumptions of this model are the existence of a borrowing and lending rate, r, no bequest motive, and perfect certainty about wages, R, and T. Furthermore, it requires that individuals, at least with respect to their retirement decisions, are able to compare the costs and benefits of different work and retirement alternatives in present value. There is some evidence that this isn't always the case. Reimers and Honig (1996) find that many individuals are "myopic" with respect to their decisions about Social Security, indicating that either workers are extremely risk averse or face borrowing constraints. Jianakoplos, Menchik, and Irvine (1996) further find evidence of aux-iliary savings for the purposes of insurance (in a world where length of life is uncertain) and intergenerational transfers.

Determinants of Retirement Age

Employer and employee-driven theories aside, why do people actually retire? Wide ranges of studies have presented results from surveys where the respondent was asked to give the reason for retirement. Parnes and Nestel (1981) allege, however, that retrospectively reported reasons for retirement are suspect because often respondents are not able to answer objectively due to the personal and sometimes even traumatic nature of the event. Nevertheless, there are four main reasons people give for why they retired. First, is that they were forced to retire. Even though this is no longer legal, many people still feel forced out of their job, and hence give this reason. Second, is health reasons. Third, is feeling discouraged by the labor market. Fourth, is voluntary.

Parnes and Less (1985) found that fewer than 5% of retired men age 60–74 in 1981 were removed from their jobs involuntarily. Poor health accounted for about one-third of the retirees' decisions, and a liberal estimate of discouraged workers would be about 10%. Sammartino (1987) finds that the importance of health as a reason for retirement is probably overstated, since many of those who give this answer actually find part-time work after retirement. This is one of the advantages of using a self-reported measure: one gets some sense of what people actually do after they claim that they are retired.

An alternative strategy to researching self-reports would be to develop a model for understanding why people retire, and then observing whether or not people's behavior is consistent with the model. This is how the majority of studies looked at here assess the determinants of retirement. The elimination of mandatory retirement policies has motivated much research on the economics of the voluntary retirement decision. Models of consumer/worker choice lend themselves particularly to a discussion of the costs and benefits of retiring. This literature started as very simple, static (one–period) model of work choice that asked the question "why would someone choose not to work?" Quinn (1977) showed that poor health and sufficient assets both reduce the age of retiring and that job characteristics, independent of wages, explain much of the variation in retirement ages. Boskin (1977) used a one-period model to show that increases in Social Security entitlements should cause retirement ages to occur closer to the age of eligibility. Possibly the main result that comes out of these static models is that high asset levels induce retirement.

The next generation of economic literature on retirement was in a framework where the worker compared the costs and benefits (in terms of wages and pension accrual) of staying at work for another year with those of retiring (Burkhauser, 1979; Fields & Mitchell, 1984). Kotlikoff and Wise (1989) use this type of framework to understand the various incentives inherent in a pension scheme, and in a way confirm Hutchens' (1986) contention that pensions are being used as a way to get people to retire earlier. Nevertheless, the main result coming from these models is that, in general, higher wages lead to later retirement and richer pensions lead to earlier retirement. The latest in retirement literature has been dynamic-programming models where individuals are assumed to look across their entire expected life and make their decisions in the context of everything they know (or don't know) about the future.

Approximately 10% of people who retire say that they did so because they were "discouraged." This suggests that the labor market (employers) affected their decision. Straka (1992) concludes that the options facing older workers might not be sufficient to justify the kinds of labor-supply driven models above. Hutchens (1991) further hypothesizes that firms with high fixed costs of training would rationally prefer younger workers for older ones, and finds some support for this hypothesis, consistent with Lazear's model above. Therefore, there is significant evidence that retirement might, in many cases, mean unemployment.

In addition to purely empirical models of retirement decision making, there is another subset of literature that starts with a theoretical model of the retirement decision and attempts to estimate either the model's implications for retirement behavior, or the model directly. In the majority of this literature, it is first assumed that an individual attempts to maximize his satisfaction (utility) subject to a constraint. The utility "function" usually comprises consumption (expenditures) and leisure, or both. The constraint is usually an income constraint (you cannot have more consumption than you have money to spend) or a time constraint (there are only so many hours in a day, month, year, etc.), or some combination of the two Often, solving this rudimentary mathematical exercise (maximize the utility function subject to its constraints) yields testable hypotheses regarding human (in this case, human retirement) behavior.

Individual Static Model. Consider a Cobb-Douglas Utility specification:

$$U(C, L) = C^\alpha L^{1-\alpha} \qquad (5)$$

where C is consumption, L is Leisure, and a is a utility parameter. Equation 5 says that the more goods and services an individual consumes (C refers to the consumption of goods and services), and the more leisure an individual consumes (L), the happier is the individual (U). The utility parameter tells us how good consumption is relative to leisure (the higher the utility parameter, the higher the relative importance of goods and services relative to leisure). The individual maximizes this function subject to the constraint PC = W(T-L) + V, where W is the market wage, P is the price of consumption, T is total time available, and V is unearned income. The budget constraint, in plain English, says that the amount you spend on goods and services (PC) must be equal to the amount you received working (W(T-L))—time is either spent in leisure or working so ((T-L) is time spent working) plus any savings you had to begin with (V).

The mathematical solution to this optimization problem gives the following demand functions for leisure and consumption:

$$L^* = \frac{(WT + V)(1 - \alpha)}{W} \qquad (6)$$

$$C^* = \frac{(WT + V)\alpha}{P} \qquad (7)$$

This is essentially the way in which the early literature on the retirement decision framed the worker's problem. The model proposed by Fields and Mitchell (1984), for example, outlined the decision as one between the "Present Value of Future Asset Income (Consumption)" and "Expected Length of Retirement (Leisure)."

Three main hypotheses with respect to the determinants of retirement result from the "leisure demand" Equation 6. First, the number of hours you choose to supply to the labor force may be positively related to your wage (a positively sloped labor supply curve). Using the Fields and Mitchell analogy, this would imply that people with higher wages should demand a shorter expected length of retirement, and therefore retire later, or at an older age. While this result is unique to this particular utility specification, it has nevertheless been verified empirically by Fields and Mitchell, and originally by Burkhauser (1979). This empirical result has been prevalent in most of the retirement literature: *ceteris paribus,* people with higher wages will retire later. Another theoretical result from Equation 6 is that the higher the unearned income level V, the higher leisure demand. In a real-world setting, unearned income is not endogenous but based on past labor force participation (and hence wages). Nevertheless, the positive correlation between assets and probability of retiring was first confirmed by Boskin (1977), who was particularly interested in wealth from the Social Security program. It has since been confirmed by Fields and Mitchell (1984) and Kotlikoff and Wise (1989), both of whom take this question a step further by trying to understand how year-by-year increases in pension wealth (which are a function of employer pension policy, and therefore exogenous) influence the decision to retire. Endogeneity issues aside, this is perhaps the most universally accepted empirical fact regarding retirement: people with more assets retire earlier.

The last hypothesis that comes from this simple model is that someone with high α, i.e. someone for whom consumption plays a more important role in utility relative to leisure, will work more or retire later. Although Fields and Mitchell (1984) estimate a model which estimates an aggregate α for their sample, the analogous empirical results that are driven from this hypothesis have come from the literature on job characteristics and retirement, the rationale being that individuals who "enjoy leisure more" would tend to be those in more strenuous jobs or jobs that require less education, controlling for wages. Quinn (1977) was the first to identify the strong relationship between job characteristics and retirement, claiming that occupational status (professional, clerical, production worker, etc.) explains most of the explainable variance in retirement ages. Chirikos and Nestel (1991) find that men in sedentary work are more likely than men in physically demanding jobs to retire at a later age. This is an important economic result, mainly because they also find that "projections of the fractions of workers in physically strenuous versus sedentary job categories that are likely to encounter physical difficulty in staying in the labor force do not differ greatly." The implication of this result is that what one does for a living, and the degree to which one "enjoys" the job, impact one's probability of retirement, perhaps more than any other individual observable characteristics.

The following Stone Geary specification:

$$U(C,L) = (C - \gamma_1)^{\alpha} (L - \gamma_2)^{1-\alpha} \qquad (8)$$

yields results similar to Cobb-Douglas with respect to wages, un-earned income, and the utility parameter α. However, it can also be shown, using the logic above, that someone with a higher $\gamma 1$ would retire later and that someone with a higher $\gamma 2$ would retire earlier, *ceteris paribus*. $\gamma 1$ may be interpreted as a constraint on consumption, or subsistence level of consumption. Even though we are in a one-person setting, the addition of a dependent to the decision maker (a child or an elderly parent, for example) may be interpreted as an increase in $\gamma 1$, suggesting that people with dependents retire later than they would if they did not have dependents. $\gamma 2$, or subsistence levels of leisure, would probably be influenced most greatly by one's health status, suggesting that those in poor health would retire earlier, which has been established empirically by, among others, Sammartino (1987), and Fields and Mitchell (1984).

Two-Person Static Model. Unfortunately for the above model, assets are usually pooled within the household. The above models also fail to account for the impact of another autonomous (or otherwise) decision maker within a household. Hurd (1990), for example, estimates that for every year difference in the age of a couple, their retirement ages differ by about .25 (zero would indicate that couples are retiring at the exact same time, 1 would indicate that the differences correspond exactly to age, and hence, no retirement correlation among couples). This would suggest that we need to incorporate more than one decision maker into the model. As Hurd suggests, of particular importance is the household that consists of two married decision makers with shared wealth but individual labor force participation. The easiest way to incorporate two people into the model is to assume that individuals treat their spouse's income as unearned. It will also be assumed that the spouse's hours worked is in response to the reference person's labor supply as well. So in this way the two person model is a form of a static bargaining model, where equilibrium is achieved when the individual's labor supply (given their spouse's labor supply) corresponds to the spouse's labor supply (given that of the individual). This model more formally looks like the following maximization problem in Cobb-Douglas form:

$$\text{Max } U_O(C, L_O) = C^\alpha L_O^{\beta o} \text{ subject to } PC = W_O(T-L_O) + W_S(T-L_S) + V$$

where o (own) subscripts denote the characteristics of the utility maximizer, s denotes the characteristics of the spouse. Ls is determined simultaneously from the analogous maximization decision:

$$\text{Max } U_S(C, L_S) = C^\alpha L_S^{\beta s} \text{ subject to } PC = W_S(T-L_S) + W_O(T-L_O) + V$$

Leisure demanded by the first individual (own) can be solved by first solving for his/her spouse's leisure demand, taking the own's leisure as given, then plugging that equation into the first constraint under Ls. This gives you the Nash equilibrium leisure demand curve for the first individual (Nash, 1950). It can be shown that an exogenous increase in a spouse's wage is analogous to an increase in the unearned income of the individual in question, which should induce retirement. Recall that we should expect this change to delay retirement of the spouse because of the wage change. This would mean that, *ceteris paribus,* couples close in age or life expectancy with large wage differences should also have large differences in the time at which they retire. Similar hypotheses with respect to the other characteristics of the spouse can be generated. Whatever impacts the labor supply of the spouse should impact the unearned income of the individual in question, thereby impacting their retirement decision.

Household Production. The results from the previous model are based upon the assumption that the two individuals' quality of leisure time is unaffected by whether their spouse is working or not. One way to incorporate the concept of complementary leisure time between spouses would be to create a family utility model, where the family gets utility from consumption and the two spouse's leisure. This could be taken a step further by differentiating leisure between leisure time spent alone and leisure time spent by the couple together (for an example of this type of model, see Bryant & Wang (1990)). The utility function would look something like:

$$U(C, L_O, L_S, S) = C^{\alpha} L_O{}^{\beta_O} L_S{}^{\beta_\sigma} S^{\theta}$$

where C is consumption which costs prices p, L_O is leisure time of the first individual as before, which costs the own wage, L_S is the leisure time of the spouse, which costs the spouse's wage, and S = shared time, which costs the sum of both individuals' wage, as shown by the following budget constraint:

$$PC = W_O T + W_S T - W_O L_O - W_S L_S - W_O S - W_S S$$

If there exists sufficient amounts of utility from shared time, then the negative relationship between an individual's retirement age and his/her spouse's wage rate need not hold. Christensen and Gupta (1994) provide some evidence that there is some complementarity in leisure between couples, particularly with respect to the retirement decision. This phenomenon presumably pulls the retirement dates of spouses closer together, independent of wages, as Hurd (1990) showed empirically.

Dynamic Models of Labor Supply. Static models above can be used to make analogies regarding retirement and life cycle labor supply only if you are willing to make rigid assumptions regarding the indivisibility of hours worked and the irrevocability of the retirement decision. For example, Fields and Mitchell's "Years of Retirement" conceptualization of leisure implicitly assumes that you either work, or you don't work (rigid hours). It also assumes that once you "don't work," you do not go back to work in the future. The last section offered some reasons for why this *may* be (productivity probably decreases more when you are not working). However, the increasing popularity of partial retirement and "bridge jobs"—jobs taken between a career job and full retirement—suggest that these assumptions may be, in some cases, *too* rigid. Dynamic models of labor supply simply break the entire life cycle into distinct periods of time. One of the first examples is MaCurdy (1981), who uses the following "dynamic" utility function, where time is represented by discrete periods:

$$\sum_{t=0}^{T}\left(\frac{1}{\left(1+\rho^{i}\right)}\right)U[C(t),L(t)] \qquad (9)$$

Here, the t subscripts denote time, $C(t)$ is consumption in period t, $L(t)$ is Leisure in period t, and ρ is a time preference parameter. $U[C(t), L(t)]$ can be any of the static utility functions, including those from above. The budget constraint for the maximization problem is the following:

$$A(0) + \sum_{t=0}^{T} R(t)N(t)W(t) = \sum_{t=0}^{T} R(t)C(t) \qquad (10)$$

where $R(t)$ is a present value factor, $N(t)$ is the hours worked in period t (total time in the period less $L(t)$), and $W(t)$ is the wage in period t.

Although these types of models tend to have lots of data requirements and do not yield fundamentally different hypotheses than their more simple static-model counterparts, one major advantage of using dynamic modeling has been estimating utility parameters for the purposes of simulation. Gordon and Blinder (1980) conclude, after estimating age-specific marginal rates of substitution between leisure and consumption, that the increase in this parameter is the major factor leading to retirement (as opposed to decreasing market opportunities). Gustman and Steinmeier (1986) simulations account for peaks in labor force exit between 62 and 65 that are consistent with what we find in the U.S. Stock and Wise (1989) and Rust (1989), find that increasing uncertainty about the future leads to later retirement, which is a result that previous models were not capable of investigating.

The two main points from the economic literature on retirement have been the following. First, pension and Social Security rights should be interpreted as assets accrued to households. Second, the changes in those assets over time that result in postponing retirement should be interpreted as compensation. The changes in these accruals, particularly the negative accruals after normal ages at retirement, significantly influence the decision to retire.

Opportunities for Future Research

It is without question that, to some extent, individuals act as rational economic agents with respect to their impending retirements. Many of the questions left unresolved in the retirement economics literature focus on apparent inconsistencies between theoretical models of retirement behavior and actual retirement experiences of American workers. That the collective members of the baby-boom generation (Americans born between 1945 and 1960) are not saving enough to generate retirement consumption at their current level of consumption is well-documented (Mitchell & Moore, 1998; Montalto, Yuh, & Hanna, 1998). What is not known, however, is whether undersaving is due primarily to uninformed financial planning or personal preference. In other words, are boomers undersaving because they do not understand how much they need to retire, are they are choosing to live with less consumption in retirement, do they expect to save more in the future, or some combination of the three?

The answer to these questions depends on a deeper understanding of the role consumption plays in the retirement planning process. The Life-Cycle Income Hypothesis (Ando & Modigliani, 1963) implies that the asset levels of an individual should peak at her retirement date. Before retirement, she is saving for it, and after retirement, she is spending her assets down to zero at the time of death. However, there is an abundance of evidence that individuals do not tend to spend down their assets until well into their retirement years. (Menchik & David, 1983; Kurz, 1984; Jianakoplos, Menchik, & Irvine, 1996). One possible explanation for this is that a retiree's wealth is often made up of housing wealth, which they might not be able to spend down without moving (Venti & Wise, 1990). Another reason is that the effect of expected inflation on an optimal retirement plan is fairly straightforward: you need to save more if you expect prices to go up during retirement. This means that one would expect the nominal dollar value of consumption to be lower during one's first year of retirement than one's last, even if the actual *level* of goods and services consumed stayed constant. Yet another reason why we might find the elderly not spending down their assets is for protection—from a bad economy, poor investment performance, or an unexpectedly long life (Leland 1968). Last, an individual may have a bequest motive, either for altruistic reasons (Becker, 1974), or strategic reasons (Yagi & Maki, 1994).

Essentially, there are two seemingly contradictory stories: the current generation of older workers seem not to be saving enough as the Life Cycle Income Hypothesis says they should, while their parents seem to save more. What accounts for the difference? Do the parents of the baby boom engage in more precautionary savings? Are they simply better financial planners? Perhaps the older generation is planning large future bequests (in effect, the older generation is saving for the younger)? Whatever the answers, these anomalies to the Life Cycle model hinder the links between any theoretical model and empirical facts with respect to individual savings behavior. To reconcile them, we need to better understand the relationship between how much a person saves and what they intend to consume.

REFERENCES

Ando, A., & Modigliani, F. (1963). The 'life-cycle' hypothesis of saving: Aggregate implications and tests. *American Economic Review, 5,* 55–84.

Becker, G. S. (1974). A theory of social interactions. *Journal of Political Economy, 82,* 1063–1093.

Boskin, M. (1977). Social security and retirement decisions. *Economic Inquiry, 15,* 1–25.

Bryant, W. K., & Wang, Y. (1990). Time together, time apart: An analysis of wives' solitary time and shared time with spouses. *Lifestyles: Family and Economic Issues, 11,* 89–119.

Burkhauser, R. (1979). The pension acceptance decision of older workers. *Journal of Human Resources, 14,* 63–75.

Chirikos, T., & Nestel, G. (1991). Occupational differences in the ability of men to delay retirement. *Journal of Human Resources, 26,* 1–26.

Christensen, B., & Gupta, N. (1994). A dynamic programming model of the retirement decisions of married couples. Unpublished manuscript.

Fields, G., & Mitchell, O. (1984). *Retirement, pensions and social security.* Cambridge, Massachusetts: The MIT Press.

Gordon, R. H., & Blinder, A. S. (1980). Market wages, reservation wages, and retirement decisions. *Journal of Public Economics, 14,* 277–308.

Gustman, A., & Steinmeier, T. (1986). A structural retirement model. *Econometrica, 54,* 555–584.

Hurd, M. (1990). The joint retirement decisions of husbands and wives. In D. A. Wise, (Ed.), *Issues in the economics of aging* (pp. 231–254). Chicago: University of Chicago Press.

Hutchens, R. (1986). Delayed payment contracts and a firm's propensity to hire older workers. *Journal of Labor Economics, 4,* 439–457.

Hutchens, R. (1991). *Job opportunities, job search, and the older worker.* Paper presented at the "New Jobs for an Aging Workforce" conference, Cornell University, Ithaca, New York.

Ippolito, R. (1994). Pensions and indenture premium. *Journal of Human Resources, 29,* 795–812.

Jianakoplos, N. A., Menchik, P. L., & Irvine, F. O. (1996). Saving behavior of older households: Rate-of-return, precautionary, and inheritance effects. *Economic Letters, 50,* 111–120.

Kotlikoff, L., & Wise, D. (1989). *The wage carrot and the pension stick.* Kalamazoo, Michigan: W. E. Upjohn Institute on Employment Research.

Kurz, M. (1984). Capital accumulation and characteristics of private intergenerational transfers. *Economics, 51,* 1–22.

Lazear, E. (1979). Why is there mandatory retirement? *Journal of Political Economy, 87,* 1261–1264.

Leland, H. E. (1968). Savings under uncertainty: The precautionary demand for savings. *Quarterly Journal of Economics, 82,* 465–473.

MaCurdy, T. (1981). An empirical model of labor supply in a life-cycle setting. *Journal of Political Economy, 89,* 1059–1085.

Menchik, P., & David, M. (1983). Income distribution, lifetime savings, and bequests. *American Economic Review, 73,* 672–690.

Mitchell, O. S., & Moore, J. F. (1998). Can Americans afford to retire? New evidence on retirement saving adequacy. *Journal of Risk and Insurance, 65,* 371–401.

Montalto, C. P., Yuh, Y., & Hanna, S. (2000). Determinants of planned retirement age. *Financial Services Review, 9*(1), 1–15.

Murphy, K. M., & Welch, F. (1990). Empirical age-earnings profiles. *Journal of Labor Economics, 8,* 202–229.

Nash, J. (1950). Equilibrium points in n-person games. *Proceedings of the National Academy of Sciences, 36,* 48–49.

Parnes, H. S. & Less, L. J. (1985). The volume and pattern of retirements, 1961–1981. In H. S. Parnes, J. E. Crowley, R. J. Haurin, L. J. Less, W. R. Morgan, F. L. Mott, & G. Nestel (Eds.), *Retirement among American men.* Lexington, Massachusetts: Lexington Books.

Parnes, H. S. & Nestel, G. (1981). The retirement experience. In H. S. Parnes (Ed.), *Work and retirement: A longitudinal study of men.* Cambridge, Massachusetts: MIT.

Quinn, J. F. (1977). Microeconomic determinants of early retirement. *Journal of Human Resources, 12,* 329–347.

Reimers, C., & Honig, M. (1996). Responses to Social Security by men and women. *Journal of Human Resources, 31,* 357–382.

Rust, J. (1989). A dynamic programming model of retirement behavior. In D. Wise (Ed.), *The economics of aging* (pp. 359–398). Chicago: University of Chicago Press.

Sammartino, F. (1987). The effect of health on retirement. *Social Security Bulletin, 50,* 31–47.

Stock, J., & Wise, D. (1990). Pensions, the option value of work, and retirement. *Econometrica, 58,* 1151–1180.

Straka, J. W. (1992). *The demand for older workers: The neglected side of a labor market.* Studies in Income Distribution, Paper No. 15, Office of Research and Statistics, Social Security Administration. Washington, D. C.: U.S. Department of Health and Human Services.

Venti, S. F., & Wise, D. A. (1990). But they don't want to reduce housing equity. In D. Wise (Ed.), *Issues in the economics of aging* (pp. 13–32). Chicago: University of Chicago Press.

Yagi, T., & Maki, H. (1994). Costs of care and bequests. In T. Tachibanaki (Ed.), *Savings and bequests* (pp. 39–62). Ann Arbor, Michigan: The University of Michigan Press.

Zorn, P., & Gerner, J. (1986). Incorporating the permanent income hypothesis in applied demand analysis: Advantages and implications. *CEH Working Paper, RP86–6,* Cornell University.

7

Beyond Health and Wealth: Attitudinal and Other Influences on Retirement Decision-Making

Janet L. Barnes-Farrell

Why do workers choose to retire? As described in previous chapters, there is substantial support for the position that two classes of personal variables, economic resources and health status, consistently influence retirement decisions. Specifically, the availability of sufficient economic resources to meet one's financial responsibilities may be a determining factor in allowing a worker to move into retirement; thus, it affects both the decision and the timing of the decision. Health status, on the other hand, plays a key role in allowing workers to continue full-time employment. A retirement decision that would otherwise not be considered may be prompted by health concerns. Thus, it is clear that both health and wealth play important roles in the decision to retire and the timing of retirement, largely because they place important constraints on a worker's ability to carry out a preferred path of action. However, in some ways health and wealth operate in the same manner as social policies such as mandatory retirement; that is, they mitigate the influence of other individual and contextual variables that would otherwise lead workers to remain on the job or retire from the workforce.

In this chapter, we shift our attention to the issue of retirement preferences and intentions. We look beyond health and wealth to a number of individual and contextual factors such as worker attitudes, job conditions, organizational climate, and societal pressures that have the potential to influence whether and when adults who are currently employed prefer to continue working or prefer to retire from full-time employment. Although such preferences will not always play out in terms of actual retirement behaviors, preferences serve as an important precursor to other retirement behaviors, including retirement intentions, retirement planning, and retirement decisions (Beehr, 1986). Furthermore, worker responses to the retirement role may be a function of the extent to which retirement decisions are consistent with their preferences regarding the extent and timing of the transition from work to retirement—i.e., the ability to follow one's preferences may have implications for a satisfying transition to the retirement role. Thus, there are compelling reasons to learn more about the underpinnings of worker preferences and intentions regarding work and retirement.

Theoretical Underpinnings of Work-Retirement Preferences and Intentions

There are several theoretical frameworks and mechanisms that are useful for explaining why people prefer to continue full-time employment or prefer to transition to a retirement role. These are described briefly to set the stage for discussion of attitudinal and other factors that have been studied with regard to their influences on work/retirement preferences, intentions and decisions.

PERSONAL CONTROL

One way to think of preferences for work versus retirement is to place them in the context of opportunities to maintain personal control of one's life. Life span theorists have argued that adults are motivated to maintain primary control over events in their lives (Heckhausen & Schulz, 1995). Consistent with this position, Heckhausen and Schulz (1995) reported that elderly adults with control over whether they work express higher levels of physical and psychological well being; this seems to be more important than whether they are working or retired. As they pointed out, this implies that a sense of personal control over the decision to work or retire is of primary importance.

However, consideration of perceived personal control as a primary influence on adults' reactions to their life situations also has implications for retirement preferences and retirement decisions. It suggests that, in general, individuals will prefer the role (work or retirement) that allows them to maintain a sense of personal control over their lives. To the extent that work is seen as a domain in which the worker has considerable control over both process and outcomes, it should be seen as a desirable role. Personal feelings of competence, as well as work design variables and an organizational environment of personal empowerment (in addition to the financial outcomes associated with employment), may contribute to the feeling that the work role allows the individual to maintain a sense of personal control over life events.

On the other hand, personal variables such as the sense that one is no longer able to "keep up" and larger scale events, such as organizational downsizing, may reduce the sense of personal control provided in the work role, and this should reduce the attractiveness of the work role. When this happens, secondary control mechanisms, such as reevaluation of the value of retirement, allow the individual to regain a sense of control. This should result in a shift in preference toward the retirement role. Likewise, if retirement is seen as a role in which the individual will have little control over life events, it should be seen as relatively less desirable and the individual will prefer to continue working. Collectively then, this suggests that worker preferences to continue the work role or shift to a retirement role should be influenced by personal perceptions of the degree to which work and retirement roles, respectively, provide them with opportunities to maintain personal control in their lives.

SELF-IMAGE

A second theoretical vehicle for understanding the psychological underpinnings of work and retirement preferences is rooted in the notion that adults are motivated to maintain a positive self-image and a consistent identity (Mitchell, Rediker, & Beach, 1986). Thus they make choices that are consistent with their personal identities. For example, a worker whose self-identity is closely associated with his/her work or profession should generally prefer to continue in that role, even when attractive alternatives—such as a financially compelling early retirement incentive—present themselves (Feldman, 1994). To the extent that continued work allows an individual to maintain a positive self-image, continued work should remain the desired role.

On the other hand, perceptions of waning work skills, acceptance of age-related stereotypes, or deviation from age norms for career progression may impinge on the ability to maintain a positive self-image. Should this happen, continuation in the work role will be inconsistent with maintenance of a positive self-image. To the extent that retirement provides opportunities to restore and maintain a positive self-image, it should become increasingly attractive.

ROLE ATTACHMENT

Closely related to the concepts of self-image and personal identity is the idea of role attachment. To the extent that one is highly invested in a particular role, feelings of self-worth tend to be associated with the ability to carry out that role in an effective manner (Ashforth, 2001). Furthermore, retirement represents a role transition that has a different meaning with respect to the ability to carry out each of the various roles that a worker enacts. To understand how this is likely to affect the kinds of psychological variables that are relevant to work and retirement preferences, it is important to consider the various identities that adults have and the roles associated with those identities. Some prominent roles include those of worker, organizational member, careerist, family member, and community member. Consider the attachments associated with each of these roles and the meaning of retirement when from the perspective of each role:

- The *worker* role is tied to the notion of being productively employed, although it is not necessarily associated with a particular organization. In this context, choosing to retire means choosing to leave a job and the social network associated with that job.
- The *organizational member* role is organized around the contributions and rewards associated with a particular organization. Thus, the attachment is to the organization rather than to any particular job within the organizational structure.

Choosing to retire in this context means choosing to leave the organization.

- The *career* role is probably most relevant to individuals with professional identities that are tied to their occupations rather than any particular organization. In this context, it is possible to retire from a job in an employing organization without retiring from one's profession. For example, it is fairly routine for academics to formally retire from their university posts, but to continue productive scholarly careers for many years after they have retired. This is of particular relevance to early retirement decisions and the notion of bridge employment discussed elsewhere in this book.

- The role of *family member,* which is enacted concurrently with other roles, is associated with the rewards and responsibilities of being a parent, spouse, sibling, son, daughter, etc. Attachment to this role is often in conflict with activities and responsibilities associated with various work roles. Thus, choosing to retire in this context generally means choosing to spend more time in the role of family member.

- The role of *community member* is likewise one that is primarily executed outside the work-related roles, although some community involvement may be tied to an individual's organizational or professional involvements. As such, retirement is generally an activity that frees one to engage more highly in the role of community member. However, for some individuals, retirement from an organization or a career may represent withdrawal from the role of community member as well, unless they choose to replace current role activities with other kinds of community-oriented activities.

When considered in this way, two issues emerge. First, workers should generally prefer to maintain attachments that are important to them and that provide them with positive outcomes (Adams, Prescher, Beehr, & Lepisto, 2002; Carter & Cook, 1995). Second, a worker's preference for retirement over continued employment should be most influenced by factors relevant to those roles in which the worker is most heavily invested.

RETIREMENT AS A DEVELOPMENTAL AND AGE-NORMED ROLE TRANSITION

Career transitions such as the transition from work to retirement can be loosely interpreted in the framework of normal developmental stages that have been described by life span theorists (Super, 1990; Levinson, 1986). For example, Super suggests that an individual within the fourth of his/her five life stages (the decline stage) move from an active to a more passive "spectator" role in the workplace. This is accompanied by increased examination of alternative identities and roles, e.g., the retirement role. Likewise, Levinson suggests that the fourth of his four "seasons" of life is characterized by movement to activities and roles that involve less responsibility to others and fewer opportunities for exerting control over the lives of others. The stages described by Super and Levinson represent developmental stages, although they are also generally associated with somewhat flexible age spans during which adults typically pass through these stages. They imply a natural movement toward a preference for retirement, suggesting that the relative valence associated with the work/career and retirement roles will shift in the direction of preference for the retirement role in a fairly universal fashion. Thus, the preference to retire should be largely a function of worker age and developmental stage. Other personal variables that are associated with increased preference for the retirement role are seen as consequences of the natural unfolding of life stages.

Others have criticized this linear developmental perspective on the transition from work to retirement as a preferred role. For example, Sterns and Kaplan (this volume) and Sterns and Huyck (2001) argue that career self-management is a process that continues throughout the adult life span; it may include movement into and away from retirement. Although they do not dismiss the developmental changes that accompany aging, they emphasize that individual differences in personal values, life goals, and life experiences play an important role in guiding individuals through choices that may include investing more or less time and effort in their work roles and activities. Such choices are not an inevitable function of chronological aging and may be heavily influenced by the demands and rewards of an individual's nonwork roles as well as his/her effectiveness in managing the work role. Likewise, Hall and Mirvis (1995) make the distinction between career age and chronological age. From this perspective, it can be argued that career age—which is largely a reflection of effective career self-management—is the defining feature with respect to shifting preferences for continued career role engagement compared with transition to a nonemployed role.

Others have proposed a somewhat different function for age in the determination of preferences to continue employment or transition to retirement. It has been well documented that age grading exists within many occupations and organizations (Doering, Rhodes, & Schuster, 1983). As discussed later, there are expectations held by older workers and those around them about ages at which various role transitions such as the transition from worker to retiree *should* take place (Ekerdt, 1998; Joulain, Jullet, Lecomte, & Prevost, 2000; Moen, Fields, Quick, & Hofmeister, 2000). Because the action of norms is to encourage behaviors consistent with normative behavior patterns, such norms should exert pressure on workers who are either "ahead of schedule" or "behind schedule" to conform to these expectations.

RETIREMENT AS A FORM OF ORGANIZATIONAL WITHDRAWAL

Another way of thinking about factors that should influence the preference to work or retire was introduced by Hanisch and Hulin (1990, 1991). They argued that retirement represents one of several ways that workers can withdraw from the job; specifically, they cast it as a form of voluntary turnover. Seen in this light, many of the factors that encourage or discourage voluntary turnover should also influence retirement preferences and decisions.

Other researchers have argued that retirement is sufficiently distinct from other forms of organizational withdrawal that it should not be considered as a subset of the same behaviors. Adams and Beehr (1998) agreed that some antecedents (for example, job satisfaction and organizational commitment) should operate similarly for retirement intent and other forms of voluntary turnover (binding the worker to the organization and reducing both voluntary turnover and retirement intent). However, they also argued and provided evidence for differential relationships of retirement and voluntary turnover with such variables as perceived work alternatives, age, and marital status.

DISTINCTION BETWEEN PUSH AND PULL FORCES

It is also useful to keep in mind the theoretical distinction that has been made between those forces that "push" an individual to prefer retirement (negative features of the work role or the work environment) and those forces that "pull" an individual toward retirement (positive features of the retirement role or the retirement environment). Push factors include those forces that lead a worker to believe that he/she *should* retire (e.g., feeling unable to keep up with the work, societal expectations regarding "normal" retirement age, etc.) or that he/she finds the work role dissatisfying (e.g., low job satisfaction). In this case, retirement essentially represents the lesser of two evils; it is a means of leaving the work role. Pull forces are those forces that lead a worker to believe that the retirement role is a desirable one because of its positive features (e.g., the opportunity to spend more time with family, the opportunity to engage in leisure activities). In this case the preference to retire is seen as the greater of two goods.

Of course, push and pull factors act concomitantly, so it is the combination of pushes and pulls that produces preferences and intentions regarding continued employment compared with retirement. However, the extent to which a retirement decision is dominated by push forces as opposed to pull forces should have consequences for the perception that the retirement decision is a voluntary one (Shultz, Morton, & Weckerle, (1998). This, in turn, has implications for adjustment and satisfaction with the retirement role (Hanisch, 1994).

Although it is discussed less often, it should be recognized that the same reasoning can be applied to the work role. The expressed preference to remain in the work role is the outcome of push and pull forces as well. Thus, an expressed preference/intention to continue work is the outcome of pull forces generated by the continued attractiveness and rewards of one's job and role in the organization (e.g., status, financial rewards, intrinsic satisfaction associated with the nature of work performed) as well as push forces that contribute to the desire to avoid retirement (e.g., anxiety about how one will spend one's time, anticipated decrease in social contacts, reduced financial security, loss of structure, reduced status).

Psychological Models of Retirement Preferences and Decisions

In the industrial and organizational psychology literature, models of retirement decision making developed by Beehr (1986) and Feldman (1994) have received considerable attention. They provide important articulations of the nature of the retirement decision process and suggestions regarding the classes of variables that are likely to influence retirement decisions.

Beehr's conceptualization of the process of retirement distinguishes among three dimensions that characterize the retirement decision: *timing* (early vs. "on-time," reflected in age at retirement), *completeness* (partial vs. complete), and *perceived voluntariness* (voluntary vs. involuntary). Until fairly recently, retirement was generally described and studied primarily in terms of complete, on-time, involuntary retirement as the default position. For example, in the U.S., this type of retirement would be characterized as follows: Workers retire completely from employment at approximately age 65, regardless of a preference to leave the workplace at an earlier age, to continue employment longer, or to continue working in a part-time capacity.

Beehr's model also makes distinctions among three chained events in the retirement process: *preference to retire* (thoughts), *decision to retire* (intentions), and the *act of retirement* (which, as explained above, can be characterized with respect to its voluntariness, completeness, and timing). When retirement is treated as an enacted decision that has the potential to vary along all three dimensions, it is clear that retirement preferences have the potential to play a significant role in determining when and how completely a worker chooses to retire. Beehr identified two primary classes of variables that are likely to contribute to retirement preferences: personal factors such as personality variables, skill obsolescence, health, and financial resources; and environmental forces emanating from job and nonjob sources, e.g., job characteristics and family life. He developed several propositions relating various personal and environmental factors to retirement decisions, and encouraged a research agenda that would provide empirical evidence regarding those propositions. Furthermore, he emphasized the importance of identifying and testing moderators of the many main effects that have been reported in the conflicting body of evidence that exists with respect to predictors of retirement decisions.

Feldman's model focuses specifically on factors that are likely to influence the decision to retire "ahead of schedule" (i.e., before age 65). His model also emphasizes the idea that retirement decisions vary in terms of their perceived voluntariness, and the retirement act does not necessarily conclude with complete withdrawal from the workforce. Feldman's conceptualization presents the early-retirement decision as one piece of a decision making process that includes interconnected decisions about whether to continue work in some capacity (i.e., bridge employment) and whether to continue work in the same industry or occupation (e.g., second career). Primarily informed by Beach's image theory as the theoretical basis for explaining the kinds of factors that should be relevant to these decisions, Feldman presented an array of hypotheses regarding individual-level, organizational-level, and environmental-level variables that should influence early retirement and bridge employment decisions. Many of those hypotheses are closely tied to psychological variables such as the centrality of work in one's self-identity, perceptions of age discrimination in the workplace, and perceptions of work effectiveness.

To summarize, there are a variety of perspectives that provide ways of identifying variables that may contribute to workers' preferences to continue working and preferences to retire. Furthermore, potential influences on retirement decisions can be classified into those that primarily emanate from differences among persons (personal variables), and those that primarily emanate from differences among situations (organizational variables and environmental variables).

In the following section, empirical evidence regarding factors that have been theoretically linked to work-retirement preferences, intentions, and decisions is summarized with a particular emphasis on psychological variables that play a role in retirement decision making. I will continue the distinction between person-centered sources of influence and external sources of influence. The review is organized in terms of individual-level variables, job and organizational variables, and contextual-environmental variables outside the job and organizational domain.

Evidence Regarding Predictors of Work-Retirement Preferences, Intentions, and Decisions

There have been several recent, thorough reviews of the relationships between retirement status and critical demographic variables (Hansson, DeKoekkoek, Neece, & Patterson, 1997; Kim & Moen, 2001; Shultz & Taylor, 2001). As documented in those reviews and in other chapters in this book, health, wealth, socioeconomic variables, as well as other demographic variables such as age consistently predict propensity to retire and the timing of retirement decisions. Generally speaking, poor health speeds retirement and limited resources coupled with financial responsibilities delay retirement (Beehr, 1986; Kim & Moen, 2001). In addition, age exhibits a strong positive relationship with propensity to retire (Taylor & Shore, 1995), although there are a variety of potential underlying reasons for this relationship. However, a host of psychological variables have also been identified as influences on retirement preferences, decisions, and timing. These are the focus of the review that follows.

Before reviewing the outcomes of this research, a few issues are worth noting. First, the decision to retire is closely intertwined with the decision to stop full-time employment. Thus, studies of psychological variables that affect retirement decisions have sometimes focused on positive and negative feelings toward continued work and plans to continue work; at other times they have focused on positive and negative feelings toward retirement and plans to retire from the workforce. Furthermore, as Shultz and Taylor (2001) pointed out in their recent meta-analysis of predictors of retirement decisions, a problem in aggregating and interpreting the extant literature on retirement decision making is that there is not substantial consistency in dependent variables that have been studied. Outcomes of interest have included preference to continue (or discontinue) working and preference to retire (or to avoid retirement), intentions to retire and age of planned retirement, actual decisions to accept retirement opportunities, age at retirement, and "earliness" or "lateness" of retirement. In addition, although they are certainly related, there are theoretical reasons to expect that preferences, intentions, and decisions are not interchangeable (Beehr, 1986). Because influences on preferences may be different from influences on plans and actual decisions, to avoid confusion I will point out the dependent variables used in studies cited in the following sections.

Individual Level Variables:
Personal Characteristics and Attitudes

WORK AS A SOURCE OF SELF IDENTITY AND MEANING

At the most basic level, it has been observed that some individuals feel a strong, stable preference to work that is fairly independent of the nature of the work performed. The impact of this preference can be seen in such measures as a preference to continue working, even when there are no financial incentives to do so (Harpaz, 2002; Harpaz & Fu, 2002), in negative attitudes toward retirement (Dobson & Morrow, 1984; Erdner & Guy, 1990), in failure to take advantage of early retirement opportunities, and in decisions to delay or even to shun retirement.

For example, Parnes and Sommers (1994) described characteristics and labor force participation of a large population sample of men in their seventies and eighties. Consistent with the notion that attachment to the role of worker should play an important part in determining retirement preferences, they argued that there are individual differences in the extent to which paid employment is important to self-fulfillment. They found that "strong psychological commitment to work and a corresponding distaste for retirement are among the most important characteristics related to continued employment into old age" (p. S117). In a similar vein, studies reported by Kilty and Behling (1985) and Richardson and Kilty (1992) offered evidence from two samples of professional workers that work alienation, which was largely composed of measures of the meaning of work in one's life, was a significant predictor of age of planned retirement and the preference to avoid retirement. Professional workers who felt that work gave their lives meaning planned later retirements and preferred to avoid retirement.

It is also important to remember that there are gender differences in the role that work plays in one's personal and social identity; the work role is more central to the personal identity and self-image of men than it is for women. This has the potential to explain gender differences that have been observed in retirement status (Talaga & Beehr, 1995) and retirement timing (Han & Moen, 1999). As noted later, gender differences in retirement preferences and decisions are also likely to reflect contextual features of the nonwork environment that tend to exert somewhat different forces in the lives of men and women.

RETIREMENT AS A SOURCE OF ANXIETY

Other factors that contribute to delayed retirement are more closely associated with fears about retirement rather than a desire to work. Fletcher and Hansson (1991) focused on the concept and predictors of retirement anxiety. They reported that anxiety about transitioning to a retirement role was associated with feelings about both work and retirement roles. Specifically, they found that both job involvement and fear of retirement were positively related to retirement anxiety, while retirement attitude was negatively related to retirement anxiety. More recently, Taylor and Shore (1995) examined predictors of planned retirement age among a sample of workers from a multinational firm. In addition to age and health, they found that self-perceptions of the ability to adjust to retirement accounted for variance in planned retire-ment age: Those who felt uncomfortable about their ability to adjust to retirement planned to retire at a later age.

RETIREMENT AS A RESPONSE TO (UN)HAPPINESS WITH ONE'S JOB AND CAREER

Other work-related attitudes, such as job satisfaction and career satis-faction have also been identified as possible influences on retirement preferences and retirement decisions. However, the direction and magnitude of influence of such variables on retirement preferences and behaviors has not been consistent. For example, Dobson and Morrow (1984) examined a constellation of career orientation vari-ables including job satisfaction, work commitment, and work ethic. Although career orientation was related to attitudes toward retirement, it was not associated with anticipated retirement age or engagement in retirement planning activities. Likewise, Schmitt and McCune (1981) found no difference in job satisfaction between individuals who retired early and those who chose not to respond to an early retirement opportunity. More recently, Adams and Beehr (1998) reported a non-significant relationship between job satisfaction and retirement intent in a field study that included nonfaculty university staff, workers in a manufacturing facility, and members of a software development firm. Likewise, Adams (1999) found no evidence of a relationship between job satisfaction and planned retirement age in a sample of nonfaculty university staff members who participated in a large organizational survey.

In contrast, several studies have reported significant relationships between various affective responses to work and retirement plans and decisions. In a comparison of retired and nonretired faculty members, Durbin, Gross, and Borgatta (1984) indicated that those with strong feelings of job alienation retired earlier than those with positive feelings about their jobs. Kilty and Behling (1985) reported that career satisfaction was associated with an older planned retirement age. Similarly, Goudy, Powers, and Keith (1975) observed a positive correlation between work satisfaction and suggested age for retirement. In a pair of studies presenting evidence for conceptualizing retirement as a form of voluntary job withdrawal, Hanisch and Hulin (1990, 1991) examined the relationship between anticipated retirement age and differences between current job satisfaction and expected retirement satisfaction. They found that later planned retirement age was a positive function of job satisfaction relative to expected retirement satisfaction. Taylor and Shore (1995) also found evidence that job and organizational variables representing affect toward the work setting had a significant relationship with planned retirement age; in particular, organizational commitment was positively related to age of planned retirement. Most recently, Shultz and Taylor (2001) conducted a meta-analysis of demographic, financial, health, and psychosocial predictors of planned retirement age and retirement intentions. They reported small to medium effect sizes for job satisfaction on both outcomes (weighted average correlations of .13 and -.17, respectively).

A recent study by Adams (1999) turned attention to the potential influence of worker attitudes toward their careers and career success on planned retirement age, rather than focusing on reactions to the current job. He proposed that career-related variables such as career commitment, which focuses on attitude toward one's career, and occupational attainment, which should contribute to positive feelings about one's career, would be positively correlated with planned retirement age. Consistent with these expectations, career commitment and occupational attainment accounted for significant variance in planned retirement age in a field study of employed adults over the age of 45 years.

Some of the conflicting findings regarding the role of work attitudes such as job satisfaction in the retirement decision may be a function of relevant individual circumstances that alter expectations and priorities in a worker's life. For example, there is evidence that the retirement decision making process is somewhat different for men and women because of differing expectations about work and non-work roles, such as care giving (Talaga & Beehr, 1995). The outcome should show gender differences in the extent to which retirement decisions are primarily driven by the "pull" influence of opportunities to carry out family role responsibilities vs. the "push" influences of negative affect toward the job and the organization.

Another case in point is age, and particularly nearness to "normal" retirement age. Age can affect planned retirement age directly, but it may also affect which psychological variables enter into workers' thoughts and plans about retirement. Taylor and Shore (1995) reported that job and organizational affect variables had more impact on planned retirement age for those who were not yet eligible to retire than it had on those who had actually entered the window of eligibility for retirement from the organization. One viable explanation for this finding is that those for whom the retirement role is more distal envision retirement as a response to job conditions, whereas those for whom retirement is a proximal reality envision retirement primarily in terms of the desirability/undesirability of the new role.

Perceptions of personal efficacy at work represent another aspect of happiness with one's work-life that have been linked to retirement decisions, based on the reasoning that workers who perceive themselves as declining in work effectiveness or as no longer competitive in their careers are likely to experience an array of feelings regarding their job situation that would encourage them to give serious consideration to retirement. These include threats to one's positive self-image, implicit messages that they are no longer valued, recognition that extrinsic rewards for their performance are unlikely, and increased feelings of vulnerability to economic instabilities such as downsizing efforts. As noted above, perceived occupational attainment has been linked to planned retirement age in this fashion (Adams, 1999); lower occupational attainment was associated with a younger planned retirement age in that study. In addition, Kim and Feldman (1998) reported a significant negative relationship between university faculty recent productivity and likelihood of accepting an early retirement offer.

RETIREMENT AS A PROXIMAL OR DISTAL PHENOMENON

Ekerdt, Kosloski, and DeViney (2000) examined the impact of worker beliefs about the proximity of retirement (the difference between current age and anticipated retirement age) on their engagement in retirement planning and thinking about retirement. They argued that thinking about and talking about retirement (what they referred to as retirement consideration) serves as a mediator of retirement. The question then becomes, what encourages/discourages workers from active engagement in retirement consideration activities? Ekerdt, Kosloski, & DeViney analyzed responses to the 1992 baseline wave of the Health and Retirement Study, which includes a nationally representative sample of approximately 12,000 adults between the ages of 51 and 61 years. They found evidence that perceived temporal proximity to retirement (as opposed to chronological age) was associated with increased consideration of retirement. This was true even after statistically adjusting for a wide variety of situational and personal factors that might direct a worker's attention to retirement issues (e.g., pay, occupational position, work and retirement attitudes, job demands, etc.) They argued that this provides evidence for the importance of normative anticipation of retirement as a feature in the retirement consideration and retirement decision making process. They also pointed out that, within the group of older workers who participated in this study, the relationship between perceived temporal proximity of retirement and retirement consideration was linear, in contrast to the suggestion by Atchley (1976) that there is an abrupt transition from a distal (remote) phase to a proximal (near) phase of retirement anticipation.

ATTACHMENTS TO WORK, CAREER, AND ORGANIZATION

In the study of career-related variables by Adams (1999) described earlier, Adams reasoned that career commitment should be inversely related to plans and behaviors to withdraw from that career. Since retirement implies leaving a career behind, he anticipated a positive relationship between career commitment and planned retirement age; data from the study provided evidence to support this hypothesis.

Arguing from the stance of work-role attachment theory, Adams, Prescher, Beehr, & Lepisto (2002) provided support for the hypothesis that affective organizational commitment, which should strengthen ties to the work role, would be negatively associated with retirement intentions. Thus, attachments to work that are specifically associated with positive affect toward the organization appeared to reduce intentions to leave the work role (or, perhaps more accurately stated, they reduce intentions to leave the organization that is associated with the work role).

However, contrary to expectations, indicators of work role attachment associated with the job (i.e., job involvement) were positively associated with retirement intent and career identification was unrelated to retirement intent in this study. In a discussion of these seemingly counterintuitive findings, Adams and his colleagues suggested that high job involvement may also be associated with behaviors that increase levels of stress and conflict on the job. Thus, high job involvement could actually produce conditions leading to a desire to transition to the retirement role, as a means of reducing stress and conflict.

It might also be useful to distinguish between job involvement and job satisfaction. High job involvement may function to increase the salience and importance of job satisfaction as an affective reaction to which workers respond. In other words, it is reasonable to think that job involvement might serve as a moderator of the proposed negative relationship between job satisfaction and preference to retire: The relationship between job satisfaction and preference to retire should be stronger (i.e., more negative) among those who are highly involved in their jobs than it is for those who express relatively low job involvement. Adams, Prescher, Beehr, & Lepisto (2002) further suggested that the relationship between career identification and retirement intent may be somewhat more complex than originally anticipated because those with strong attachments to their careers may plan ways of continuing their careers through bridge retirement.

PERSONAL BELIEFS ABOUT AGING AND PERFORMANCE

Another set of attitudes that may be relevant to retirement decisions is tied to workers' beliefs and feelings about themselves vis à vis the aging process. Bailey and Hansson (1995, as reported in Hansson, DeKoekkoek, Neece, & Patterson, 1997) reported that individuals who held negative attitudes about their own aging saw greater obstacles to career change. It might be inferred that such individuals would be more likely to seek the safety of retirement from a work environment that demands considerable career flexibility.

Several age-related perceptions, such as perceptions of one's age relative to the age of others in the work environment and the perception that retirement is a proximal role transition, have also been identified as relevant individual difference variables. For example, Cleveland and Shore (1992) studied the incremental influence of psychological construals of worker age on variables that have been identified as relevant to retirement preferences. They found that workers who perceive themselves to be older than others in their work group tend to report higher levels of job involvement, job satisfaction, and organizational commitment. Consistent with the work cited earlier on the relationships between job attitudes and retirement decisions, this would suggest that the perception of "oldness" relative to one's peers may be associated with decreased preference to retire and delayed retirement.

Job and Organizational Level Variables: Characteristics of the Work Environment

JOB DESIGN AND JOB DEMANDS

Conditions of work and organizational settings have also been found to contribute to workers' desire to retire and decisions to retire early. In a comparison of early retirees and nonretirees, Schmitt, (Schmitt, Coyle, Rauschenberger and White 1979) found a small but significant relationship between the way people describe their jobs and the decision to retire early, even when health, demographic factors, and work experience had been statistically controlled. Specifically, those who chose to retire early described their jobs as lower in autonomy, skill variety, opportunity to deal with others, and intrinsically satisfying tasks; while also describing their jobs as higher in feedback from others. Schmitt and his colleagues argued that early retirement decisions may represent positive attempts to pursue more interesting, challenging activities. Consistent with this, in the study by Schmitt and McCune (1981) cited earlier, workers who chose to retire early viewed their jobs as less involving and less challenging. It is also worth noting that early retirees in these studies described their jobs as providing relatively few opportunities for personal control over their work lives. Thus it is possible to interpret many of these findings as providing additional evidence regarding the value that people place on opportunities to control their lives and activities.

More recently, Herzog, House, and Morgan (1991) reported that the nature of work plays an important role in worker preferences regarding continued work. They found that workers in stressful or unrewarding jobs preferred to reduce their work commitments or retire completely. Similarly, Lin and Hsieh (2001) found that stressful work conditions associated with increased workload were related to increased intention to take early retirement.

Likewise, jobs that are structured so that they provide little opportunity for upward movement with continued tenure in the organization and jobs that are perceived as "younger worker" jobs do not provide an incentive to stay on, thus, apparently increasing the attractiveness of retirement as an alternative to a frustrating, and ego-deflating work situation. However, contrary to expectations based on this kind of argument, evidence regarding the impact of opportunity structures in an organization that was not actively offering early retirement incentives did not find the anticipated positive relationship between career growth opportunities and planned retirement age (Adams, 1999).

AVAILABILITY OF SOCIAL NETWORKS AT WORK

Henkens and Tazelaar (1997) were particularly interested in understanding discrepancies between workers' retirement intentions and their actual retirement behaviors. They studied early retirement decisions of a sample of civil servants in the Netherlands. As others have reported, they found that those with poor work conditions and nonchallenging work were more inclined to retire early. However, they also found support for the position that social embeddedness—the availability and importance of social networks in the workplace—contributes to worker evaluations about the relative attractiveness of continuing to work versus retiring. Furthermore, they pointed out that social embeddedness may be particularly important for single individuals, for whom the expected loss of social contacts when they transition to retirement may be more dramatic.

AGE-COMPOSITION OF JOBS AND AGE-RELATED NORMS FOR CAREER PROGRESS AND RETIREMENT TIMING

The age composition of the workplace has the potential to influence social embeddedness as well as perceptions of the age-appropriateness of continued employment. As described earlier, Cleveland and Shore (1992) have provided evidence that worker perceptions of age demography are also likely to influence some of the individual work attitudes that have been linked to retirement preferences, intentions, and decisions.

Workplace norms and expectations about appropriate career trajectories (i.e., the sense that an individual is "on schedule" or "stalled" with respect to career advancement) and occupational expectations about appropriate retirement age produce another set of pressures that affect retirement preferences and plans. Workers who are on target or ahead of schedule with respect to their careers receive the personal satisfaction of knowing that they are meeting standards for career success, which tends to increase job attachment (Ekerdt & DeViney, 1993). This tends to decrease the attractiveness of alternative roles and is associated with delayed retirement (Settersten & Hagestad, 1996). In contrast, workers who have plateaued are more likely to respond to pressures to exit the organization via acceptance of early retirement offers. Recent work by Settersten (1998) provides evidence that norms for "late" retirement timing rarely have negative personal consequences.

Beyond the Organization: Environmental and Societal Variable

FAMILY AND FRIENDS

Just as social embeddedness at work has been identified as a factor influencing preferences to continue work or retire, worker retirement preferences cannot be divorced from the proximal social networks of family and friends that operate outside the workplace. Szinovacz, DeViney, and Davey (2001) examined evidence from the National Survey of Families and Households for the impact of family obligations and kin salience on the retirement decisions. They found that the salience of family ties, particularly ties to children, is associated with the decision to retire from the workforce. However, they pointed out that the relationship is complex, in that kin salience (operationalized in terms of frequency of interaction with kin) reflects both social ties and the perception of financial obligations to family members. Feelings of financial obligation to kin tend to produce delayed retirement, while strong social ties outside the workplace tend to encourage earlier retirement. Gender differences in the way the competing forces of financial obligations and social ties are interpreted and managed are also reflected in retirement decisions. For men, decisions about retirement in light of high kin salience tend to emphasize meeting financial obligations; for women, such decisions tend to emphasize maintaining social ties. A reduced social network outside the workplace (and increased reliance on workplace social networks) is also used to explain the generally delayed retirement plans of unmarried workers. Szinovacz, DeViney, and Davey also suggested that there are cultural differences in response to the pull of family and friends that are reflected in differential ethnic patterns of retirement decisions when family considerations come into play.

The other aspect of family ties that has been studied fairly closely is the impact of partners' work/retirement plans on individual workers' retirement decisions. There is some evidence that partners are inclined to time their retirement plans to coordinate with spouse retirement plans, presumably because companionship is one of the attractions of retirement, and lack of companionship is a disincentive for retirement. For example, Kim and Feldman (1998) reported that university faculty with working spouses were less likely to accept early retirement offers than faculty with nonworking spouses. Likewise, Moen and colleagues provide evidence from the Cornell Retirement and Well-Being Study that retirement is a "coupled transition" that must be coordinated with family and spouse plans (Kim & Moen, 2001; Moen, Fields, Quick, & Hofmeister, 2000).

SOCIETAL AND CULTURALLY TRANSMITTED BELIEFS

Earlier it was pointed out that individual attitudes toward retirement influence its attractiveness. However, it is also true that external pressures regarding the status and acceptability of the retirement role contribute to willingness to enter the retirement role. Some of these pressures are uniquely associated with the cultural milieu in which retirement decisions take place. For example, American culture tends to encourage a strong work orientation and emphasizes the rewards that derive from the work role (Burrus-Bammel & Bammel, 1985).

The influence of culturally transmitted beliefs about the meaning and attractiveness of retirement leads to predictions about global differences in retirement preferences and intentions (particularly with respect to timing), but they also suggest patterns of change in behavior within a particular societal setting that should follow from gradual changes in societal endorsement of retirement as desirable role. In particular, Quadagno and Hardy (1996) observed that societal attitudes toward retirement have become increasingly positive. Hansson, DeKoekkoek, Neece, and Patterson (1997) cite this as contributing to worker decisions to retire at an earlier age. Theoretically, this is consistent with the view that workers are willing to engage in roles that allow them to maintain a positive self-image. Furthermore, social pressures to retire that emanate from fluctuations in the economy may provide a more negative "push" influence on worker retirement decisions (Greller & Stroh, 1995).

A cultural press toward work may be exacerbated by gender differences in the interpretation of work as an essential part of one's self-image. Moen, Fields, Quick, and Hofmeister (2000) have clearly described the different life courses of men and women, and argue that gender role expectations and the differential experiences that typify men's and women's lives have an impact on whether retirement is seen as self-image affirming or threatening to one's self-image. So, for example, men in a work-oriented culture will delay retirement when family responsibilities mount; women are more likely to plan early retirement in order to meet care-giving responsibilities.

Some Observations: What Can We Take From This Work? Where Do We Go From Here?

In the past decade, there has been a decided increase in attention to the variety of psychological processes that are called into play when workers make decisions about whether, when, and how to make a transition from work to retirement. However, many unanswered questions remain, and several deficiencies in the extant literature limit our ability to get a clear picture of how this process works for today's workers. There are a number of directions in which future research efforts could be profitably directed. It is important to recognize that several of the suggestions I make here actually represent reiterations of points made by Beehr (1986) and Talaga and Beehr (1989) in the 80s and again by Feldman in 1994—but still largely unattended to in the empirical literature.

DEPENDENT VARIABLES

A full understanding of retirement decision making would benefit from researchers more clearly distinguishing between different aspects of the retirement decision that have already been proposed: preference, intention, partial/full, early/on-time/late. There are good reasons to think that preferences, intentions, timing, and extent of retirement may respond to somewhat different influences, but these kinds of differences have not been systematically explored. Furthermore, it would be valuable to build measures of retirement timing that explicitly recognize the important conceptual and psychological distinctions that may be implied by early vs. late timing of the retirement decision. In addition, the dependent variables under consideration may need to be reconsidered as the meaning and structure of retirement continues to evolve.

IDENTIFICATION OF KEY MODERATOR VARIABLES

Perhaps a more important question than which work-related attitudes are relevant and which work conditions affect retirement decisions is the question of *when* these attitudes and conditions are likely to play an influential role in retirement decision making. So it may be more useful to ask: When does job satisfaction affect retirement intentions and decisions? When does career commitment affect retirement decisions? When do feelings about the organization play a role in individual retirement decisions? Under what conditions do workers ignore health and wealth considerations in their retirement decision making?

It seems important to recognize that the relevance or importance of psychological variables probably depends on the context in which they exist. Gender, age, ethnicity, occupation, and family situation can all be conceived of as variables that play a critical role in providing social and personal context for retirement decisions. Retirement is a personal decision that has quite different ramifications for people from different generations, different gender role sets, different cultures, different family situations, and different socioeconomic contexts. To the extent that they impact variables such as work attachment, career attachment, and work centrality, it is likely that they will also help to provide boundary conditions for some of the relationships between psychological variables and work-retirement preferences that have been proposed.

RESEARCH DESIGNS

It is fairly common to remind researchers concerned with age-related processes that longitudinal research designs provide critical information about the issues at hand. Retirement decision making is no exception. A number of studies have creatively examined data from longitudinal panel studies to track the path of retirement predictors for cohorts of workers. However, many studies (particularly those that include the kinds of work attitude measures that are the focus of this chapter) rely on cross-sectional comparisons of workers who differ with respect to cohort membership and other cohort-associated variables. Studies that track individual job attitudes and role commitments over time as workers approach and deal with retirement decisions would offer valuable information about the dynamics of retirement decisions.

ADDITIONAL THEORETICAL FRAMEWORKS

Another theoretical perspective that may be useful in thinking about retirement preferences and decisions is organizational justice, which is concerned with perceptions of fair distribution of outcomes and fair treatment in organizational settings. Although this framework has not been used widely to conceptualize the thinking and reactions of those who are considering retirement, worker perceptions of fair treatment may have a significant impact on their decision making and on their feelings about how the retirement process was handled. In the context of early retirement decisions, questions of equitable treatment, informational justice, and interpersonal justice may play a role in determining whether workers choose to pursue early retirement, and are likely to affect their feelings about the retirement process. Similarly, retirement decisions should be reconsidered from the perspective of changing psychological contracts and the implications that they have for feelings of entitlement and fair treatment.

Concluding Comments

Retirement preferences and decisions have been fruitfully examined from a variety of theoretical perspectives. Researchers in the fields of gerontology, sociology, and economics have devoted substantial attention to this significant work role transition, although, surprisingly, it has been relatively neglected by researchers in the field of industrial/organizational psychology. However, recent empirical work that treats retirement decisions as a process that is primarily psychological in nature demonstrates that individual attitudes, characteristics and perceptions of the work and organizational environment, as well as the broader social and societal context in which workers make these decisions, play roles in influencing workers' desires, intentions, and decisions about whether and when to transition to a retirement role. Furthermore, the potential for growth in our understanding of how worker attitudes and other psychological variables affect retirement decisions is great. Systematic attention to the complex nature of the dependent variable under study, thoughtful identification of moderators and important context variables, development of creative approaches to research design and analysis, and consideration of alternative theoretical frameworks that have been used to study psychological phenomena in the workplace all represent areas in which much work remains to be done.

REFERENCES

Adams, G. (1999). Career-related variables and planned retirement age: An extension of Beehr's model. *Journal of Vocational Behavior, 55,* 221–235.

Adams, G., & Beehr, T. (1998). Turnover and retirement: A comparison of their similarities and differences. *Personnel Psychology, 51,* 643–665.

Adams, G., Prescher, J., Beehr, R., & Lepisto, L. (2002). Applying work-role attachment theory to retirement decision-making. *International Journal of Aging and Human Development, 54,* 125–137.

Ashforth, B. (2001). *Role transitions in organizational life: An identity-based perspective.* Mahwah, New Jersey: LEA.

Atchley, R. (1976). *The Sociology of Retirement.* Cambridge, Massachusetts: Schenkman.

Beach, L. R., & Fredrickson, J. R. (1989). Image theory: An alternative description of audit decisions. *Accounting, Organizations, and Society, 14,* 101–112.

Beehr, T. (1986). The process of retirement: A review and recommendations for future research. *Personnel Psychology, 39,* 31–55.

Burrus-Bammel, L. L., & Bammel, G. (1985). Leisure and recreation. In J. Birren & K. W. Schaie (Eds.), *Handbook of the psychology of aging, 2nd edition* (pp. 848–863). New York: Van Nostrand Reinhold.

Carter, M., & Cook, K. (1995). *The Career Development Quarterly, 44,* 67–82.

Cleveland, J., & Shore, L. (1992). Self- and supervisory perspectives on age and work attitudes and performance. *Journal of Applied Psychology, 77,* 469–484.

Dobson, C., & Morrow, P. (1984). Effects of career orientation on retirement attitudes and retirement planning. *Journal of Vocational Behavior, 24,* 73–83.

Doering, M., Rhodes, S., & Schuster, M. (1983). *The aging worker: Research and recommendations.* Beverly Hills, California: Sage Publications.

Durbin, N. E., Gross, E., & Borgatta, E. F. (1984). The decision to leave work: The case of retirement from an academic career. *Research on Aging, 6,* 572–592.

Ekerdt, D. (1998). Workplace norms for the timing of retirement. In K. W. Schaie & C. Schooler (Eds.), *Impact of work on older adults* (pp. 101–142). New York: Springer Publishing.

Ekerdt, D., & DeViney, S. (1993). Evidence for a preretirement process among older male workers. *Journal of Gerontology, 48,* S35–S43.

Ekerdt, D., Kosloski, K., & DeViney, S. (2000). The normative anticipation of retirement by older workers. *Research on Aging, 22,* 3–22.

Erdner, R., & Guy, R. (1990). Career identity and women's attitudes toward retirement. *International Journal of Aging and Human Development, 30,* 129–139.

Feldman, D. (1994). The decision to retire early: A review and conceptualization. *Academy of Management Review, 19,* 285–311.

Fletcher, W., & Hansson, R. (1991). Assessing the social components of retirement anxiety. *Psychology of Aging, 6,* 76–85.

Goudy, W., Powers, E., & Keith, P. (1975). Work and retirement: A test of attitudinal relationships. *Journal of Gerontology, 30,* 193–198.

Greller, M., & Stroh, L. (1995). Careers in midlife and beyond: A fallow field in need of sustenance. *Journal of Vocational Behavior, 47,* 232–237.

Hall, D., & Mirvis, P. (1995). The new career contract: Developing the whole person at midlife and beyond. *Journal of Vocational Behavior, 47,* 269–289.

Han, S., & Moen, P. (1999). Clocking out: Temporal patterning of retirement. *American Journal of Sociology, 105,* 191–236.

Hanisch, K. (1994). Reasons people retire and their relations to attitudinal and behavioral correlates in retirement. *Journal of Vocational Behavior, 45,* 1–16.

Hanisch, K., & Hulin, C. (1991). General attitudes and organizational withdrawal: An evaluation of a causal model. *Journal of Vocational Behavior, 39,* 110–128.

Hanisch, K., & Hulin, C. (1990). Job attitudes and organizational withdrawal: An examination of retirement and other voluntary withdrawal behaviors. *Journal of Vocational Behavior, 37,* 60–78.

Hansson, R., DeKoekkoek, P. D., Neece, W., & Patterson, D. (1997). Successful aging at work: Annual review, 1992–1996: The older worker and transitions to retirement. *Journal of Vocational Behavior, 51,* 202–233.

Harpaz, I. (2002). Expressing a wish to continue or stop working as related to the meaning of work. *European Journal of Work and Organizational Psychology, 11,* 177–198.

Harpaz, I., & Fu, X. (2002). The structure of the meaning of work: A relative stability amidst change. *Human Relations, 55,* 639–667.

Heckhausen, J., & Schulz, R. (1995). A life-span theory of control. *Psychological Review, 102,* 284–304.

Henkens, K., & Tazelaar, F. (1997). Explaining retirement decisions of civil servants in the Netherlands: Intentions, behavior and the discrepancy between the two. *Research on Aging, 19,* 139–173.

Herzog, A. R., House, J., & Morgan, J. (1991). Relation of work and retirement to health and well-being in older age. *Psychology and Aging, 6,* 202–211.

Joulain, M., Jullet, E., Lecomte, C., & Prevost, R. (2000). Perception of "appropriate" age for retirement among young adults, middle-aged adults, and elderly people. *International Journal of Aging and Human Development, 50,* 73–84.

Kilty, K., & Behling, J. (1985). Predicting the retirement intentions and attitudes of professional workers. *Journal of Gerontology, 40,* 219–227.

Kim, S., & Feldman, D. (1998). Healthy, wealthy, or wise: Predicting actual acceptances of early retirement incentives at three points in time. *Personnel Psychology, 51,* 624–641.

Kim, J., & Moen, P. (2001). Moving into retirement: Preparation and transitions in late midlife. In M. Lachman (Ed.), *Handbook of midlife development* (pp. 487–527). New York: John Wiley.

Levinson, D. J. (1986). A conception of adult development. *American Psychologist, 41,* 3–13.

Lin, T-C., & Hsieh, A-T. (2001). Impact of job stress on early retirement intention. *International Journal of Stress Management, 8,* 243–247.

Mitchell, T., Rediker, K., & Beach, L. (1986). Image theory and organizational decision-making. In H. Sims, Jr., & D. Gioia (Eds.), *The thinking organization* (pp. 293–316). San Francisco: Jossey-Bass.

Moen, P., Fields, V., Quick, H., & Hofmeister, H. (2000). A life-course approach to retirement and social integration. In K. Pillemer, P. Moen, E. Wethington, & N. Glasgow (Eds.), *Social integration in the second half of life* (pp. 75–107). John Hopkins University Press: Baltimore, Maryland.

Parnes, H., & Sommers, D. (1994). Shunning retirement: Work experiences of men in their seventies and early eighties. *Journals of Gerontology: Social Sciences, 49,* S117–S124.

Quadagno, J., & Hardy, M. (1996). Work and retirement. In R. H. Binstock & L. K. George (Eds.), *Handbook of aging and the social sciences* (3rd ed., pp. 307–327). San Diego: Academic Press.

Richardson, V., & Kilty, K. (1992). Retirement intentions among black professionals: Implications for practice with older black adults. *The Gerontologist, 32,* 7–16.

Schmitt, N., Coyle, B., Rauschenberger, J., & White, J. K. (1979). Comparison on early retirees and non-retirees. *Personnel Psychology, 32,* 327–340.

Schmitt, N., & McCune, J. (1981). The relationship between job attitudes and the decision to retire. *Academy of Management Journal, 24,* 795–802.

Settersten, R. (1998). Time, age, and the transition to retirement: New evidence on life-course flexibility? *International Journal of Aging and Human Development, 47,* 177–203.

Settersten, R., & Hagestad, G. (1996). What's the latest. Cultural age deadlines for educational and work transitions. *The Gerontologist, 36,* 602–613.

Shultz, K., Morton, K. , & Weckerle, J. (1998). The influence of push and pull factors on voluntary and involuntary early retirees' retirement decision and adjustment. *Journal of Vocational Behavior, 53,* 45–57.

Shultz, K., & Taylor, M. A. (2001, August). The predictors of retirement: A meta-analysis. In K. S. Shultz and M. A. Taylor (Co-chairs), *Evolving concepts of retirement for the 21st century.* Symposium conducted at the 109th annual meeting of the American Psychological Association, San Francisco, California.

Sterns, H., & Huyck, M. H. (2001). The role of work in midlife. In M. Lachman (Ed.), *Handbook of midlife development* (pp. 447–486). New York: John Wiley.

Super, C. E. (1990). A life-span, life-space approach to career development. In D. Brown (Ed.), *Career choice and development,* 2nd ed., (pp. 197–261). San Francisco: Jossey-Bass.

Szinovacz, M., DeViney, S., & Davey, A. (2001). Influences of family obligations and relationships on retirement: Variations by gender, race, and marital status. *Journals of Gerontology: Social Sciences, 56B,* S20–S27.

Talaga, J., & Beehr, T. (1995). Are there gender differences in predicting retirement decisions? *Journal of Applied Psychology, 80,* 16–28.

Talaga, J., & Beehr, T. (1989). Retirement: A psychological perspective. In D. L. Cooper & I. Robertson (Eds), *International review of industrial and organizational psychology* (pp. 185–211). New York: John Wiley & Sons.

Taylor, M., & Shore, L. (1995). Predictors of planned retirement age: An application of Beehr's model. *Psychology and Aging, 10,* 76–83.

8

Self-Management of Career and Retirement

Harvey L. Sterns and Jerome Kaplan

In response to changing social and organizational environments, self-management has emerged as a major theme. With workers changing employers, occupations, or jobs within their current company, individual responsibility is required for maintaining and updating knowledge, skills, and abilities (Farr, Tesluk, & Klein, 1998; Sterns & Sterns, 1995). Similar to work, retirement has moved into the realm of self-management. The individual has become the focal point of when and how to retire. Retirement is still evolving as can be seen by changing transition patterns and labor force exits. The transition from work to retirement can take many forms including bridge jobs, part-time work, or new careers (Sterns & Gray, 1999).

Multiple pathways from work to retirement highlight retirement as a process. Changing economic environments have had a dramatic affect on individual financial well-being and have altered individual approaches to when and how individuals plan to retire. Another aspect is that individuals may have to work longer than they had planned, or they may have to accept an early buyout package rather than risk being laid off or fired at a later date. Individual characteristics, work-related, and not work-related factors impact work and retirement choices. These factors influence anticipatory retirement planning and decision processes.

Brief History of Retirement Education in the United States

A brief history of retirement in the United States illustrates the continual evolution of this life transition. Through the 1700s and the mid 1800s, retirement was rather uncommon and about 70 percent of older men remained in the labor force. Many of these older workers held high status and prestigious positions (Atchley, 1976; Graebner, 1980). Older adults were valued for wisdom and experience, and forced retirement was not supported by the social ideology of the time.

The growth of retirement was influenced by two trends—the emergence of labor unions and mandatory retirement. Labor unions sought worker privileges based on seniority and, in response, management's position was that older workers were both less able and more expensive. Prevailing theories of older adults as worn out and useless reinforced policies that said older adults were too incompetent to work (Richardson, 1993).

Mandatory retirement emerged as a reflection of these polices and became a mechanism for removing older workers while simultaneously generating opportunities for younger workers. A 1934 union-sponsored railroad bill that promoted compulsory retirement was unanimously passed by the U.S. Senate. One outcome of this bill was that many retirees were left in poverty due to the nonexistence of private pensions. Workers who were mandatorily retired had little hope of finding another job and often had insufficient financial resources to support their retirement. In general, retirement was seen in an unfavorable light as it was associated with poverty and uselessness. The Social Security Act of 1935 was passed in response to the growing number of older adults in poverty (Richardson, 1993).

The Age Discrimination and Employment Acts (1967, 1978, 1986) over a period of years have, in general, eliminated mandatory retirement in the United States. Our ideas about retirement have undergone an evolution over the last forty years; a major theme of the 1971 White House Conference on Aging was to convince people that retirement was a good thing and that people deserved a period of rest and relaxation at the end of the life span. There were people who chose to work longer. Ideas about mandatory retirement were pervasive. The ADEA legislation of 1967 created a protected class of people 40+ but maintained mandatory retirement at age 65. In the revisions of 1978, mandatory retirement was raised to age 70 and there was an uncapping of federal workers. In the 1986 revisions, there was an uncapping of mandatory retirement with the exception of commercial airline pilots, air traffic controllers, age authenticity in actors, military, diplomatic core, and individuals in key leadership positions with pensions greater than $44,000 per year.

Gerontology in the 1970s placed a great deal of emphasis on the fact that most people had little difficulty making the transition to retirement status (Atchley, 1976). Often it was stated that 12% of older adults had difficulty with the transition, but most did not. Much of the focus was on subgroupings of individuals in retirement such as reported by Neugarten, Havighurst, and Tobin (1968). Much discussion focused on "activity theory" and retirement and on "disengagement theory" and retirement.

Retirement education further developed in this period. Often the initial focus was on finances; however, much more extensive programs were developed to include legal issues, family relationships, housing and where to live, use of leisure time, health promotion, nutrition, health care benefits, etc. The context for this approach was that the company was facilitating a planned exit so that the employee would feel positive about leaving and the company would have positive imagery with the former employee. This was the period of paternalism—if you're good to the company, then the company will be good to you. There were issues emerging with the closing of Studer-baker-Packard Automobile Company, which led to ERISA legislation with protection for employees in pension programs by the federal government. Pension vesting was an issue—many people were not fully vested until 25 years of service and many were let go at 24 and one-half years. Vesting was changed to a much more reasonable period of time. Recent issues with company-based 401K pension programs are leading to new pensions regulations and a renewed interest in employee protections.

Self-Perception and Retirement

Physical and psychological changes, which emerge in midlife and older adulthood, may be less dramatic than those of childhood, adolescence, and advanced old age as recently discussed by Sterns and

Huyck, (2001). Wrinkles, gray hair, reduced sensory capacities, altered fat distribution, and even menopause signal to the self and to others that one is moving along the life span. These changes may provide cues to others about one's age. The extent that others respond to a person differently because they are thought to be "middle aged or older" may force the person to acknowledge changes (Neugarten, 1968). This may lead to increased awareness of potential ageism in the work place (McCann & Giles, 2002).

Some theories emphasize the awareness of health issues and personal death as a crucial "marker" of midlife and older adulthood, an awareness which is not based upon the actual nearness of death so much as the recognition that underlying biological changes are occurring (Jacques, 1965; Levinson, Darrow, Klein, Levinson, & McKee, 1978; Colarusso & Nemiroff, 1981). Biological changes become central when they are diseases, many of which emerge in midlife and have the potential to dramatically redirect the course of life.

The impact of biological changes on work depends substantially upon the individual and the context. In times and settings where stereotypes persist that midlife and older persons are less desirable workers, individuals will strive to mask external signs of age (through hair coloring, plastic surgery, systematic exercise, fashion, avoiding references to earlier experiences which would "date" them, etc.). Men and women who work in physically demanding jobs often seek relief in early retirement; men and women who have a chronic disease or disability may be forced to withdraw from employment, or they may find settings which accommodate their altered capacities (Sterns & Huyck, 2001). Vaillant (1977, 2002) reported that the men in the longitudinal Grant Study (all Harvard graduates of 1942–44) showed a maturing of defense mechanisms. By age 35, these men were four times more likely to use dissociation, suppression, sublimation, and altruism than as young adults, and they were far less likely to use projection, masochism, or hypochondriasis. The net effect is to make cognitive and emotional perceptions less marked by defensive distortions.

Another shift often described in models of midlife is of self-in-the-world, with an overall shift from outer-world orientation to an inner-world one. Buehler (1935) described this shift on the basis of her studies of biographies. Levinson, Darrow, Klein, Levinson, &

McKee, (1978) and Levinson & Levinson (1996) emphasize the BOOM/BOOW—Becoming One's Own Man/Woman—as a critical thrust signaling a preparation for middle age. Gutmann (1994) assumes that young adults repress aspects of the self in the service of the social-psychological demands of parenting, and that midlife offers the opportunity to reclaim these aspects to become more individualized and whole. The concept is clearly heralded as an opportunity and even a mandate in many of the popular books on midlife, for example, Sheehy's model of a second adulthood where one can "choose your own path" (Sheehy, 1995; Sher, 1998).

The impact of these changes on work is discussed in several of the models. Generally, middle-aged persons are perceived as potentially better workers because they have a more complex, holistic view of issues, and are more attuned to their own contributions to both problems and solutions. On the other hand, the increased focus on self-determination may lead individuals to withdraw investment in career building in favor of greater attention to family, friends, or self-development. This clearly conflicts with current expectations that all workers remain engaged, ambitious, eager to update, and flexible in meeting the changing demands of their workplace (Sterns & Huyck 2001).

Self-Management—Career and Retirement

Conceptualizations of work and retirement continue to evolve. In the 1990s three very important publications were released by Hall and Mirvis (1995a, 1995b) and by Hall and Associates (1996). *The Career is Dead: Long Live the Career* (Hall & Associates, 1996) presents the strongest statements regarding the protean careers that are referred to throughout the chapter. The emphasis is on self-management of career in a dramatically changing work environment.

Sterns and Gray (1999) emphasize the challenge faced by midlife and older workers in terms of self-management. As organizations transition from pyramids to flatter, more streamlined configurations through downsizing and restructuring, employees may experience job loss, job plateauing, and skills obsolescence (Farr, Tesluk & Klein, 1998; Sterns & Miklos, 1995). Older workers may be singled out in downsizing efforts on the basis of stereotypic traits, such as being unsuitable for retraining or fast-paced work environments (Hall & Mirvis, 1995a, 1995b; Mirvis & Hall, 1996). Furthermore, depending on age of career entry, middle-aged and older workers may be more likely to occupy the mid-level managerial positions that are often the focus of downsizing and restructuring strategies. Additionally, slow company growth may lead to less opportunity for advancement (Farr, Tesluk, & Klein, 1998). These changes suggest older workers may need to take increased involvement and responsibility in terms of career management.

Organizational changes are also altering the nature of the relationships between organizations and employees (Hall & Mirvis, 1996). Employers' commitment to employees may last only as long as there is a need for their skills and performance. Similarly, employees' commitment to the employer may last only as long as their expectations are being met. These changes place greater emphasis on employees' adaptability and abilities in learning to learn (Hall & Mirvis, 1996).

Career self-management is carefully analyzed by Hall and Mirvis (1996) in their discussion of the protean career. A protean career is directed by the individual rather than the employing organization. Greater responsibility for learning, skill mastery, and reskilling is also placed on the individual (Hall & Mirvis, 1995b). The individual is in charge, in control, and able to change the shape of his or her career at will—similar to a free agent in sports (Hall & Mirvis, 1996). This perspective and the goals of this type of career (e.g., psychological success, identity expansion, and learning) also recognize the artificiality of the distinction between work and nonwork life. Personal roles and career roles are highly interrelated and the boundaries between these roles tend to be fuzzy rather than clear cut (Hall & Mirvis, 1995b). One disadvantage of protean careers is that an individual's identity is not likely to be tied to any one organization. Problems of self-definition may result in that one's personal identity is not connected to a formal organizational work role.

Mirvis and Hall (1996) also suggest that taking the responsibility of career self-management may hold special benefits for older workers. Greater tenure in a protean-type career may lead to increased value of older workers. It may be rather expensive to replace such knowledgeable, adaptable, and continuously learning employees with younger workers with less protean-type career experience. Protean careers may increase the organization's options for deploying older workers. Similarly, the options older workers may pursue in changing their careers are also increased (Mirvis & Hall, 1996). Potential alternatives include moving to a new field (i.e., second or third careers), building new skills in their present field, changing organizations, phasing into retirement, or joining the contingent workforce.

Older workers, however, may also be at a disadvantage in terms of moving toward greater career self-management. Transitioning from a typical, organizational-driven career to a protean career may be a rather daunting task—particularly if an individual initially entered the workforce with a one career-one employer ideal. Additionally, stereotypic beliefs about older workers may lead to the underutilization of this group within new relationships between organizations and employees (Mirvis & Hall, 1996).

One of the major goals of retirement education is the development of key issues of retirement. Much of the emphasis is on consciousness raising, values clarification, getting in touch with personal feelings, and awareness of viewpoints held by significant others. Staudinger (1999) and Smith (1996) have both presented important work regarding the development of planning capability, wisdom regarding life events, and the development of an approach to the art of living.

Sterns (1986), in his model of career development and training, sees the option of full or part-time retirement as part of the decision to no longer be actively involved in career development and work activities. Decisions regarding career and updating are based on many dimensions. However, individuals can move in or out of the work role. A similar multi-dimensional model is proposed for self-management of retirement.

A person's self-concept is influenced by many factors in consideration of retirement issues (see Figure 8.1). First, there is the understanding of our past selves and what values, preferences, and desires are based in our past. Examples here are returning to where our family used to live, maintaining close contact with old friends, or making use of a family summer home. This is countered and complemented by our future selves. The possibility of new lifestyles, new living environments, new friends, and new actions are options. The decision to live in the same community but carry out a new set of life activities outside of work in a familiar community environment is still another option.

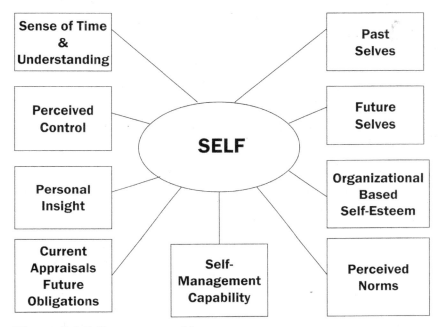

Figure 8.1 Influences on self.

Three factors are important here. One factor influencing self-concept is the understanding of change and an awareness of the passage of time. How we view change in others and ourselves over time and how we see and understand the implications of future time is a major aspect of personal cognitive integration leading to increased self-understanding. The second factor influencing self-concept is the perceived control that we have over our lives at the personal level, in relation to significant others, and in our work, career, or business situations, etc. (which will be discussed separately in a later section). We may feel in control based on financial resources, position held, or seniority, or we may feel extremely vulnerable based on the current financial situation and/or business climate. In one year we have gone from the highest level of employment to a sense of great vulnerability. The summer of 2002 made many potential early retirees come to terms with the fact that they would have to work longer based on the decline of their investments. In many cases people in retirement have had to change lifestyle or return to work for pay in order to maintain desired lifestyle. The third factor is personal insight—how well we understand ourselves, our motivations, our personal desires, our work approaches, and our relations to family, friends and organizations. Self study, education, and counseling may aide this process.

Organization-based self-esteem (OBSE) is the bridge to the world of work. How valued one feels, how one feels in relation to one's fellow workers, and the feeling of contribution that one gets from one's work are all part of OBSE. Another important area is how one perceives the work and retirement norms. One's personal social clock and one's understanding of social norms will influence self-perceptions and actions to be taken.

The orchestration of all of these influences on self and the needed interpretation, planning, sophistication, and wisdom are all part of self-management capability. An important continuing area of research will focus on how people are able to self manage their planning and execution of retirement decision-making.

Figure 8.2 focuses on the work environment. Briefly, one is concerned here with the self-evaluation of the employment situation. Part of this relates to one's appraisal of the current situation: how one believes he or she is viewed by supervisors, outcomes of performance appraisals, perceived growth opportunities within the organization, and observations of treatment received by other later career employees. Part of this is an understanding of personal strengths and weaknesses that one knows about oneself and one's approach to meeting assignments, deadlines etc.

Employment-based appraisal refers to the formal and informal feedback that is received from supervisors—outcomes of performance appraisal, salary increases, and involvement in organization planning and policy. Work opportunities refer to future plans within the work context and potential opportunities over time. New work opportunities may be an important incentive to continue to work as a bridge employee until full-time retirement. Other bridge opportunities may provide a gradual change in responsibilities to part-time employment. A major dimension is one's activities in continuous learning and maintaining professional competence. Remaining competitive with up-to-date skills may make one valuable to the organization.

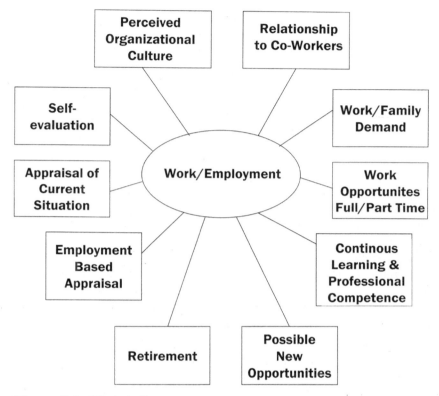

Figure 8.2 Work influences.

Relationships with coworkers may be extremely important in continued employment. How people feel about their work situation is highly influenced by coworker interactions in many cases. Middle aged and older workers value relationships on the job. A negative relationship with coworkers may lead a valuable older worker to decide to retire. Supervisors may want the employee to stay (may not be able to replace), but may not be aware of interpersonal difficulties. On the other hand, an older employee who feels the need to work longer than they really wanted to for financial reasons may be a challenge for coworkers and supervisors.

Perceived organizational culture is another dimension that provides important messages to current employees. Choices made by current organizational leadership, and how these are transmitted to current employees, provide important general information. Middle aged and older employees are usually very aware of the changing climate and treatment of long-service employees.

Another dimension is possible: new opportunities. This refers to looking for new employment opportunities within or outside the organization. This can be planned in terms of second- or third-career education and training, or may be related to chance encounters or in response to a corporate recruiter. In those cases where one is self-managing and no longer desiring to continue employment, the decision to retire may be the decision of choice. Often, middle aged and older employees may not be in a position to choose when to retire as discussed elsewhere.

Figure 8.3 focuses on marriage and other significant relationships. This area can have a major influence on decisions regarding work and retirement. One of the benefits of formal retirement education is that husbands and wives, or significant others, can engage in planning exercises that often create new awareness. Caregiving responsibilities for parents may be a major concern for many people. Corporate elder-care services have been available for over two decades to assist employees who have care responsibilities. In many cases, an employee may choose, or feel forced, to retire in order to provide care to loved ones. Many people do not expect their retirement to become a major caregiving experience for parents or a spouse. Family relationships may become more important and become a major influence in the self-management of retirement.

Choosing to be near children, grandchildren, or other important family members may be a reason to retire from one's current job, move, and reestablish one's household in a new location. New part-time or full-time employment may be a choice after such a move. Migration research tells us that approximately 80% of older adults choose to stay in their home communities to be near family and friends. This does not preclude new and exciting choices as part of a new life period.

Probably the most complex ties are the intergenerational ones (Sterns & Huyck, 2001) Some 90% of adults age 35–64 are parents.

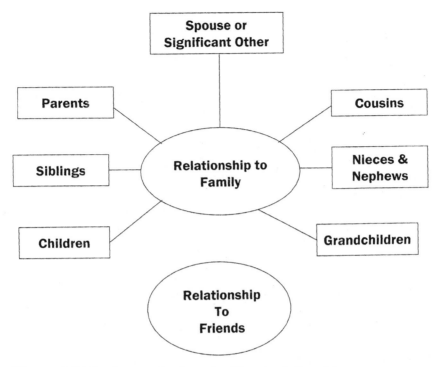

Figure 8.3 Marriage and other significant relationships.

According to a recent review of some of the research, "no single trajectory is characteristic of all or even most families during the middle years of parenthood" (Seltzer & Ryff, 1994). It is, thus, impossible to generalize neatly about the "midlife family" given the changes in timing of births, marriage, divorce, remarriage, or blended families. Instead, parenting experiences vary by social class, gender, life events and transitions, and psychological functioning in both generations. Generally, whites, married couples, and unmarried fathers have more material resources than do minority group parents, unmarried parents, and single mothers. Divorced parents report more strain and less support from parenting and are generally less satisfied with parenting during these years. The majority of parents need to tend both to work and parenting: 81% of fathers and 64% of mothers age 35–44 have children at home and are employed (Seltzer & Ryff, 1994).

Grandparenting is a relationship, which has many meanings and varied enactments (Robertson, 1977). In contrast to the stereotyped images of sedentary, cookie making, or fishing grandparents, many are very involved in vigorous, complex lives of their own. With the rise in unwed maternity, divorce, and substance abuse, more grandparents—especially grandmothers—have found themselves playing an active parental role with grandchildren, and many grandparents have fought for legal recognition of "grandparents' rights." While some grandparents have little contact with their grandchildren, others are thrust into responsibilities they thought they had left behind.

Many middle-aged children have living parents and the wish and/or the need to be involved in their parents' lives can pose another balancing challenge. For comparison, in 1800 a 60–year-old woman had only a 3% chance of having a living parent; by 1980 that had risen to 60% (Watkins, Menken, & Bongaarts, 1987). The increased longevity of elders means that four- and five-generation families are increasingly common. As we have previously discussed, many of the elders are still involved in nurturing younger generations. However, the increased longevity, the relatively low fertility of women who are now elderly, and changes in the health care system mean that families are providing more care and more difficult care over longer periods of time than ever before in history (Brody, 1990). Family members even provide around 80% of the care provided to bedridden elders.

Brody described the situation of "women in the middle" (Brody, 1990), with the recognition that "women" included others who provide care. A 1992 Harris survey of adults over 55 found that 29% of men and 29% of women are caregivers for spouses, parents, other relatives, friends, and neighbors (The Commonwealth Fund, 1993). The heroic balancing efforts of family caregivers have been well documented. Many caregivers feel pulled between spouse, children, parents, and employment. Work may be, in such cases, a relief from otherwise relentless pressures. Some women, however, find they must reduce work to part-time or withdraw altogether.

Figure 8.4 relates to what keeps people in their home communities or what aspects of community may be important in providing a meaningful context and sense of belonging. Much of the classical retirement literature has focused on these dimensions of community. What is important here is how these dimensions relate to our self-

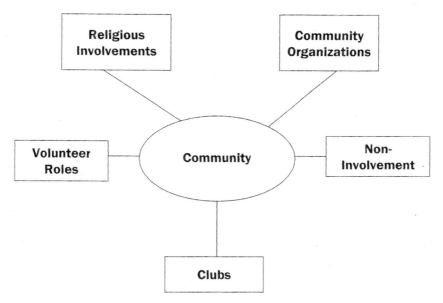

Figure 8.4 Community influences.

concept and how this influences our decisions to continue to work or retire. Some individuals feel alienated by their community relationships and wish to reestablish themselves in a new community context. Others may have more than one residence and move back and forth between the new and the old empowered by both locations, whereas others totally enjoy being a part of roles and involvements that are longstanding.

Self-concept is influenced in many of the ways described above. What is critical is our ability to bridge from the individual level to the broader work and societal context.

Work and Retirement in Middle and Later Life

Psychosocial definitions of older workers (Sterns & Doverspike, 1989) are based on social perceptions including age typing of occupations, perceptions of the older worker and the aging of knowledge, skill, and ability sets. The individual's self-perception is also considered. How individuals perceive themselves and their careers at a given age may be congruent or incongruent with societal image. Relatively little research has addressed the quite basic question of how we know when workers will perceive themselves, or be perceived by others, as old. Timing norms are discussed as prescriptions about when and how one retires, influenced by level of commitment to the work organization, modes and styles of exiting, and pension incentives. Timing norms become the bearer of societal, firm level, or reference group preferences for retirement (Ekert, 1998). His analysis of the Health and Refinement Study 1992 base-line wave (age 51–61) reveals support for the concept of a usual age for retirement, which may vary in different work settings and occupational categories. Plan incentives clearly influence timing of retirement behavior and 85% of workers reported that they planned to leave at or prior to the local, typical age for retirement. In addition, over 80% of respondents did not plan to work beyond the typical age.

Lawrence (1987) broadly defines age effects as outcomes within an organization attributed to the age of employees. In her discussion, chronological age and age distributions impact age norms. Age distributions are the actual age distributions in the organization while the age norms are shared perceptions of the normal ages with an organization or role. Individual age expectations are also important, as they reflect the degree to which the individual applies the social norm to him/herself. Age norms are likely to occur when the range of perceived ages is narrow and agreement on typical ages is high. Organizational tenure is expected to increase recognition of age group distinctions as individuals of roughly the same age and organizational tenure will have shared history and experience. These age norms may provide a context that influences judgments about individuals.

One can look to parents and peers for models, but each person's circumstances, feelings and situations may be very different. Recent discussions of the future of retirement (Morris, 1996) tell us that nothing less than a paradigm shift is underway that will affect how people will have to save and invest and how they will fantasize about and plan for the future. Uncertainty regarding what present and future employment will offer is true for individuals who presently have job security, stable working conditions, and choices about their retirement. This can change quickly with corporate buyouts, new public policies, and changing attitudes on the part of workers themselves.

The possibility of losing one's job, being faced with an early buyout, or uncertainty regarding future prospects are all part of the current scene. At the same time, there are capable people continuing in fairly traditional careers. Others may lose jobs but are re-entering the job search finding that it is a major challenge to find a new position at the same or better salary. Often the person has to settle for reduced salary and benefits, if any. It appears that somewhere between 10–20% of older adults want to work beyond traditional retirement age. In any case, it is important to focus on individuals who will continue to work.

Sterns and Sterns (1995) have stated that people may not only wish to work longer, they may have to. All of these individuals, regardless of their health and disability status, are believed to feel the financial pressure to continue working. Until recently, many people, now ranging in age from the 40s to the mid-60s, felt that they would have a choice about working after the normal retirement age. This belief was based on the expectation of an expanding economy and a strong economic climate. Many middle aged and older workers are surprised that the large numbers of early buyouts and layoffs, and the general trend of downsizing, have continued even by successful companies and most recently economic forces have diminished investments leading to changes in plans for early retirement.

It is apparent that the relationship between employer and employees no longer promises lifelong employment. This places middle aged and older workers in the position of having to be responsible for their own careers, maximizing the employment opportunities presented to them, and competing with people of all ages in finding new employment. People will have to fight harder to remain in the workforce longer. The present 50- and 60–year-olds were hired at a time when they could choose among jobs. They were a part of the work force when there was accelerated growth and numerous promotions. They had to deal with the slower promotions and salary increases of the 1980s but still expected that they would have control over how long they worked and when they exited the workforce. At the peak of their careers, they now have much less control or no control at all.

Employment benefits, especially retirement benefits, have changed from defined benefit programs to defined contribution. Many employees were told that they would receive the same level of benefit with these conversions but this has definitely not turned out to be the case. Individuals now pay or copay into pension and health benefit programs both before and after retirement. This has been devastating for many individuals who had 401k plans and/or stock portfolios resulting in fewer discretionary resources in retirement and the need on the part of many individuals to return to full-time work.

As a result, baby boomers may need or desire to supplement their pension or benefits. Dychtwald and Flower (1989) propose that the baby boomers are more likely "to do their own thing" and will be comfortable breaking the retirement norm. A new trend toward more cyclic lifestyles (multiple periods of training, work, and leisure) is, and will continue to become, more common. The increasing pressures of changing technology and the need for continuous training to remain competitive in the job market are the forces that will drive multiple-cycle careers (Sterns, 1986).

Older adults have many different reasons for remaining in the work force longer. They want to earn money and have health insurance, and they seek other intrinsic benefits, such as developing new skills, using time productively, and feeling useful and needed. Work allows people to stay in touch with current developments; it provides structure to older people and helps them retain a sense of doing something worthwhile. People who enjoy work will want to continue to maintain the social interactions and relationships they enjoyed with coworkers, and they will want to continue to participate in meaningful activity. The work one does contributes to identity and a sense of self (Sterns, Matheson, & Schwartz 1990). An increasing concern for health and youthfulness may also contribute to longer career patterns. Being retired may conflict with a person's youthful image, leading to postponing retirement. We can expect older workers who have expertise to take advantage of additional training in their own or related disciplines and take on new challenges, such as working in new small businesses or in a consulting role.

Many women, having entered the work force in midlife, may want to work longer for many of the same reasons mentioned above. They may need to work longer to receive benefits in retirement. A majority of older adults are women and 60% of women age 45 to 60 are employed. Women's participation varies by industry. It now estimated that 75% of women were in the workforce by the year 2000.

Women have become a major component of the work force and will become a larger component within the next decade.

Middle aged and older workers of today have to reconsider their plans based on recent economic events. Clearly, people are trying to make meaningful decisions about their futures. The decision to continue to work, modify work, or retire is influenced by many factors. Time left (at work or in the labor force) is part of a decision process influenced by eligibility for Social Security, employer pension, and norms (Sheppard, 1991). This is as described an "extended stream of decision-making for retirement that can be observed in the changing plans and intention toward retirement that workers entertain over time" (p. 130).

Potential working years range from approximately age 18 to the end of the life span. Sterns and Alexander (1987) reviewed the issues relating to industrial gerontology by emphasizing the decisions of workers throughout the life span. They emphasize that career decisions are not limited to a specific age or stage; decisions are not age-specific. Forteza and Prieto (1994) examined the changes that occur in the life cycle and the implications for the labor cycle. They include an international flavor by considering industrial countries as opposed to only the U.S. By adopting a life span orientation, these reviews consider a range of ages and issues. A life span perspective emphasizes the continuity and change as individuals move through adulthood and older adulthood.

One of the most notable social perspectives of life course decisions was offered by Neugarten and her colleagues in the description of the power of age norms to shape behaviors in all domains (Neugarten, Moore, & Lowe, 1965; Neugarten & Hagestad, 1976). One consequence is the development of a "social clock" by which progress is charted—according to one's personal timetable and according to the one held by others in the social system. In this perspective, jobs and career progress are both governed by age norms (as well as gender norms). There are "young men's jobs" and "midlife jobs". Neugarten (1968) described the shift in relations between generations as particularly evident in the workplace; the shift from "apprentice" to becoming part of the "command generation" and "mentor" to the younger workers was an important marker of feeling middle aged among high achieving adults. Neugarten later deemphasized age norms and argued that America had become a largely "age irrelevant" society (Neugarten, 1996).

The social role model has clear applications to the work realm, since role defines one's place in social structures. A review of career development literature and first person accounts make it clear that many persons who are now middle aged and older came of age when "career ladders" were anticipated, and expectations of progress were tied to age. By age 35–40, men "knew" whether they were likely to be promoted in their line of work, or sidelined, and this awareness had significant repercussions (e.g., Howard & Bray, 1988; Huyck, 1970; Levinson, Darrow, Klein, Levinson, & McKee, 1978). Personal identity was heavily invested in the work role, and the degree of competence, authority, and power implied in titles (such as journeyman, master craftsman, assistant vice-president, Lt. Col., CEO) was an important element. In addition, social relationships, within the workplace and even in the wider community, were governed by work role status. In the current era, when adults are likely to change careers several times, organizational structures are less hierarchical, and promotion is based more upon expertise than tenure, the previous notions of "appropriate work roles for middle age" have been challenged. The models developed on earlier realities may not fit in the future.

Barth, McNaught, and Rizzi (1995) and McNaught, Barth, and Henderson (1989) have raised the issue of where the future labor supply should be drawn from now that the workforce expansion may no longer be fueled by the baby-boom generation and women shifting into working roles. The 1991 Commonwealth Fund Productive Aging Survey (CFPAS), which interviewed 2,999 older Americans, indicated that 9% (75 and older) to 12% (65 to 74) of nonworking older adults were willing and able to work. Depending on assumptions made about the health of older Americans and acceptable working conditions, the CFPAS results indicated that between 1.9 million and 5.4 million older adults are capable, available, and interested in working. This is a preview of the future.

The CFPAS was conducted in order to understand the interest level and circumstances that older adults would be willing to work under. It examined daily activities, employment, and work attitudes of men and women over the age of 55. Twenty-seven percent of the respondents reported having a job for which they were paid. Those employed worked an average of 37.4 hours (median = 39.9) per week. In order to determine if respondents were satisfied with the hours worked, they were also asked how many hours they would like to work. The average (29.5 hours) was considerably lower than actual hours worked (median = 34.0 hours); 22% of respondents wanted to work less than 15 hours per week, while 29% wanted to work more than 40 hours per week.

A majority of older adults seemed content to have retired and wanted to remain retired. For the 72% of the sample who were not employed, 73% of that group had not worked since 1985. The unemployed group was asked if they would prefer to be working: 31% responded "yes" and 4% responded "not sure." The 31% who indicated they would work were asked "if a suitable job were available in your area, would you be able to work or would it not be possible for you to work?" Forty-six percent said "yes, it would be possible." Fifty-one percent responded, "no, it would not be possible" and 3% responded "not sure." The large percentage of "not possibles" may be due to health or caretaker responsibilities, or other competing activities. Of those willing and able to work, two-thirds were willing to work part-time and one-third wanted more than 35 hours of work.

The CFPAS data implied that those older adults who are working would like to continue to work, but work fewer hours per week. Most older adults who were not working said they would like to remain retired. However, approximately 14% of those nonworking older adults said they would like to return to work. Based on this percentage, of the 32 million older adults who are currently not in the work force, some 4.5 million are potential full or part-time older adult employees.

Over the past two decades, employees' attitudes toward working have become increasingly more important to organizations in their efforts to predict worker behavior (Warr, 1994). General attitudes about work contribute to a desire to continue to work and to maintain the skills required to excel. The work environment itself also influences employees' attitudes about their job performance and whether they want to continue to work.

The desire to continue working in an organization has been researched under the topic of organizational commitment. Meyer and Allen (1997) distinguish between two dimensions of organizational commitment that affect work attitudes in different ways. The first, continuance commitment, is the employee's perceived cost of leaving or a perceived lack of alternatives to make up for investments in the benefits of the current job. Individuals remain at work because they are not willing to risk loss of salary, health benefits, or pension investment. This aspect of organizational commitment is especially relevant to older adults. As workers increase their tenure with an organization, they may feel increasing continuance commitment because they have established a home and friendships in the area, have become specialized in a skill that they feel cannot be transferred, or believe that they could not get the same salary or benefits if they moved to a new organization.

Affective commitment, the second dimension of organizational commitment, refers to the employee's affective, or emotional, orientation to the organization. Affective commitment is concerned with the individual's interest in the work and loyalty to the organization and its goals. This emotional tie to the organization motivates them to remain, not because they cannot afford to leave, but because they feel a sense of contribution and growth by staying with the organization. Other things being equal, an organization that encourages maintenance at one's job, provides challenging work, and offers opportunities to inject new ideas will not only be more likely to stay ahead of competitors but will also reduce turnover and retain more productive employees.

An organization can measure the success of its efforts to improve the work environment by examining organization-based self-esteem (Pierce, Gardner, Cummings, & Dunham, 1989). Organization-based self-esteem is measured by the degree to which organization members believe they are valuable, worthwhile, and effectual employees (Pierce, Gardner, Cummings, & Dunham, 1989).

Evidence is mounting that the intrinsic rewards of work—satisfaction, relationships with coworkers, and a sense of participating in meaningful activity—become more important as an individual ages. The abolishment of the mandatory retirement age allows working older adults to continue to participate in these benefits until they feel that they have the financial resources and personal network outside the workplace to retire (Brady, Fortinsky, Norland, & Eichar, 1989). Contemporary research has established that financial incentives influence retirement behavior, although the relative importance of economic factors compared to affective and social factors is not known (Ruhm, 1990). There is considerable disagreement about the effect of economic factors (Quinn and Burkhauser, 1990).

Job satisfaction shows consistently that work-related attitudes are more positive with increasing age in surveys of employed adults (Rhodes, 1983). Older adults may have a different perspective on work than younger adults. For older workers, survival needs are less likely to be urgent as they will probably have reached a maximum income for their jobs. Desire for more control over the job is still strong. However, older workers have seen less evidence that hard work leads to promotions, salary increases, or other rewards. Goals may not change with age but expectations of achieving these outcomes can diminish.

The life span approach to older workers (Sterns & Doverspike, 1989) advances the possibility for behavioral change at any point in the life cycle. Substantial individual differences in aging are recognized as vital in examining adult career patterns. Three sets of factors are seen as affecting behavioral change during the life cycle. The first set includes normative, age-graded biological and/or environmental determinants. These bear a strong relationship to chronological age. The second set of factors is normative, history-graded influences which affect most members of a cohort in similar ways. The third set of events is nonnormative. This includes unique career and life changes, as well as individual health and stress-inducing events. The unique status of the individual is the result of the joint impact of these factors. According to this approach, there are more individual differences as people grow older (Baltes, Reese, & Lipsitt, 1980).

These differences create difficulty in developing theories that adequately address the broad range of differences. Late careers are often more difficult to study than early careers because there is less consistency in the developmental tasks. For example, in early career, individuals must choose a career. In late career, a person may continue a career, start a new career, modify a career, or retire.

Bronte (1993) interviewed individuals having long careers into their 80s and 90s. The participants are proof that it is possible to continue being creative and productive past age 65. They present a positive view of what can be accomplished late in one's career or even early in a career started late in life. While it is not a rigorously designed study, it provides portraits of individuals who break the stereo-types of older adult careers.

While Bronte found a great deal of variety in careers, she identi-fied three basic career patterns. The "homesteaders" are individuals who stay in the same job or profession for their entire careers. Many of these individuals are in artistic or scientific fields. They are still deeply engaged in their careers and feel that they have more potential for growth.

The second group, the "transformers" change jobs once. Early transformers change careers shortly after starting an occupation. This process seems to be part of the trial-and-error process. In contrast, late transformers tended to be well established financially and personally, giving them the freedom to pursue another interest later in life.

The third group, the "explorers" changed careers from as few as three to as many as ten times. The reasons for the shifts were varied, as were the career paths. The book illustrates the variability in career pattern and ages of career peaks and contributions. Early models of career development were linear models, which assumed individuals moved through predictable career stages and then retirement. For old-er adults, maintaining skills for a period of time and then declining was the predicted pattern. This notion that career stages are linked to age will lead practitioners to incorrectly develop career development opportunities that are congruent with the age and stage of various cohorts. These models ignore individual differences and the contribu-tions that older workers make. People may be aware of norms and expectations regarding their expected retirement. At the same time, workers may have the options of part-time or full-time work in the same career or in a new career or new job in their later part of life.

REFERENCES

Atchley, R. C. (1976). *The sociology of retirement.* Cambridge, Massachusetts: Schenkman.

Baltes, P. B., Reese, H. W., & Lipsitt, L. P. (1980). Life-span developmental psychol-ogy. *Annual Review of Psychology, 31,* 65–110.

Barth, P. B., McNaught, W., & Rizzi, P. (1995). Older Americans as workers. In S. Bass (Ed.), *Older and active* (pp. 35–70). New Haven: Yale University Press.

Brady, E. M., Fortinsky, R, H., Norland, S., & Eichar, D. (1989). *Predictors of success among older workers in new jobs.* Final report. Human Services Development Institute, University of Southern Maine.

Brody, E. M. (1990). *Women in the middle: Their parent-care years.* New York: Springer Publishing.

Bronte, L. (1993). *The longevity factor.* New York: Harper-Collins.

Buehler, C. (1935). The curve of life as studied in biographies. *Journal of Applied Psychology, 19,* 405–409.

Colarusso, C. A., & Nemiroff, R. A. (1981). *Adult development.* New York: Plenum.

Dychtwald, K., & Flower, J. (1989). *Age wage: The challenges and opportunities of an aging America.* Los Angeles: Jeremy P. Tarcher.

Ekerdt, D. J. (1998). Workplace norms for the timing of retirement. In K. W. Schaie & C. Schooler, (Eds.), *Impact of work on older adults* (pp. 101–123). New York: Springer Publishing.

Farr, J. L., Tesluk, P. E., & Klein, S. R. (1998). Organizational structure of the workplace and the older worker. In K. W. Schaie & C. Schooler, (Eds.), *Impact of work on older adults* (pp. 143–185). New York: Springer Publishing.

Forteza, J. A., & Prieto, J. M. (1994). In M. Dunnette, L. Hough, & H. Triandis (Eds.), *Handbook of industrial and organizational psychology* (Vol. 4, pp. 447–483). Palo Alto, California: Consulting Psychologists Press.

Graebner, W. (1980). *A history of retirement.* New Haven and London, Yale University Press.

Gutmann, D. L. (1994). *Reclaimed powers: Toward a new psychology of men and women in later life* (2nd ed.). Evanston, Illinois: Northwestern University Press.

Hall, D. T. (1996). *The career is dead: Long live the career.* San Francisco: Jossey-Bass.

Hall, D. T., & Mirvis, P. H. (1995a). The new career contract: Developing the whole person at midlife and beyond. *Journal of Vocational Behavior, 47,* 269–289.

Hall, D. T., & Mirvis, P. H. (1995b). Careers as lifelong learning. In A. Howard (Ed.), *The changing nature of work* (pp. 323–361). San Francisco: Jossey-Bass.

Hall, D. T., & Mirvis, P H. (1996). The new protean career: Psychological success and the path with a heart. In D. T. Hall (Eds.), *The career is dead—long live the career: A relational approach to careers.* San Francisco: Jossey-Bass Publishers.

Howard, A., & Bray, D. W. (1988). *Managerial lives in transition: Advancing age and changing times.* New York: Guilford.

Huyck, M. H. (1970). *Age norms and career lines in the military.* Unpublished doctoral dissertation, University of Chicago.

Jacques, E. (1965). Death and the mid-life crisis. *International Journal of Psychoanalysis, 66,* 502–515.

Lawrence, B. S. (1987). An organizational theory of age effects. *Research in the Sociology of Organizations, 5,* 37–71.

Levinson, D. J., Darrow, C. N., Klein, E. B., Levinson, M. L., & McKee, B. (1978). *The seasons of a man's life.* New York: Knopf.

Levinson, D. J., & Levinson, J. D. (1996). *The seasons of a woman's life.* New York: Knopf.

McCann, R., & Giles, H. (2002). Ageism in the workplace: A communication perspective. In T. D. Nelson (Ed.), *Ageism—stereotyping and prejudice against older persons.* Cambridge, Massachusetts: The MIT Press.

McNaught, W., Barth, C. B., & Henderson, P. H. (1989). The human resource potential of older Americans. *Human Resource Management, 28,* 47–64.

Meyer, J. P., & Allen, N. J. (1997). *Commitment in the workplace: Theory, research, and application.* Thousand Oaks, California: Sage.

Mirvis, P. H., & Hall, D. T. (1996). New organizational forms and the new career. In D. T. Hall and associated (Eds.), *The career is dead—long live the career: A relational approach to careers.* San Francisco: Jossey-Bass.

Morris, B. (1996). The future of retirement: It's not what you think. *Fortune, 86–94.*

Neugarten, B. L. (1968). The awareness of middle age. In B. L. Neugarten (Ed.), *Middle age and aging* (pp. 93–98). Chicago: University of Chicago Press.

Neugarten, B. L. (1996). The young-old and the age-irrelevant society. In D. A. Neugarten (Ed.), *The meanings of age: Selected papers of Bernice L. Neugarten* (pp. 47–71). Chicago: University of Chicago Press.

Neugarten, B. L., & Hagestad, G. O. (1976). Age and the life course. In R. H. Binstock & E. Shanas (Eds.), *Handbook of aging and the social sciences.* New York: Van Nostrand Reinhold.

Neugarten, B. L., Havighurst, R., & Tobin, S. (1968). Personality and patterns of aging. In B. Neugarten (Ed.), *Middle age and aging.* Chicago: University of Chicago Press.

Neugarten, B. L., Moore, J. W., & Lowe, J. C. (1965). Age norms, age constraints, and adult socialization. *American Journal of Sociology, 70,* 710–717.

Pierce, J. L., Gardner, D. G., Cummings, L. L., & Dunham, R. B. (1989). Organization-based self-esteem: Construct definition measurement and validation. *Academy of Management Journal, 32,* 622–648.

Quinn, J. F., & Burkhauser, R. V. (1990). Work and retirement. In R. H. Binstock & L. K. George (Eds.), *Aging and social sciences* (pp. 308–327). San Diego: Academic Press.

Rhodes, S. R. (1983). Age-related differences in work attitudes and behavior: A review and conceptual analysis. *Psychological Bulletin, 93,* 328–367.

Richardson, V. E. (1993). *Retirement counseling.* New York: Springer Publishing.

Robertson, J. F. (1977). Grandmotherhood: A study of role concepts. *Journal of Marriage and the Family, 39,* 165–174.

Ruhm, C. J. (1990). Determinants of the timing of retirement. In P. B. Doeringer, (Ed.), *Bridges to retirement* (pp. 23–32). Ithaca, New York: Cornell University Press.

Seltzer, M. M., & Ryff, C. D. (1994). *Parenting across the life span: The normative and non-normative cases.* In D. L. Featherman, R. M. Lerner, & M. Perlmutter (Eds.), *Life-span development and behavior* (Vol. 12, pp.1–40). Hillsdale, New Jersey: Erlbaum.

Sheehy, G. (1995). *New passages: Mapping your life across time.* New York: Random House.

Sheppard, H. L. (1991). The United States: The privatization of exit. In J. Quadagno & D. Street (Eds.), *Aging for the twenty-first century: Readings in social gerontology* (pp. 351–377). New York: St. Martin's Press.

Sher, B. (1998). *It's only too late if you don't start now: How to create your second life after 40* (1st ed.). New York: Delacorte Press.

Smith, J. (1996). Planning about life: A social-interactive and life-span perspective. In P. B. Baltes & U. M. Staudinger (Eds.), *Interactive minds: Life-span perspectives on the social foundation of cognition* (pp. 242–275). Hillsdale, New Jersey: Lawrence Erlbaum Associates.

Staudinger, U. M. (1999). Social cognition and a psychological approach to an art of life. In T. M. Hess & F. Blanchard-Fields (Eds.), *Social cognition and aging*. San Diego, California: Academic Press.

Sterns, H. L., & Alexander, R. A. (1987). Industrial gerontology: The aging individual and work. In K.W. Schaie (Ed.), *Annual review of geriatric medicine and gerontology* (Vol. 7, pp. 243–264). New York: Springer.

Sterns, H. L., & Doverspike, D. (1989). Aging and the training and learning process in organizations. In I. Goldstein & R. Katzell (Eds.), *Training and development in work organizations* (pp. 299–332). San Francisco: Jossey-Bass.

Sterns, H., & Gray, H. (1999). Work, leisure and retirement. In J. Cavanaugh & S. Whitbourne (Eds.), *Gerontology* (pp 355–390). Oxford: Oxford University Press.

Sterns, H. L., & Huyck, M. H. (2001). Midlife and work. In M. E. Lachman (Ed.), *Handbook of midlife development* (pp. 447–486). New York: John Wiley.

Sterns, H. L., Matheson, N. K., & Schwartz, L. S. (1990). Work and retirement. In K. Ferraro (Ed.), *Gerontology: Perspectives and issues* (pp. 163–178). New York: Springer.

Sterns, H. L., & Miklos, S. M. (1995). The aging worker in a changing environment: Organizational and individual issues. *Journal of Vocational Behavior, 47,* 248–268.

Sterns, H. L., & Sterns, A. A. (1995, November 17). *Training and careers: Growth and development over fifty years.* For BSS section history symposium: Aging and work: Fifty years of labor. Scientific Meeting of the Gerontological Society of America, Los Angeles, California.

Sterns, H. L., & Sterns, A. A. (1995). Age, health and employment capability of older Americans. In S. Bass (Ed.), *Older and active* (pp. 10–34). New Haven, Connecticut: Yale University Press.

Sterns, H. L. (1986). Training and retraining adult and older adult workers. In J. E. Birren, P. K. Robinson, & J. E. Livingston (Eds.), *Age, health, and employment* (pp. 93–113). Engelwood Cliffs, New Jersey: Prentice-Hall.

The Commonwealth Fund (1993, November). *The untapped resource: The final report of The Americans Over 55 at Work Program.* New York: Author.

Vaillant, G. (1977). *Adaptation to life.* Boston, Massachusetts: Little, Brown.

Vaillant, G. E. (2002). *Aging well.* Boston, Massachusetts: Little, Brown.

Warr, P. (1994). Age and employment. In H. C. Triandis, M. D. Dunnette, & L. M. Hough (Eds.), *Handbook of industrial and organizational psychology* (2nd edition, Vol. 4, pp.485–550). Palo Alto, California: Consulting Psychologists Press, Inc.

Watkins, S. C., Menken, J. A., & Bongaarts, J. (1987). Demographic foundations of family change. *American Sociological Review, 52,* 346–358.

9

Bridge Employment: Work After Retirement

Kenneth S. Shultz

Historical Background, Recent Research, and Future Directions

An interesting paradox has occurred over the course of the last century, namely, individuals are living longer and healthier, yet they continue to retire at earlier ages. For example, Kinsella and Velkoff (2001), using data from 15 member countries of the Organization for Economic Cooperation and Development (OECD) showed that "in 1960, men on average could expect to spend 46 years in the labor force and a little more than 1 year in retirement. By 1995, the number of years in the labor force had decreased to 37 while the number of years in retirement had jumped to 12" (p. 111). Women's average number of years in the labor force, of course, has been increasing in that time frame, however, "at the same time, the amount of time women live after reaching retirement age increased greatly, from 9 years in 1960 to more than 21 years in 1995" (p. 111). Consequently, retirement is taking a larger portion of our lives, and therefore the concept of retirement itself is being redefined.

For example, not too long ago, retirement was synonymous with the absence of paid employment among elderly people. Today, however, many retirees (particularly those in their 50s, 60s, and early 70s) engage in some form of paid employment. Much of this work can be classified as bridge employment. Bridge employment refers to the labor force participation patterns observed in older workers between their career jobs (e.g., held 10 plus years) and complete labor force withdrawal (Doeringer, 1990; Feldman, 1994; Quinn, 1999). Economists have documented its prevalence, however we know little about its antecedents and consequences. In order to understand bridge employment better, its historical background is first presented. Then, recent research on bridge employment is reviewed. Finally, directions for future research are provided.

HISTORICAL BACKGROUND

Until the late 1800s, most men simply worked until they were no longer physically able to work. Then, slowly, men's labor force participation began to decline after age 65. In the last half-century, labor force participation rates for men 55–64 have also declined (Costa, 1998). For example, in 1950 more than 70% of all 65–year old men were in the labor force. By 1985, fewer than half the early percentage (roughly 30% of 65–year-old men were in the labor force. Similarly, in 1950, half of men 70 years old were in the labor force, whereas by 1985 that percentage had shrunk to less than 16% (see Quinn, 2000, Table 1, for more detailed analyses).

However, recent analyses indicate that this declining trend may in fact be leveling out, if not reversing (Quinn, 1997a, 1997b, 1999, 2000). In addition, as noted above, while labor force participation rates have fallen, life expectancy continues to rise. Thus, younger workers in their 20s and 30s can now expect to spend up to one-third of their life in retirement. What will these individuals do in retirement? Many will travel and volunteer, while others may pursue informal education and hobbies (Moen, Plassmann, & Sweet, 2001). A sizable portion though, will likely be seeking full- and part-time wage and salary employment, as well as self-employment, in what are commonly referred to as bridge jobs (Quinn, 1999).

For instance, in 1998, 3.7 million adults over the age of 65 were either working or seeking work (AARP, 1999a). In addition, a 1997 Retirement Confidence Survey of baby boomers conducted by the Employee Benefits Retirement Institute (EBRI) (reported by AARP,

1999b) showed that about 75% of older boomers (born between 1946–1955) plan to continue working at least part-time in retirement, while just over 70% of younger boomers (born between 1956–1964) anticipate working at least part-time in retirement. Less than 5% of both groups did not know whether they would work in retirement. A similar study conducted by Roper Starch Worldwide (1999) found that 55% of baby boomers intend to continue working part-time and 32% full-time after retirement. Finally, an analysis of first-wave data from the Health and Retirement Study (HRS) (1992) showed that most (73%) of preretirees (age 51–61) say they want to work in retirement (AARP, 1999b).

Hence it appears that many individuals in their 50s and 60s want to work when they retire, but not in full-time, career jobs. Instead, many plan to seek bridge jobs. This increasingly prevalent transition employment status allows older workers to exit the labor force gradually. It often consists of employment in a new line of work, typically part-time wage and salary jobs, or self-employment and/or full-time work of relatively short duration (Quinn, 1999, 2000). Ruhm (1994) showed, however, that 75% of bridge employment in a 1989 survey of older adults 50–64 years old was on a full-time basis. Regardless of whether it is more likely to be part-time or full-time, given the increasing prominence of bridge employment, the question becomes, what would compel researchers and policy makers interested in retirement issues to devote limited research time and money to studying bridge employment?

TRANSITIONING FROM CAREER EMPLOYMENT TO RETIREMENT

As Beehr (1986) hypothesized over a decade and a half ago, retirement is not a single event as much as it is a process. Quinn's (2000) analysis of three waves of the Health and Retirement Study (HRS) data (1992, 1994, and 1996) clearly demonstrates this process empirically. Using the HRS data, Quinn conservatively suggests that about one-third of men and almost half of all women transition out of the labor force gradually by engaging in bridge employment. This includes moving from career jobs (of at least 10 years in duration) to part-time or short term jobs and/or self-employment jobs. Thus, bridge employment is clearly becoming a more prominent feature at the end of individuals' careers, thus blurring the transition between work and retirement (Elder & Pavalko, 1993; Herz, 1995; Mutchler, Burr, Pienta, & Massagli, 1997).

Henretta (2001) discusses some of the reasons why we are seeing increased late career heterogeneity. He notes that late career trajectories are varying more widely due to individual, organizational, and societal level changes. For example, we are seeing increased reentry rates where retirees are continuing to move in and out of the workforce after retirement (Elder & Pavalko, 1993; Hayward, Crimmins, & Wray, 1994; Herz, 1995; Hurd, 1996). Hayward, Crimmins and Wray show that the majority of the increase in reentries is at relatively young ages (i.e., less than 65 years old). Also, individuals are less likely to stay with the same employer their entire career. As a result, they are less likely to build sufficient pension wealth to completely withdraw from the workforce after retirement. Consequently, they end up "retiring" from their current employer and seeking new employment opportunities to bridge the gap between their current job and permanent retirement.

On the employer side, early retirement pension offers are now commonplace. In fact, such offers represent an increasingly important component of many employers' strategic human resource initiatives. In addition, many employers are more likely to offer their employees defined benefit contribution pensions plans (Dulebohn, Murray, & Sun, 2000). Such plans offer employees increased flexibility in planning the timing and nature of their retirement (see Feldman's chapter in this volume for more details on such plans). Thus, we see both individual and employer influences on bridge employment levels.

At the societal level, O'Rand (1996) discusses some of the broader structural reasons for the increasing variability in late-life trajectories. In particular, she notes that "trajectories of variability in retirement wealth savings increase the likelihood for larger segments of cohorts to be employed later in their lifetimes, whereas others exit the labor force earlier" (p. 204). Thus, O'Rand notes that a "universally experienced 'retirement'" is increasingly becoming a thing of the past (p. 204).

A model depicting the bridge employment process is presented in Figure 9.1. In this model we see that contextual (societal level) factors directly affect the bridge employment decision and experience. In addition, these contextual factors also influence both the individual

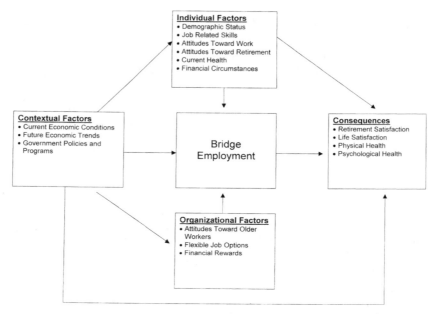

Figure 9.1 Model of antecedents and outcomes of bridge employment.

and the organizations that employ older workers. Usui's (1998) discussion of Japanese gradual retirement policies provides a nice analogy for examining contextual level influences on individuals and organizations, although with regard to retirement. In turn, these individual and organizational factors directly impact bridge employment. Finally, bridge employment results in a variety of consequences for the individual and their family. This model is by no means presented as a comprehensive depiction of the antecedents and consequences of bridge employment. Instead, it is presented simply as an organizing framework for examining some of the more prominent antecedents and consequences of bridge employment that are discussed next.

CYCLICAL AND STRUCTURAL FACTORS IMPACTING BRIDGE EMPLOYMENT

Quinn (1999, 2000) delineates some of the cyclical (e.g., historically low unemployment) and structural (e.g., fewer pension disincentives to remain employed past age 65) factors that have prompted an apparent end to the downward trend in employment rates at older ages. In particular, Quinn is able to show that even controlling for cyclical factors such as the strong economy of the 1990s, broader structural changes to the incentives for older adults to work past age 65 are still relatively strong.

According to Quinn (2000), cyclical factors include, until recently, our robust economy and low unemployment levels that coaxed many older adults to either stay in the labor force longer or to return to the labor force after retirement. As a result of these abundant economic conditions, bridge employment levels continued to increase throughout the 1980s and 1990s for both men and women. While these temporal cyclical factors influence bridge employment levels, more permanent structural factors, such as the recent removal of Social Security earnings limits for those 65 to 69 years old, can and do influence labor force participation rates among older adults. Thus, additional structural changes (i.e., prowork policies) are discussed in the second part of this chapter in order to promote employment for older adults.

Ruhm (1990a) examined six waves of data (1969 to 1979) from the Retirement History Longitudinal Survey (RHLS) at two-year intervals to investigate bridge employment and partial retirement patterns. Ruhm's analysis of the RHLS data (a precursor to the more recent Health and Retirement Study—HRS) on over 6,500 working heads of household (age 58–63 in 1969) showed that by age 60 over half of all older adults had left their career jobs and were engaging in bridge employment. Thus, a majority of individuals actually permanently retire from bridge jobs, not career jobs. In addition, those who depart their career job before age 60 are likely to stay in their bridge jobs for two or more years. These individuals are also fairly unlikely to change bridge jobs (i.e., their job mobility is low). Finally, Ruhm showed that the movement from career to bridge employment typically involves either a switch in occupation, industry, or both (p. 484–486).

Ruhm (1990a) also found clear demographic differences in bridge employment patterns. For example, white, well educated, pension-eligible men were more likely to stay in their career employment. However, if they did exit their career employment at a relatively young age, they were more likely to be able to continue in their career employment industry and/or occupation—which has important implications for increased earnings potential. Overall, Ruhm was able to demonstrate that bridge employment is much more common than most researchers and policy makers believe, and that there are clear differences across demographic groups in how (and if) bridge employment is experienced.

In a second study, Ruhm (1994) used data from a 1989 Louis Harris telephone survey to study the "job-stopping" process among 3,509 older adults (age 50–64 years old). Ruhm found similar results to his earlier study summarized above, in that retirement often occurs gradually over time and for many individuals includes a stint of bridge employment. In particular, he found that demographic variables such as age, race, sex, education, marital status, and employment history all impact one's likelihood of engaging in bridge employment. For example, Ruhm (1994) notes that, "Women, nonwhites, high-school dropouts, and workers in poorly compensated occupations are most likely to leave their longest jobs at relatively young ages. After doing so, they rarely obtain or retain bridge jobs" (p. 95). One nondemographic factor studied, enjoyment of the bridge job, rather than pay, was a more important factor in determining how long someone stayed in that bridge job.

Economists (e.g., Gustman & Steinmeier, 1984; Herz, 1995; Honig & Hanoch, 1985; Quinn, 1997a, 1997b, 1999, 2000; and Ruhm, 1989, 1990a, 1990b, 1994) have conducted much of the research on bridge employment. Not surprisingly, efforts to describe and understand bridge employment have focused primarily on macroeconomic, structural, and demographic factors, rather than psychosocial factors related to participation in bridge employment. Psychosocial factors such as job-related self-efficacy and social support also, no doubt, influence older individuals' willingness to seek out and engage in bridge employment (Adams & Lax, 2002). However, a few sociologists, psychologists, and management scholars have examined bridge employment from a conceptual and/or empirical standpoint. Therefore, the more prominent psychosocial factors that have been hypothesized and/or investigated in relation to bridge employment are discussed next.

PSYCHOSOCIAL FACTORS IMPACTING BRIDGE EMPLOYMENT

Adams and Lax (2002) recently theorized that job seeking among older workers looking for bridge employment is impacted by biographical, self-evaluation, motivational, and situational variables. They suggest that younger, more educated men will be more likely to seek bridge employment and should have an easier time obtaining bridge employment. However, even when such demographic variables are controlled, Adams and Lax hypothesize that self-evaluation factors (i.e., job- and work-specific self efficacy) will still impact older adults' likelihood of seeking out and obtaining bridge employment. In addition, they propose that situational variables, such as emotional and instrumental social support, and motivational variables, such as work commitment, retirement negativity, and financial hardship, will all influence individuals' likelihood of seeking bridge employment and their ultimate success in obtaining it.

Feldman (1994) proposed a decision-tree framework to examine bridge employment. The first in a series of questions in his decision tree framework was, "Should I leave my current employer before age 65?" If yes, then "Should I take a bridge job?" If yes, then "Should I change to a different industry or occupation?" Feldman hypothesized four levels of variables that influence the decision to retire early and/ or to engage in bridge employment. The first level includes individual difference variables such as work history and marital, demographic and health status, as well as attitudes toward work and retirement. The next level of variables includes opportunity structures, which encompass the type of industry individuals are in, whether they are in the primary or secondary labor market, age-related performance decrements, and whether individuals have experienced age-related discrimination.

A third level of variables includes organizational factors such as financial rewards, exposure to early retirement counseling programs, and the organization's flexibility in managing older workers. Finally, the external environment is also hypothesized to influence individual's likelihood of retiring early and/or engaging in bridge employment. This factor includes uncertainty about the macroeconomic environment, social security and pension regulations, as well as the availability of governmental programs to assist older workers. While Feldman (1994) did not provide any empirical evidence for his propositions, his theoretical work has helped to guide several recent empirical investigations of the bridge employment concept.

For example, Weckerle and Shultz (1999), analyzing first-wave data from the Health and Retirement Study (HRS) (1992) data set, examined the factors that distinguished older workers based on their desire to retire early, continue work, obtain bridge employment in the same job, and obtain bridge employment in a different job. Using discriminant function analysis, Weckerle and Shultz tested Feldman's (1994) hypotheses regarding the factors that distinguish different types of bridge employment. In particular, the research addressed whether voluntariness of retirement, flexibility in current employment, retirement planning, and anticipated financial reward distinguished working within the four categories. Weckerle and Shultz found that those individuals who wanted to continue in their current position were much more satisfied with their financial situation, had flexible jobs, and felt the decision to retire would be voluntary, than individuals in the other three groups. Conversely, few anticipated financial rewards and lack of flexibility in one's current employment were important predictors of those individuals who desired early retirement. Thus support was found for three of the organizational factors that Feldman (1994) proposed as influencing bridge employment decisions.

In a somewhat similar study, Heindel, Adams, and Lepisto (1999) also tested Feldman's (1994) hypotheses regarding different types of bridge employment. Analyzing data from 223 workers age 50 and over using hierarchical regression, Heindel, Adams, and Lepisto found that retirement income satisfaction, work opportunities, job involvement, organizational commitment, and career commitment all predicted plans for bridge employment in one's current field. More specifically, the job involvement, and organizational and career commitment variables added unique variance beyond the retirement income satisfaction and work opportunities scales when predicting older workers' intentions to engage in bridge employment in the same career. However, only retirement income satisfaction predicted plans for bridge employment in another field. Thus, Feldman's (1994) hypotheses were partially supported by Heindel, Adams, and Lepisto.

In a series of studies, Kim and Feldman (1998, 2000) and Feldman and Kim (2000) examined the bridge employment experience of faculty from the University of California (UC) system who experienced a series of early retirement incentive offers. In the first study, Kim and Feldman (1998) looked at the predictors of acceptance of a series of three early retirement incentive offers. While a variety of factors influenced the early retirement incentive acceptance decision (e.g., age, poor health, a working spouse), of relevance to this chapter was that Kim and Feldman found that those individuals who anticipated working part-time in retirement were more likely to accept an early retirement incentive than those individuals who did not anticipate working in retirement. This should not be surprising as bridge employment helps to fill the gap between full-time work and permanent retirement by supplementing one's pension before Social Security payments begin, and psycho socially by allowing for a more gradual transition out of the labor force by providing structure and connection to valued activities (Kim & Feldman, 1998).

Looking more specifically at bridge employment, Feldman and Kim (2000) found that early retirees who were older, healthier, and had higher salaries and seniority, as well as those who had spouses who were still working and children at home or in college, were much more likely to engage in bridge employment either within or outside the UC system. In addition, those who engaged in bridge employment were also more likely to be satisfied with retirement as well as life in general. In fact, those retirees who engaged in full-time bridge employment were even more satisfied on both fronts than those engaged in part-time bridge employment, possibly suggesting that most of these individuals were not ready to begin the transition out of the labor force.

Feldman and Kim (2000) also provided interesting qualitative descriptions of the benefits and downsides of both engaging in bridge employment and of not engaging in bridge employment, that were provided by retired UC faculty members. For example, those who did not engage in bridge employment, but were satisfied with their retirement, wanted to reconnect with family, desired less hectic (e.g., no commute) lifestyles, and wanted to pursue leisure and travel activities without the interruption of work. However, those who did engage in

bridge employment were thankful for the daily structure that postretirement work provided, welcomed the chance to "give back" to their
employer and/or profession, and were happy to have a reduced level
of work and stress. So, at least part of the benefit of engaging in
bridge employment may well be the need to match an individual's
desired level of employment to their actual level of employment (Shultz,
Morton, & Weckerle, 1998). That is, if an individual really does not
want to work but feels compelled to engage in bridge employment
(e.g., because he/she needs the money), that individual is more likely
to be dissatisfied with retirement. Conversely, an individual who feels
the need to structure his or her daily life, but is unable to obtain
satisfactory bridge employment, is also likely to be dissatisfied in
retirement.

In one of the few truly theoretically based empirical studies of
bridge employment, Kim and Feldman (2000) used Atchley's "continuity theory" of aging to examine bridge employment. Using the same
sample of faculty from the UC system as reported in Feldman and
Kim (2000), Kim and Feldman used hierarchical regression to examine the extent of total bridge employment, as well as bridge employment both within and outside the UC system. Kim and Feldman found
that individual difference factors (e.g., health and age) accounted for
about 5.5% of the variance in who sought bridge employment. Job
factors (e.g., tenure, salary, declining a previous early retirement of-
ficer) accounted for an additional 7.5% of the variance, while family
status (e.g., having a working spouse or dependent children) accounted for an additional 5.1% of the variance in who sought bridge employment. Comparable figures were obtained for bridge employment
both within and outside the UC system.

Kim and Feldman (2000) also used hierarchical regression analysis to examine retirement and life satisfaction. They found that engaging in some form of activity (e.g., bridge employment, volunteer work,
or leisure activity) accounted for 9.2% of the variance in retirement
satisfaction. In the next step they added the individual difference factors (noted above) and accounted for an additional 3.7% of the variance in retirement satisfaction. Job factors accounted for an additional
5.1% of variance, while family status variables accounted for an addition 3.7% of variance in retirement satisfaction (for a total of 21.7%
of variance accounted for by all variables). Surprisingly similar re-

sults were obtained for life satisfaction, even though retirement and life satisfaction only correlated at r = .09.

Moen, Plassmann, and Sweet (2001) recently reported results from *The Cornell Midcareer Paths and Passages Study* consisting of 887 residents of upstate New York in which they "employ a life course, contextual perspective" to understand the transition to retirement (p. 4). Moen, Plassmann, and Sweet note that, "Men with school-age children and older women with no children are the most likely to consider a post-retirement career" (p. 6). Almost 40% of these two groups were planning postretirement careers, compared with less than 28% of respondents overall. Similarly, 35% of male managers and 37% of male professionals plan postretirement careers, whereas female managers were the most likely to pursue postretirement careers (31%) among women. Moen, Plassmann, and Sweet (2001) also found that desired work hours and alternative pathways to retirement are at least partially a function of individual's current life stage. Specifically, younger cohorts of workers wanted to retire earlier (late 50s) than older workers, yet surprisingly they were less likely to be planning for a postretirement career.

In summary, we see that economists have done a good job of documenting the existence of bridge employment. In addition, they have been able to delineate many of the broader cyclical and structural factors, as well as demographic factors, that appear to impact the prevalence of bridge employment. Psychologists, sociologists, and other social scientists, however, are just beginning to understand the major psychosocial antecedents and consequences of bridge employment. Therefore, future research needs, both in terms of factors that should be examined and methods of doing so, are discussed next.

FUTURE RESEARCH NEEDS

While some descriptive studies (Quinn, 2000; Ruhm, 1990a) have used longitudinal data sets, most of the work on bridge employment has used cross-sectional data. If retirement truly is a process and not an event, then longitudinal data is essential to studying the retirement process. The Health and Retirement Study (HRS) data provides some of the largest and most current data available to study the process of retirement, and bridge employment as a phase of that process, from a longitudinal framework. In addition, a longitudinal data set with the size and scope of the HRS would allow for more powerful statistical techniques (e.g., growth curve modeling, see Zickar and Gibby's chapter in this volume) in examining what intra-individual changes occurring within older adults predict engagement in a variety of forms of bridge employment.

In addition, researchers also need to take a multilevel approach (Klein & Kozlowski, 2000) to studying bridge employment. That is, while psychologists have focused on psychosocial factors, sociologists on social factors, and economists on demographic and macroeconomic factors, no researchers have looked across multiple levels of variables to simultaneously examine individual, group, family, organizational, and society-wide factors that impact bridge employment antecedents and outcomes. Feldman (1994) suggests influence at the various levels of analysis, but not how they might interact to affect bridge employment. Once again, the HRS data set provides at least proxies for many of these variables and thus would serve as an ideal data set to tease apart the independent and joint effects of various levels of influence on the bridge employment process.

Hagestad and Dannefer (2001) discuss a multilevel approach to studying the life course that fits well with the concept of bridge employment. They delineate four levels of analysis: individual, micro, meso, and macro. While the latter levels are more distal to individuals' attitudes and behaviors, changes in those distal levels create new opportunities and/or constraints at the lower levels. Thus their model emphasizes the strong interplay between the individuals and their sociohistorical context. In doing so, we can study bridge employment as an evolutionary process (similar to retirement itself) and not just as a certain stage in one's life. Feldman (1994) and Kim and Moen (2001) both emphasize the need to look at the family unit when examining retirement, and in turn, bridge employment. This would be within the realm of the much neglected "meso" level of analysis that Hagestad and Dannefer discuss. Much of the prior research has focused on individuals' decision making with regard to retirement, and subsequently about bridge employment. However, as Kim and Moen note, retirement is very much a "coupled" experience. For example, whether one's spouse is currently engaged in work or is in need of care can strongly influence the other partner's intentions to seek out, obtain and maintain bridge employment.

The issue of bridge employment is not unique to the United States. For example, a recent summary of international aging statistics by Kinsella and Velkoff (2001) notes that, "gradual retirement is still relatively uncommon [for men] in industrialized nations. The strongest tendency toward part-time work was seen in Japan, Sweden, and the United States" (p. 105). However, Kinsella and Velkoff also note that there is a consistent pattern in developed countries (e.g., Australia, European Union, United States) of women being more likely to be working part-time in old age than men. Unfortunately, most of the research on bridge employment has focused on U.S. based samples by U.S. researchers. Many European countries and several Asian countries are experiencing even greater shortages of workers as well as older and more rapidly aging populations. As a result, the need to encourage work at older ages, particularly in the form of bridge employment, is even more pressing for these countries. Usui (1998), for example, provides an interesting description of Japanese strategies that have been employed to allow older workers to retire gradually, thus providing an "internalized" bridge path to complete retirement (i.e., phased retirement). Accordingly, cross-national studies, or at least cross-national comparisons, are needed to study the issue of bridge employment more fully (see Henkens and Van Dalen's chapter on international issues in retirement in this volume).

In addition, Feldman and Kim (2000), Quinn and Kozy (1996), and Ruhm (1989) all clearly demonstrate that certain demographic groups (i.e., minorities, women, lower SES) are less likely to engage in bridge employment, and if they do, they are more likely to take jobs outside the industry in which they spent their careers. This typically results in reduced wages and benefits. Therefore, to the extent that bridge employment has more positive versus negative consequences for later retirement adjustment and satisfaction, groups that were disadvantaged throughout their careers and lifetimes will continue to feel the burden of that disadvantage in retirement as well via a lack of bridge employment opportunities (O'Rand & Henretta, 1999).

In summary, given that work after retirement (i.e., bridge employment) appears to have more positive than negative consequences

(Feldman & Kim, 2000), we need to find ways to encourage and promote bridge employment for those older adults who are willing and able to engage in postretirement work. Thus, strategies for fostering bridge employment are presented next. First, however, the changing societal context that will foster bridge employment is discussed. Then, possible strategies for promoting bridge employment at the societal, organizational, and older worker levels, respectively, are delineated.

Fostering Postretirement Employment

AGE DIFFERENTIATED VERSUS AGE INTEGRATED SOCIAL STRUCTURES

Sociologist Angela O'Rand (O'Rand, 1996, 2001; O'Rand & Henretta, 1999) has discussed how the life course has traditionally been stratified into school when we are young, work in middle age, and leisure in old age. However, theorists such as O'Rand and Matilda White Riley have suggested a gradual progression from an age differentiated society (as noted above) to an age integrated society. In an age integrated society, education, work, and leisure occur simultaneously, in close proximity, or in much shorter, repeated cycles of education, work, and leisure. If in fact this transformation is occurring, then it is not surprising that bridge employment is becoming more prominent, in that bridge employment typically consists of part-time, short-duration, or self-employment, which by its very nature, allows older individuals time to concurrently engage in employment, leisure, and/or education. As a result, we should continue to foster opportunities for bridge employment across many levels. Therefore, how we can foster bridge employment at societal/governmental, organizational, and individual (i.e., older worker) levels is discussed next.

SOCIETAL/GOVERNMENTAL RESPONSES TO FOSTER BRIDGE EMPLOYMENT

Burkhauser and Quinn (1997) trace the historical progression from anti to neutral work policies, with regard to employment of the elderly, which has occurred over the course of the last quarter century. They then go on to discuss how we can further progress to actual pro-work policies for the elderly by delineating five key legislative policy changes that will promote employment of older individuals. First, they recommend restoring the Social Security early retirement age from 62 to age 65—its pre-1962 level. The normal Social Security retirement age is already slowly increasing from age 65 to age 67 over the next few decades. They contend that returning early retirement to age 65 would create a strong incentive for older workers to remain in the workforce to age 65. Although not fostering bridge employment specifically, it would encourage those between the ages of 63 and 65 to remain in the workforce. However, a small percentage of minorities, in particular, would suffer adverse economic consequences if required to forgo retirement until age 65, in that African American and Hispanic older workers have a disproportionate number of health limitations, compared with Caucasians, making work at older ages prohibitive.

A second policy change would be to allow workers age 65 and over to opt out of additional Social Security contributions. Since Social Security is paid jointly by the employee and the employer, this would not only be a strong incentive to older workers to continue working (especially with the recent repeal of the Social Security earnings test for those aged 65 to 69), but would also reduce the cost of these employees for employers, thus making older workers more attractive to employers.

A third suggested policy change by Burkhauser and Quinn (1997) is to amend the Employee Retirement Income Security Act (ERISA) so that fringe benefits can be prorated based on the number of hours worked. Currently, part-time employees who work less than 1,000 hours per year get no benefits, while those working more than 1,000 hours per year get full benefits. The current rules thus encourage employers to keep part-time employees' hours to the statutory minimum. Since bridge employment often consists of part-time or temporary work, making such an adjustment could increase the prominence of bridge employment, particularly now that the Social Security earnings limits have been repealed for those 65 to 69 years old.

Because health care costs are a major concern of employers with regard to employment of the elderly, a fourth suggested policy change is to make Medicare the primary health insurance of older workers 65 to 69 years old, rather than employer-based health insurance. Such a change would inevitably increase Medicare expenses, but would, like the second suggested policy change above, make older workers more attractive to employers. Finally, Burkhauser and Quinn (1997) suggest expanding the Earned Income Tax Credit to include workers age 65 and older, who do not have qualifying dependents. Doing so, they propose, would encourage low-income older workers to continue in lower wage, contingent, or bridge jobs.

Shultz, Sirotnik, and Bockman (2000) propose similar governmental and legislative initiatives to reduce barriers and encourage work at older ages. While their initiatives were targeted more specifically to the state of California, most could be applied more widely. For example, Shultz, Sivotnik, and Bochman focus on the need for retraining and updating of job skills. They propose building partnerships between public universities, organizations, and older worker advocacy groups (e.g., AARP) in order to provide skill enhancement training for older workers. In addition, they suggest offering tax credits to employers who provide training targeted at older workers. Furthermore, they suggest offering individual level incentives in the form of tuition subsidies, need-based tuition wavers, or tax rebates that could be offered to older adults who engage in skills upgrading. Other suggestions include support for community outreach efforts, promotion of basic and applied research, as well as demonstration projects on issues of importance to older workers (e.g., training needs, retirement planning).

A recent publication by the Committee for Economic Development (CED) (1999) also provides a "pro-work" agenda for the employment of older workers. Their recommendations fall into six broad categories. In this section, several of the broad policy and societal level initiatives are discussed. The first deals with the financial incentives, including pension and social security reforms like those discussed above. In addition, the CED report discusses the need for changes in federal laws governing employee benefits similar to Burkhauser and Quinn's (1997) suggestion above. In doing so, the report suggests that phased retirement would become a more viable option. The CED report, similar to Shultz, Sivotnik, and Bochman (2000) above, also urges "higher education and other training institutions to recognize the need for work-oriented learning among older Americans and expand their offerings to this largely untapped customer market" (p. 4). Finally, the CED report also recommends bolstering Social Security Disability Insurance (DI) to promote work by DI recipients, many of whom are older Americans.

A recent Government Accounting Office (GAO) (2001) report makes recommendations similar to those provided above, but also cautions that sweeping legislative changes may well have unintended consequences. "For example, amending the ADEA to facilitate the expansion of phased retirement programs might result in some older workers losing legal protection against age discrimination in ways not previously recognized or understood" (p. 33). Therefore, the GAO report recommends formation of a broad-based advisory council or task force to examine such recommendations for potential unintended consequences. This council could include Department of Justice and Labor Department representatives, as well as other "experts" who could provide critical assessment and input to make sure any changes were carefully crafted and represented sound public policy.

Finally, Ruhm (1994) notes that whatever public policy initiatives are pursued to assist the elderly in obtaining bridge employment, they should be targeted at disadvantaged groups, rather than providing "general incentives" to all older adults. This is because nontargeted assistance, like the recent removal of the Social Security earnings test for those 65 to 69 years old, is more likely to assist advantaged groups. Ruhm also suggests that any intervention should be targeted at younger and younger ages, since many individuals now have opportunities to exit the labor force well before traditional retirement ages (i.e., early to mid 60s). Finally, Ruhm cautions policy makers to be aware that broad efforts to delay retirements may actually worsen the lot of some older workers.

The above suggestions, while all worthwhile, are somewhat controversial and would require lengthy legislative and political debate. However, more timely and targeted changes can be implemented more expediently by organizations in order to fit their particular, and continually changing, needs. Some of these potential employer responses are discussed below.

EMPLOYER RESPONSES TO FOSTER BRIDGE EMPLOYMENT

Burtless and Quinn (2001) note that the historical evidence for the capacity of the U.S. economy to create jobs, and thus absorb extra job seekers, is very strong. That is, as more individuals, regardless of age, enter the labor market, employers have responded rather swiftly by creating new jobs and hiring job seekers. However, if a certain class of workers, for example, highly paid and experienced older workers, becomes abundant, the laws of supply and demand would likely depress wages for this group. This might be counterbalanced by the slower pace of growth of the workforce in the future due to lower U.S. fertility rates. For example, a recent Government Account Office (GAO) (2001) report cited Bureau of Labor Statistics (BLS) figures that project "total labor force growth will slow from an average annual rate of 1.1 percent between 1990 and 2000 to an annual rate of 0.7 percent between 2000 and 2025" (p. 1). Thus, as in the past, employers will likely have to tailor jobs to the needs of the available workforce, which will increasingly include more and more older workers.

Rosen and Jerdee (1985, 1988) proposed the use of phased retirement, job sharing, job transfers, job redesign, sabbaticals, and retraining to address the issues of career burnout, plateauing, and obsolescence faced by many older workers near retirement age. Usui (1998) provides an interesting example of how Japan, as a nation, has "internalized" phased retirement for older workers. Japanese organizations provide such prowork options, and the Japanese government supports such options through public pensions to supplement wages lost through reduced work schedules. Additional alternative work arrangements such as consulting roles or permanent part-time jobs could also be implemented by employers to retain older workers, thus allowing them to bridge or phase into retirement without having to engage in an external job search (see Greller and Stroh's chapter in this volume for more examples of managing older workers).

Doeringer and Terkla (1990) suggest that instituting such flexible work arrangements would be easier to implement in small-to medium-sized firms, yet much of the public policy debate has focused on large firms. Doeringer and Terkla note that, "Small firms are less burdened by rigid job structures and are thus more quickly able to modify job opportunities to accommodate older workers seeking bridge employment" (p. 147). Doverspike, Taylor, Shultz, and McKay (2000) also note that such alternative work arrangements could be used by a variety of employers' in recruiting older workers as they end their career jobs and begin to explore bridge employment options. These same strategies may also work for recruiting recently retired workers back into the workforce.

The Committee for Economic Development (CED) (1999) also provided suggestions for employers to foster employment at older ages. For example, the report suggests that employers implement changes to company pension plans and benefits offerings (e.g., cafeteria style benefits) to allow a greater variety of work options at older ages, such as phased retirement or other flexible work arrangements such job sharing. The report also suggests that employers revise their recruitment practices with an eye toward older candidates. Finally, the CED report also "urges employers to address age discrimination in the workplace and hiring practices through training sessions and workshops" (p. 4). In doing so, organizations will serve their self-interests better by getting an "honest assessment" of the potential value that older workers bring to the table.

Sterns and Gray (1999) echo the CED report's final message when they state that, "only partial support is found for both the negative and positive aspects of the older worker stereotypes examined here . . . . [thus] each individual, regardless of age, should be evaluated (or self-evaluated) based on his or her own merits, skills, abilities, and motivation and not stereotypic characteristics of a particular age group with which he or she happens to be associated" (p. 365–366). To the extent employers heed their advice, more bridge employment opportunities will become available to older workers.

Shultz (2001) also discussed how contingent work arrangements (e.g., part-time, temporary, seasonal, contract work) could be used to bridge the gap between one's career and full-time retirement. The contingent workforce continues to increase as employers seek more flexible workforces (Lindbo & Shultz, 1998). However, many full-time employees feel threatened by contingent workers who hope to turn temporary assignments into full-time employment. Older workers, though, may be viewed as less threatening to current employees of the organization, since older workers are less likely to be seeking full-time, permanent positions. Thus, Shultz (2001) notes that, "Bridge employment (and contingent work in particular) serves as a potential conduit for both employers needing to fill critical roles and mature individuals looking for work. But how to best incorporate these contingent older workers into an integrated strategic human resource planning effort is not completely clear" (p. 254). Feldman and Kim (2000) provide several practical suggestions for attracting and retaining bridge employees, including providing clear goals and expectations, tax and financial planning, as well as clear and direct pension and fringe benefit calculations.

Adams and Beehr (1998) and Feldman and Kim (2000) note that bridge employment can be a potentially valuable experience for retirees as well as employers, in that bridge employment typically allows retirees to transition out of full-time work less abruptly. Thus, in addition to the above societal and employer responses, we must also examine the role of older workers themselves in successfully implementing bridge employment strategies. Ultimately, it is up to the older workers to successfully promote themselves in order to obtain bridge employment once it is created by the societal and organizational means noted above. The role of older workers in the bridge employment equation is examined next.

OLDER WORKER RESPONSES TO FOSTER BRIDGE EMPLOYMENT

Sullivan, Carden, and Martin (1998) hypothesize that careers in the 21st century will vary along two key dimensions, namely, transferability of competencies and level of internal work values. Clearly, as noted previously, baby boomers appear to have a strong desire to continue working, at least part-time, once retired. In some ways, this indicates high internal work values, given many will not be working primarily for the income (Sterns & Huyck, 2001). Therefore, the bigger issue becomes that of transferability of skills. As Sullivan, Carden, and Martin point out, many older workers' skills are "firm specific" and, as a result, will not transfer as readily to other employers. Thus, older workers will be much more likely to have to start over again if they choose to change jobs or, worse yet, careers just prior to retirement.

Spiegel and Shultz (in press) examined transferability of skills in a sample of military retirees, the majority of whom began second careers, to determine if it affected adjustment to retirement from the military. Spiegel and Shultz (in press) found that "those naval officers who were able to readily transfer their knowledge, skills, and abilities (KSAs) to the civilian labor market were satisfied with, and adjusted well to, their [military] retirement." Thus, in this case, it appears that military retirement is analogous to those individuals in the civilian labor force who begin second careers and/or engage in bridge employment after their primary careers.

In another somewhat idiosyncratic sample, Feldman and Kim (2000) showed that college professors accepting early retirement incentives who were able to use existing skills in new settings showed much better adjustment to retirement, and to bridge employment, than those who did not have transferable skills. Consequently, it would behoove older workers, regardless of whether they are in the civilian labor market or the military, to obtain and foster KSAs before retirement that are readily transferable across a wide variety of possible bridge jobs.

Drucker (2001) noted, "The next society will be a knowledge society. Knowledge will be its key resource, and knowledge workers will be the dominant group in its workforce" (p. 2). These knowledge workers will include not only highly educated individuals (e.g., medical doctors, lawyers, engineers), but also "knowledge technologists" (e.g., computer technicians, paralegals). That is, those individuals who work primarily with their hands, but such work requires extensive formal training. Thus, an increasing proportion of workers will need to engage in continued training and retraining to remain competitive for postretirement employment opportunities in order to avoid "starting over" (Shultz, Sivotnik, & Bochman (2000).

However, as Maurer has recently noted, most employers are unwilling to invest in older workers by providing valuable employer-sponsored training to update and improve their skills (Maurer, 2001; Maurer, & Rafure, 2001). Therefore, it becomes incumbent on the older workers themselves to seek out training and development opportunities to make themselves as marketable as possible in the ever-changing job market (Hansson, DeKoekkoek, Neece, & Patterson, 1997; Sterns & Huyck, 2001). The CED (1999) report notes that, "Older workers themselves have the primary responsibility to acquire and maintain their own skills" (p. 4). In addition, the CED report also notes that older workers searching for new employment need to not only update their job skills, but also their computer-based job search skills. Sterns and Gray (1999) note that this need to "self-manage" one's career, and potentially one's postretirement second career, can be a daunting challenge for many older workers.

Hansson (Abraham & Hansson, 1995; Hansson, DeKoekkoek, Neece & Patterson, 1997) has extensively discussed the concept of "successful aging at work" using Baltes and Baltes (1990) selective optimization with compensation (SOC) model. Using their framework, Hansson proposes that older workers engage in a variety of compensating mechanisms to remain up-to-date and employable. The basic issue becomes one of, "How do older workers adapt with age?" Unfortunately, most research examining age issues and adaptability at work has focused on age differences in adaptability rather than how individuals actually adapt as they age. Shultz and Morton (2000) delineate some of the methodological issues in examining successful aging at work and how older workers adapt by differentiating how researchers can tease apart age, cohort, and time effects. Of relevance to the present discussion, is that to the extent older workers adapt (i.e., age successfully) in terms of their work-related competencies, they are more likely to seek and obtain bridge employment. Thus, another fruitful area for future research is examining to what extent older workers can and do successfully age at work (Shultz & Morton, 2000).

Summary and Conclusions

Ruhm (1990b) noted more than a decade ago that "the process by which individuals move from stable career employment to retirement remains poorly understood, and the gaps in our knowledge lead to inadequately focused analysis, poorly constructed theories, and questionable policy recommendations" (p. 92). While important descriptive, empirical, and theoretical research has emerged in the last decade to improve our understanding of the transition from career employment to permanent retirement (i.e., the job-stopping process, to use Ruhm's terminology), much more work is still needed. For example, we need to better understand the psychosocial antecedents and consequences of engaging (or not engaging) in bridge employment. Feldman's work (Feldman, 1994; Feldman & Kim, 1998; Kim & Feldman, 1998, 2000) has begun to address some of the theoretical and empirical shortcomings of past work. In addition, we also need to better understand the barriers that historically disadvantaged groups face with regard to bridge employment and how we can help these individuals overcome such barriers (Ruhm, 1994). Cross-cultural comparisons are also severely lacking and need to be addressed.

In terms of Ruhm's (1990b) complaint of past research having "inadequately focused analyses," several suggestions are provided at the end of the first part of the chapter. These include making better use of longitudinal data by employing multivariate techniques such as structural equation, multilevel, and growth curve modeling. Doing so would allow us to simultaneously estimate the joint effects of a variety of antecedents and consequences of bridge employment that are measured at an assortment of levels.

Finally, in the second part of this chapter a plethora of suggestions were presented to address Ruhm's (1990b) admonition regarding "questionable policy recommendations." While additional research from a variety of sources will be needed to strengthen our resolve in the policy options currently being put forth, to the extent that the recommendations for future research presented earlier are heeded, such resolve should be forthcoming. However, we must keep in mind that public policy is only one piece of the puzzle to increasing employment options for older workers. We must also continue to work to strengthen employer initiatives, as well as provide older workers themselves opportunities to improve their attractiveness to potential employers. By doing so opportunities for bridge employment will be maximized for all older adults wishing to engage in postretirement work.

REFERENCES

AARP (1999a). *A profile of older Americans: 1999.* New York: Author.

AARP (1999b). *Boomers approaching midlife: How secure a future?* New York: AARP Public Policy Institute.

Abraham, J. D., & Hansson, R. O. (1995). Successful aging at work: An applied study of selection, optimization, and compensation through impression management. *Journals of Gerontology: Psychology Sciences, 50B,* P94–P103.

Adams, G. A., & Beehr, T. A. (1998). Turnover and retirement: A comparison of their similarities and differences. *Personnel Psychology, 51,* 643–665.

Adams, G. A., & Lax, G. A. (2002, April). Job seeking among retirees seeking bridge employment. In K. S. Shultz (Chair), *Addressing projected workforce shortages by recruiting and retaining older workers.* Symposium conducted at the 17th annual conference of the Society for Industrial and Organizational Psychology (SIOP), Toronto, Ontario.

Baltes, P. B., & Baltes, M. M. (1990). Psychological perspectives on successful aging: The model of selective optimization with compensation. In M. M. Baltes & P. B. Baltes (Eds.), *Successful aging: Perspectives from the behavioral sciences* (pp. 1–34). Cambridge: Cambridge University Press.

Beehr, T. A. (1986). The process of retirement: A review and recommendations for future investigation. *Personnel Psychology, 39,* 31–55.

Burkhauser, R. V., & Quinn, J. F. (1997). *Pro-work policy proposals for older Americans in the 21st century.* Policy Brief No. 9, Maxwell School for Citizenship and Public Affairs, Syracuse University, Syracuse, New York.

Burtless, G., & Quinn, J. F. (2001). Retirement trends and policies to encourage work among older Americans. In P. P. Budetti, R. V. Burkhauser, J. M. Gregory, & H. A. Hunt (Eds.), *Ensuring health and income security for an aging workforce* (pp. 375–415). Kalamazoo, Michigan: W.E. Upjohn Institute for Employment Research.

Committee for Economic Development (1999). *New opportunities for older workers.* Available at http://www.ced.org/docs/older.pdf

Costa, D. L. (1998). *The evolution of retirement: An American economic history, 1880–1990.* Chicago, Illinois: University of Chicago Press.

Doeringer, P. B. (1990). *Bridges to retirement.* Ithaca, New York: Cornell University Press.

Doeringer, P. B., & Terkla, D. G. (1990). Business necessity, bridge jobs, and the non-bureaucratic firm. In P. B. Doeringer (Ed.), *Bridges to retirement* (pp. 146–171). Ithaca, New York: Cornell University Press.

Doverspike, D., Taylor, M. A., Shultz, K. S., & McKay, P. (2000). Responding to the challenge of a changing workforce: Recruiting nontraditional demographic groups. *Public Personnel Management, 29,* 445–459.

Drucker, P. F. (2001, Nov 1st). The next society. *The Economist.* Available at: http://www.economist.com/printedition/PrinterFriendly.cfm?Story_ID=770819

Dulebohn, J. H., Murray, B., & Sun, M. (2000). Selection among employer-sponsored pension plans: The role of individual differences. *Personnel Psychology, 53,* 405–432.

Elder, G. H., Jr., & Pavalko, E. K. (1993). Work careers in men's later years: Transitions, trajectories, and historical changes. *Journal of Gerontology: Social Sciences, 48,* S180–S191.

Feldman, D. C. (1994). The decision to retire early: A review and conceptualization. *Academy of Management Review, 19,* 285–311.

Feldman, D. C., & Kim, S. (2000). Bridge employment during retirement: A field study of individual and organizational experiences with post-retirement employment. *Human Resource Planning, 23,* 14–25.

Government Accounting Office (2001, November). *Older workers: Demographic trends pose challenges for employers and workers.* Available at http://www.gao.gov/cgi-bin/getrpt?GAO-02-85

Gustman, A. L., & Steinmeier, T. L. (1984). Partial retirement and the analysis of retirement behavior. *Industrial and Labor Relations Review, 37,* 403–415.

Hagestad, G. O., & Dannefer, D. (2001). Concepts and theories of aging: Beyond microfication in social science approaches. In R. H. Binstock & L. K. George

(Eds.), *Handbook of aging and the social sciences, 5th ed.,* (pp. 3–21). San Diego, California: Academic Press.

Hansson, R. O., DeKoekkoek, P. D., Neece, W. M., & Patterson, D. W. (1997). Successful aging at work: Annual review, 1992–1996: The older worker and transitions to retirement. *Journal of Vocational Behavior, 51,* 202–233.

Hayward, M. D., Crimmins, E. M., & Wray, L. A. (1994). The relationship between retirement life cycle changes and older men's labor force participation rates. *Journals of Gerontology: Social Science, 49B,* S219–S230.

Heindel, R. A., Adams, G. A., & Lepisto, L. (1999, April). *Predicting bridge employment: A test of Feldman's (1994) hypotheses.* Poster presented at the 14th annual conference of the Society for Industrial and Organizational Psychology, Atlanta, Georgia.

Henretta, J. C. (2001). Work and Retirement. In R. H. Binstock & L. K. George (Eds.), *Handbook of aging and the social sciences, 5th ed.,* (pp. 255–271). San Diego, California: Academic Press.

Herz, D. E. (1995). Work after retirement: An increasing trend among men. *Monthly Labor Review, 118 (4),* 13–20.

Honig, M., & Hanoch, G. (1985). Partial retirement as a separate mode of retirement behavior. *Journal of Human Resources, 20,* 21–46.

Hurd, M. D. (1996). The effect of labor market rigidities on the labor force behavior of older workers. In D. A. Wise (Ed.), *Advances in the economics of aging* (pp. 11–60). Chicago: University of Chicago Press.

Kim, J. E., & Moen, P. (2001). Moving into retirement: Preparation and transitions in late midlife. In M. E. Lachman (Ed.), *Handbook of midlife development* (pp. 487–527). New York: John Wiley & Sons.

Kim, S., & Feldman, D. C. (1998). Healthy, wealthy, or wise: Predicting actual acceptances of early retirement incentives at three points in time. *Personnel Psychology, 51,* 623–642.

Kim, S., & Feldman, D. C. (2000). Working in retirement: The antecedents of bridge employment and its consequences for quality of life in retirement. *Academy of Management Journal, 43,* 1195–1210.

Kinsella, K., & Velkoff, V. A. (2001). *An aging world: 2001.* U.S. Bureau of Census, Series P95/01–1, Washington, D. C.: U.S. Government Printing Office.

Klein, K. J., & Kozlowski, S. W. J. (2000). *Multilevel theory, research, and methods in organizations: Foundations, extensions, and new directions.* San Francisco: Jossey Bass.

Lindbo, T. L., & Shultz, K. S. (1998). The role of organizational culture and mentoring on mature worker socialization toward retirement. *Public Productivity and Management Review, 22,* 49–59.

Maurer, T. J. (2001). Career-related learning and development, worker age, and beliefs about self-efficacy for development. *Journal of Management, 27,* 123–140.

Maurer, T. J., & Rafuse, N. E. (2001). Learning not litigating: Managing employee development and avoiding claims of age discrimination. *Academy of Management Executive, 15(4),* 110–121.

Moen, P., Plassmann, V. S., & Sweet, S. (2001). *Cornell midcareer paths and passages study: Summary 2001*. Ithaca, NY: Bronfenbrenner Life Course Center, Cornell University. Available at http://www.lifecourse.cornell.edu/ archives/misc/ midcareer_2001.pdf

Mutchler, J. E., Burr, J. A., Pienta, A. M., & Massagli, M. P. (1997). Pathways to labor force exit: Work transitions and work instability. *Journals of Gerontology: Social Sciences, 52B,* S4–S12.

O'Rand, A. M. (1996). The cumulative stratification of the life course. In R. H. Binstock & L. K. George (Eds.), *Handbook of aging and the social sciences, 4th ed.,* (pp. 188–207). San Diego, California: Academic Press.

O'Rand, A. M. (2001). Stratification of the life course: The forms of life-course capital and their interrelationships. In R. H. Binstock & L. K. George (Eds.), *Handbook of aging and the social sciences, 5th ed.,* (pp. 197–213). San Diego, California: Academic Press.

O'Rand, A. M., & Henretta, J. (1999). *Age and inequality: Diverse pathways through later life.* Boulder, Colorado: Westview Publishing.

Quinn, J. F. (1997a). Retirement trends and patterns in the 1990s: The end of an era? *The Public Policy and Aging Report, 8 (3),* 10–14, 19.

Quinn, J. F. (1997b). The role of bridge jobs in the retirement patterns of older Americans in the 1990s. In P. R. DeJong (Ed.), *Social policy and the labour market* (pp. 91–116). Brookfield, Massachusetts: Ashgate.

Quinn, J. F. (1999). Retirement patterns and bridge jobs in the 1990s. *Employee Benefit Research Institute (EBRI) Issue Brief Number 206.* Washington, D.C.: EBRI.

Quinn, J. F. (2000). New paths to retirement. In O. S. Mitchell, P. B. Hammond, & A. M. Rappaport (Eds.), *Forecasting retirement needs and retirement wealth* (pp. 13–32). Philadelphia, Pennsylvania: University of Pennsylvania Press.

Quinn, J. F., & Kozy, M. (1996). The role of bridge jobs in the retirement transition: Gender, race and ethnicity. *The Gerontologist, 36,* 363–372.

Roper Starch Worldwide (1999). *1999 survey of Americans born between 1946 and 1964.* New York: AARP.

Rosen, B., & Jerdee, T. H. (1985). *Older employees: New roles for valued resources.* Chicago: Dow-Jones/Irwin.

Rosen, B., & Jerdee, T. H. (1988). Managing older workers careers. *Research in Personnel and Human Resource Management, 6,* 37–74.

Ruhm, C. J. (1989). Why older workers stop working. *Gerontologist, 29,* 294–299.

Ruhm, C. J. (1990a). Bridge jobs and partial retirement. *Journal of Labor Economics, 8,* 582–601.

Ruhm, C. J. (1990b). Career jobs, bridge employment, and retirement. In P. B. Doeringer (Ed.), *Bridges to retirement* (pp. 92–107). Ithaca, New York: Cornell University Press.

Ruhm, C. J. (1994). Bridge employment and job stopping: Evidence from the Harris/ Commonwealth Fund Survey. *Journal of Aging & Social Policy, 6(4),* 73–99.

Shultz, K. S. (2001). The new contingent workforce: Examining the bridge employment options of mature workers. *International Journal of Organizational Theory and Behavior, 4,* 247–258.

Shultz, K. S., & Morton, K. R. (2000). Successful aging at work: How do older workers adjust? *Southwest Journal of Aging, 16(2),* 63–72.

Shultz, K. S., Morton, K. R., & Weckerle, J. R. (1998). The influence of push and pull factors in distinguishing voluntary and involuntary early retirees' retirement decision and adjustment. *Journal of Vocational Behavior, 53,* 45–57.

Shultz, K. S., Sirotnik, B. W., & Bockman, S. E. (2000). An aging workforce in transition: A case study of California. *Southwest Journal of Aging, 16(2),* 9–16.

Spiegel, P. E., & Shultz, K. S. (in press). The influence of pre-retirement planning and transferability of skills on naval officers' retirement satisfaction and adjustment. *Military Psychology.*

Sterns, H. L., & Gray, J. H. (1999). Work, leisure and retirement. In J. C. Cavanaugh & S. K. Whitbourne (Eds.), *Gerontology: An interdisciplinary perspective* (pp. 355–390). New York: Oxford University Press.

Sterns, H. L., & Huyck, M. H. (2001). The role of work in midlife. In M. E. Lachman (Ed.), *Handbook of midlife development* (pp. 447–486). New York: John Wiley & Sons.

Sullivan, S. E., Carden, W. A., & Martin, D. F. (1998). Careers in the next millennium: Directions for future research. *Human Resource Management Review, 8,* 165–185.

Usui, C. (1998). Gradual retirement: Japanese strategies for older workers. In K. W. Schaie & C. Schooler (Eds.), *Impact of work on older adults.* New York: Springer Publishing.

Weckerle, J. R., & Shultz, K. S. (1999). Influences on the bridge employment decision among older U.S.A. workers. *Journal of Occupational and Organizational Psychology, 72,* 317–330.

10

Early Retirement Systems and Behavior in an International Perspective

Kène Henkens and Hendrik P. Van Dalen

All countries in the western world are confronted with an aging population. This demographic change is caused by a sharp drop in fertility in the late sixties, together with a steady increase in average life expectancy (United Nations, 2001; Kinsella & Gist, 1995). In spite of the continued increase in life expectancy, which can be observed across all developed countries, this trend was not accompanied by an increase in working careers or an upward shift in the retirement age. On the contrary, in most countries, there is a long-run trend of decreasing labor force participation of older workers. Although there is a fierce debate among academics whether a trend that began almost a century ago can actually be reversed, the goal of raising retirement ages seems to have obtained in almost every western society the status of a mantra in public policy circles. In this chapter we will examine the policy initiatives that have been put forward in the majority of countries of the Organization for Economic Cooperation and Development (OECD). These policy initiatives cover retirement reforms dealing with social and private arrangements to finance retirement, but also public policies with the broader goal to strengthen the position of older workers on the labor market, such as combating age discrimination and nega-

tive stereotyping. We will discuss to what extent these policy initiatives have been successful in affecting retirement behavior. The short
version of "tour d'horizon" is that policy initiatives have proven far
less effective than the claims and ambitions made at the time these
initiatives were designed. Why have these policies been successful,
and—as will be our claim—why have they failed? Is it just a case of
bad luck or do the failures have to do with faulty design choices,
reforms based on models that do not describe the way the world
works. To many policy makers, retirement seems like a simple decision problem. It is all a matter of costs and benefits if you ask the
advisors at an average pension fund or insurance company. Certainly
the financial costs and benefits matter, since no one can afford to
retire from the labor force without sufficient funds. But in everyday
life more elements come into play in making retirement choices, and
the central tenet of this chapter is to confront public policy with some
current scientific insights concerning factors affecting retirement behavior of older workers. In general, the case turns out to be that the
scientific foundation of policy measures often does not seem to be as
firm as it appears at first sight. This observation is perhaps an obvious
point which can be made at every occasion where policies are evaluated, but it is one which goes right to the heart of the retirement
policy debate. For example, in an extensive overview of the international experiences of governments, Taylor, Tillsley, Beausoleil, Wilson, and Walker (2000) concluded that policy making is proceeding
on the basis of an incomplete understanding of older workers' orienta-
tions toward work and retirement and they show how retirement behavior
may change in response to policies aimed at delaying retirement.

The set-up of this chapter is straightforward, since the overview
of international experiences has to be brief and to the point. We start
with a conventional overview of the stylized facts of (early) retirement followed directly by a summary of the policy initiatives which
have been designed in the past across countries in the OECD to deal
with the problem of reversing the early retirement trend. Following
this, the basic assumptions underlying the policies are discussed. The
final point of this chapter is that, for retirement policies to become
more effective, the policy makers and their advisors should return
first to the drawing board and draw a better picture of the retirement process.

Stylized Facts of Retirement Systems

Most retirement systems around the world were intended to provide the elderly with a reasonable income during the final stage of their life course. The Beveridge Report (1942) has perhaps been most influential in this respect, since it propounded state responsibility for individual welfare "from the cradle to the grave." The Beveridge Report offered for a number of European nations a blueprint for designing their welfare state, a state which aimed at efficiency in the use of resources, distribution in accordance with norms of justice or equity, and the preservation of individual freedom, or as Beveridge (1944) once remarked: "to use the powers of the State to avoid the five giant evils" (p. 254), those evils being: want, disease, ignorance, squalor, and idleness. Social insurance was not a novelty. As early as the 1880s Germany already offered social insurance to cover events such as industrial accidents, sickness, health expenditures and pensions. However, the grand scale at which social insurance was enacted could well be deemed a novel aspect of Western societies.

Welfare states around the world evolved and expanded after World War II to such an extent that pensioners by and large did not have to fall back to subsistence levels. For the cohorts who were present at the introduction of extensive social security programs, life expectancy generally surpassed the statutory retirement age by a few years, labor force participation was high, and early retirement was almost nonexistent. At this moment in time, things have turned around quite drastically, as the number of years spent in retirement for industrialized countries is approximately 18 years for men and 23 years for women (OECD, 2001), and labor force participation of older workers (60–64 years) has dropped almost in every OECD country. With this perspective in the back of our minds, there can hardly be any disagreement about the real concern for the early retirement trend: the sustainability of pensions and social security in an aging world. *The Economist* (2002) was rather harsh in its verdict about the state of pensions, but it summed up the consensus that most economists and policy makers would make at this juncture in time: "public pension systems do not achieve a reasonable trade-off between actuarial fairness and protection against poverty in old age. What they mainly do is redistribute income from the young (who may be poor) to the old (who may be rich) often in an inequitable way." At present, most countries are encountering aging populations, which not only increase the number of pensioners but also makes the work force a territory dominated by older workers. At the same time, most countries have to deal with an endogenous phenomenon, early retirement, which makes things even worse for future pensioners, because workers leaving the labor force too early erode the tax and premium base on which the insurance arrangements are based. Reducing the outflow of older workers on the labor market has therefore become the key policy objective in many countries in the Western world.

Blöndal and Scarpetta (1998) indicate that trends toward earlier retirement from the labor force are clearly visible in all OECD countries over the period 1950–1995, (perhaps with the exception of Japan, where a trend towards early retirement is present, but it is so small that the retirement age for both men and women remains high). Early retirement is most pronounced in the European countries such as the Netherlands where as of 1995, the average age of retirement is 58.8 for men and 55.3 for women, Belgium (men=57.6/women=54.1) and France (men=59.2 /women=58.3) and with average retirement ages in the year 1995 well below 60. The steep decline in the number of years worked in these countries is perhaps even more staggering: they range from 7 (for most men) to almost 11 years (for French women). As a consequence of this trend towards early retirement the financial sustainability of social security and early retirement schemes is at stake.

It is important to keep in mind that retirement programs in most European countries often started out as social protection programs, which had to fix labor market failures with which governments were confronted. On the one hand, government felt responsibility for the protection of unemployed youth who had limited opportunities on the labor market. On the other hand, it also had a responsibility for protecting older workers who had difficulties keeping up with the changing job demands. Increasing unemployment puts pressure on governments to protect the unemployed with low employment opportunities and to support measures that facilitate the exit of older workers via different early retirement schemes. To promote the use of early retirement by older workers so as to make room in the labor force for youth, early retirement programs were made financially attractive.

Along the way, pension designers discovered that the different retirement programs were used by employers to get rid of older workers on a far larger scale than intended. Early retirement programs were used as de facto unemployment schemes and with the downsizing of firms early retirement benefits were the next best thing to a golden handshake. It became more and more apparent that government policies and employer policies were increasingly contradictory.

During the early 1990s, the limits of abusing the social security system for policy goals it was not supposed to meet were becoming real. Taking radical steps to counter this abuse was on the minds of many a policy advisor, and politicians paid lip service to this change in attitude. The case for taking radical steps was perhaps most forcefully stated by Gruber and Wise (1999) who carried out a research program on social security and retirement effects with a number of well-known labor market experts (from the U.S., Canada, France, Germany and the Netherlands). In their "state of the nation" report they summarized data on leading indicators from each separate country. Perhaps one of the most direct measures they used to examine how retirement programs have affected retirement behavior is a measure of the unused productive capacity of older employees, which is, of course, the complement of the labor force participation rate. These data show very clearly that Belgium leaves 67% of a substantial labor market resource unused, closely followed by countries like France (60%), Italy (59%), and the Netherlands (58%), and that each leave about 60% of the productive powers of workers in the age range of 55–65 years unused. Japan, on the other hand, is far more efficient in using the capacity of older workers since only 22 percent of this age category is left unused.

Gruber and Wise (1999) also provided data that can be used to examine a number of explanatory variables. Chief among these are the financial incentives. The replacement rate (i.e., the early retirement benefit as a percentage of the final wage income) is, for example, quite high in the countries with high exit rates, in particular the Netherlands (91%) and France (91%). Similarly, the hazard or departure rates at the early retirement age (i.e., the age at which benefits are first available) are also quite high. For example high hazard rates are witnessed in France (65%) and the Netherlands (70%). Taken together, these all make it clear that early retirement programs are designed in such a manner that leaving the labor force at the early retirement age is "an offer you cannot refuse."

RETIREMENT REFORM AND THE OLDER WORKER

With the stylized history of retirement in the back of our minds, what can one conclude? There are three common elements present in the trends across different countries. First, all countries face an aging of the population and the labor force. Second, in all countries the labor force participation of older workers has decreased significantly in the last few decades. Third, the governments in all countries underscore the importance of reversing the trend toward ever earlier retirement from the labor force. Besides these trends in the labor markets, one can also observe at the turn of the century many different initiatives across countries to stimulate the labor force participation of the older worker and these differences are in part the result of different institutions and contexts with which countries start out. Still, in spite of the differences one can also detect a common thread that runs throughout the stories of policy reform. In the remainder of this section we will review these most prominent policy measures and their effectiveness. In the subsequent section we will dig somewhat deeper and to assess the plausibility of assumptions on which the policy measures hinge.

INCREASING THE RETIREMENT AGE

The first step to reverse the trend towards earlier retirement would seem to be an increase in the statutory age of pension entitlement. The ulterior motive for proposing this is quite plausible. By increasing the retirement age, one can kill two birds with one stone: the working period is extended and the retirement period is decreased. Most countries have a standard retirement age of 65 years (OECD, 2001). Japan still has an official retirement age of 60 years. Other exceptions are women in the UK, Germany, and the old Italian system who can still retire at age 60. But all the four countries mentioned have taken steps to gradually raise the standard retirement age for men and women to 65 years in the coming decades. The U.S. has decided to increase the age of entitlement to full benefits beyond the age of 65. In Sweden a proposed labor protection law would give employees the right to remain employed until the age of 67 (OECD, 2001). Moreover, in Sweden and the U.S., mandatory retirement arrangement have been abolished.

Guillemard (1999) states that the above measures signal a determination of governments to put an end to the golden age of early exit and to gradually shut down existing retirement schemes. Whether these reforms will be effective remains, however, a highly debatable issue. First of all, pension reforms do not take place overnight as the rights of existing generations are generally protected. The transition periods tend to be so long that many cohorts of older workers will fall under old regimes. Second, the fact that the large majority of workers have left the labor force well before the official retirement age in most OECD countries may jeopardize the effectiveness of raising official retirement ages. Alternative pathways such as disability programs and unemployment serve as de facto early retirement regulations in many countries by bridging the gap until workers reach the official retirement age. In addition, occupational and individual pension arrangements are used as a tool to reduce the number of older workers. Third, to date, governments everywhere in Europe have not resisted the tempting and conventional solution for fighting unemployment by stimulating older workers to exit the labor market. Even governments in their role as employers do not differ much from employers in the private sector in advocating early retirement. Especially retirement via the unemployment and disability pathways (due to health problems and/ or downsizing) is often perceived involuntary by workers. Figures from the U.S. Health and Retirement Survey suggest that "forced" retirement may account for 30% to 40% of early retirement. These figures correspond with the total outflow of older workers into unemployment and disability in other countries such as Norway (Dahl, Nilsen, & Vaage, 2000) and the Netherlands (Henkens & Siegers, 1991).

Summing up, there have been many reforms that are intended to support higher retirement ages. However, these reforms do not seem to be sufficient to reverse the trend of early retirement. In the absence of further policy changes, the OECD (2001) concludes that the existing trends still point to the likelihood of further growth in the proportion of life spent in retirement.

PROVIDING A SMOOTHER TRANSITION INTO RETIREMENT

Part-time work is often cited as a potential measure to make gradual retirement possible. By bridging a full-time career and full-time retirement, part-time work can contribute to the transfer of knowledge and experience to younger employees and, at the same time, it can help to deal with the desire of the older worker to lessen work stress or the demand for more leisure time. Part-time early retirement schemes can generally be divided into three groups: (a) schemes where part-time retirement is followed by full-time retirement (one can work part-time before one is eligible for full-time retirement); (b) schemes where only part-time retirement is possible; and (c) schemes that combine the first two types (subjects are free to choose between full- and part-time retirement (see Delsen, 1990).

Many countries have or have had part-time retirement arrangements. However, in most cases the actual use of the systems lagged way behind expected use. The desire to retire full-time is much greater than expected, although it had initially been assumed that part-time retirement would be popular. One reason why part-time retirement has not been that popular can be traced to the solidarity argument: older workers felt the social pressure to retire completely to make room for younger employees (in Denmark, part-time retirement was not supported by the unions). There is also evidence that when employees can choose between part-time or full-time retirement, the latter is chosen much more often. Experiences in various countries suggest that part-time retirement schemes trigger only those workers to reduce their working time who intended to keep on working, whereas it does not affect the intentions of workers who wanted to retire fully from the labor force. In aggregate, part-time retirement schemes have trimmed the number of full-time workers instead of full-time pensioners (Ghent, Allen, & Clark (2001) Guillemard, 1999). Given today's incentives and preferences, gradual retirement is therefore still not a very common pattern in OECD countries (OECD, 2001).

The part-time retirement schemes are just one example of costly measures that tend to "spare" older workers. Fewer obligations and more privileges are generally proposed and negotiated. Privileges such as additional leave, age-related holiday entitlements, workload reductions, age limits for irregular work, or exemptions from working over-time are quite common in OECD countries.

More Financial Incentives for the Individual Employee

Retirement reforms are to a large extent linked to the question of *who* must pay the retirement bill. Transitions from state pensions to private pensions assuming that state pensions are generally more expensive to the tax payer than private sector pensions, is one step. The problem of many retirement systems is rooted in the pay-as-you-go (PAYG) finance method where workers pay for the retirees, which allows individuals and companies to pass the financial burden of their decisions on to others. People who retire early are dependent on the solidarity of the employed who keep on working. They are the ones who pay the pension contributions necessary to finance the early retirement benefits.

Most of the new early retirement schemes—flexible early retirement (FER) arrangements—are designed to be actuarially neutral and increase the individual responsibility. (Note: A system is actuarially neutral if the present discounted value of net retirement benefits is the same for all possible retirement ages (Börsch-Supan, 1992). Such a system would not bias or distort the labor-leisure choice.) Under the new plans, pensions are no longer financed on a PAYG basis but on the basis of the principle of funding and actuarial neutrality. The FER arrangement allows individual employees to retire early, provided they pay a price that is substantially higher than the price generally paid for early retirement. The early retirement benefit is related directly to the individual employee's employment history and the contributions paid. The less time the employee has worked, the lower the pension benefit. The new plans do, however, offer employees more flexibility in choosing the age at which they wish to retire and—through additional savings—the level of the benefits they wish to receive. In addition, the individual responsibility of workers is enhanced by the shift from defined benefit to defined contribution pension plans

In order to stimulate older workers to keep on working until the statutory retirement age of 65, some pension funds have built in extra bonuses in their FER schemes if the worker makes an effort to reach this age (see for the Netherlands: Van Dalen and Henkens, 2002; and for Belgium, Denys & Simoens, 1999). There is little evidence whether this is an effective instrument in delaying the retirement date.

MORE FINANCIAL INCENTIVES FOR THE INDIVIDUAL EMPLOYER

Most policies for older workers are also focused on triggering employers into employing older workers and keeping them employed. Increasing the retirement age will be likely to have only limited effects if it is not combined with measures that stimulate employers to employ the aged worker. Most decisions about how to deal with an aging workforce will have to be taken within individual organizations, or will, at least, be implemented within these organizations. Research among employers carried out in the U.S. and several European countries show that many employers tend to be biased against older workers and there is often a lack of attention by corporate executives to older employees, reflected in an absence of programs to retain and retrain them (Barth, McNaught, & Rizzi, 1993; Guillemard, Taylor, & Walker, 1996; Taylor & Walker, 1998; Wagner, 1998). In several countries, such as Australia, Denmark, Germany and France, governments have experimented with wage subsidies and exemptions from social security contributions for firms who employ unemployed older workers. These measures have not proven to be very effective in keeping older workers in employment (OECD, 2001).

Many employers in Europe and the U.S. still consider older workers not really a force to be reckoned with, either in absolute or in relative terms. Given the labor market and social security arrangements of today, many workers prefer early retirement, and many employers prefer to have the option of laying off older workers first during periods of adverse economic conditions when firms downsize their labor force.

IMPROVING IMAGE OF OLDER WORKER AND ABATING AGE DISCRIMINATION

Another category of policies to influence employers' behaviors and attitudes are aimed at combating negative stereotyping of older workers and combating age discrimination. Educational programs and/or the support of local workplace initiatives are expected to strengthen the position of older workers within organizations and on a broader scale their position on the labor market. Taylor (2001) shows how national education programs aimed at raising awareness of the issue of age and employment have been undertaken in many countries. Their effectiveness seems, however, to be mixed and questionable. The OECD (2001) concludes that no great importance should be attached to the many promotional activities addressed to overcoming ageistm workplace practices and encourage best practice in employment of older workers. The U.S. is one of the few countries where mandatory retirement is banned from employment practices and the basic rights of the older worker are embodied in the Age Discrimination and Employment Act (ADEA) of 1967. The intent of ADEA was to ban age discrimination. Mandatory retirement would be one case of discrimination against older workers. However, age discrimination laws like ADEA have had little impact on the ability of the firm to induce retirement. First, firms have remained able to offer financial incentives to induce retirement at specific ages (see Hurd, 1990), and second, much research suggests that mandatory retirement was generally unimportant in inducing retirement for all but a small percentage of workers (Burkhauser & Quinn, 1983; Ruhm, 1990). In short, ADEA did little in eliminating mandatory retirement, except in name.

Are the Tacit Assumptions Valid?

The diagnosis of the looming pension and aging problem of many industrialized countries already seems to provide the answer for many policy makers. The population aging problem together with the vulnerable pay-as-you-go financing methods for retirement systems makes policy reform a piece of cake: counter the aging problem and make the pension finance methods shock-proof to the (long-term) shock of aging populations. Such policy initiatives were summed up above, but the ultimate question is, of course, will it work? In reviewing the possibilities for policy reforms to work we will evaluate the most important tacit assumptions regarding the retirement decision-making process, and by doing so we provide provisional answers to the effectiveness of proposed policy reforms. In general the most important tacit assumptions boil down to four: Financial incentives work, the intrinsic rewards of work are not important, the retirement decision is an individual decision, and the use of different exit routes is unrelated.

FINANCIAL INCENTIVES WORK

The logic of carrots and sticks is unambiguous, at least according to policy reformers. Employees are strongly influenced in their retirement choices by financial incentives embodied in pension and social security systems, and employers can manipulate pension plans and incentives schemes in such a manner that employees exit the firm at more or less the right moment. To a certain extent they are, of course, right. Early retirement programs are often designed in such a manner that exit from the labor force is an offer most older workers cannot refuse. The enormous spikes in hazard rates in the labor force participation of older workers are proof of the implicit intentions of those retirement programs. So financial incentives help explain the timing of retirement, but can they also explain the long-run trend in early retirement? The majority of empirical studies do not support the "blackboard economics" of most retirement policy proposals. What empirical studies about retirement show time and time again is that changing retirement incentives only explain a small part of the long-run retirement trend (Hurd, 1990). Financial incentives need to be of a considerable magnitude to induce workers to extend their retirement date (Hernæs, Sollie, & Strøm, 2000; Van Dalen & Henkens, 2002).

The reason why older workers are hard to persuade to extend their working career is perhaps most persuasively stated by Costa (1998). She provides long-run evidence about retirement behavior of several generations of Union Army Veterans. Apparently the sensitivity of older workers to financial incentives has decreased over the past century. The responsiveness of older workers to retirement income could explain 90% of the decline in the labor force participation rates of men older than 64 between 1900 and 1930, whereas the rising incomes explain none of the decline between 1950 and 1980. Of course, several factors come to mind that explain why the responsiveness to pension income has declined. First, the level of income of retirees is today far higher than subsistence level, and workers reach the retirement date with sufficient funds to satisfy their consumption needs. Second, the opportunities for enjoying leisure time have increased, and a taste for leisure has become the overriding factor in retiring from the labor force. The fraction of 65–year old retirees in the U.S. citing a preference for leisure as their main motivation for retirement has increased from 3% in 1941 to 48 percent in 1982 (Sherman, 1985). In a way, many have developed over the years a retirement lifestyle, which was in turn stimulated by income growth, and technological progress in household and transport technology has made the old a genuine leisure class. Fogel (1999) shows how the leisure time available to the typical male U.S. worker has tripled over the past century and a work year declined from about 3,100 hours in 1880 to 1,730 hours in 1995. The great attraction of retirement was further enticed by the rise of the leisure industry which was brought on, among other factors, by the declining price of transport and rapid improvements in infrastructure.

THE INTRINSIC REWARDS OF WORK ARE NOT IMPORTANT

This assumption is closely related to the previous assumption, but we nevertheless want to stress it as it goes to the heart of our argument. When financial incentives don't appear to matter, all this signifies is that workers apparently are not moved by variations in reward, but we rarely ask why they are not responsive to the rewards. The reason for looking beyond extrinsic rewards can be quite basic, however. The nature of work has changed considerably in character, and when people choose a job they not only consider the wage it pays, but also they assess whether the job has interesting and exciting aspects, substantial variation of work tasks, and opportunities for reaching higher goals in life. In short, work is not only an investment good, but it has increasingly become a consumption good (Fogel, 1999).

Work-related factors are generally found to play an important part in the retirement decision-making process. These factors not only have to do with the degree to which workers find work mentally or physically demanding, but also with the extent to which the job is intrinsically rewarding in terms of job challenge and socially rewarding in term of social support from colleagues and supervisors. As has been shown in several studies, workers in physically demanding jobs and workers who face high job pressures retire earlier (Feldman, 1994; Greller & Simpson 1999, Henkens, 1999, Lease, 1998). Many policy initiatives are aimed at reducing this workload. The underlying assumption is that reducing the demanding aspects of work will reduce older workers' early retirement propensities. Several studies show that this is only part of the story. Increasing the psychological and social rewards linked to the job is an aspect that is somewhat of a blind spot in policy initiatives. Those workers who report higher levels of career commitment and higher career growth opportunity are inclined to retire later (Greller & Simpson 1999). In addition, job challenge and support from supervisors are the best predictors of intention to extend the career (Henkens, 1999, 2000; Lease, 1998). These results suggest that many older workers do not simply retire because the workload is too high, but because the content of jobs and tasks and the work environment have nothing new or rewarding to offer anymore.

The emphasis on the demanding aspects of the job may be in line with research showing that workers generally retired because of health problems. However, at this point in time, it is widely accepted and documented that the decision-making process is far more complex. Given the importance of the rewarding aspects of the job as a reason to delay the date of retirement, much more effort is necessary to increase the opportunities for creativity, learning, and self-fulfillment at work if policy makers want to encourage a substantial extension of the working life. Of course, designing work tasks and (intrinsic and extrinsic) incentive schemes which satisfy both the interests of principals and agents—both inside and outside organizations—is a daunting and difficult task, but in Europe and the U.S., there seem to be signs of public and private management that tries to do justice to the complexity of organizations (see for an overview, Burgess & Metcalfe, 1999).

THE RETIREMENT DECISION IS AN INDIVIDUAL DECISION

Again, much of the logic surrounding retirement can be traced to the habit of invoking the logic of methodological individualism. To a large extent, this makes sense if financial incentives are the prime motivator in taking retirement choices and if one wants to trace the macroeconomic consequences of retirement decisions in a tractable manner. But, of course, there is a price to convenience in modeling when individual circumstances and discretionary power are embedded in social networks. When social interactions play an overriding part in retirement decisions, i.e., are made in conjunction with significant others, it becomes essential to model those networks explicitly and make it an integral part of policy (Durlauf, 1999). An atomized view of retirement decision making may lead to an incorrect understanding of how these decisions are made and how individual actions influence each other (Granovetter, 1988). The need for modeling labor market choices of spouses is a case in point as Hamermesh (2000) demonstrates. As noted elsewhere in this book, numerous studies indicate that spouses adjust their retirement to each other, and that they prefer to retire jointly. Joint retirement is more conducive to well-being than situations in which one spouse has retired and the other continues to work outside the home (Szinovacz, in press, 2002). Couples prefer to retire simultaneously, and responses to income changes and constraints alter their schedules to preserve joint retirement. Jiménez-Martin, Labeaga, and Martinez Granado, (1999), show for twelve E. U. countries that a working spouse is more likely to retire the more recently the other spouse has retired. Furthermore, poor health may not only increase the probability of retiring for the person concerned, it may also make it quite probable that the spouse will retire because caregiving will make such a move a necessity—although this tendency may vary between the sexes (e.g., Talaga & Beehr, 1995).

Policies differ with regard to men's and women's retirement ages and penalties for early retirement. Many countries have gender specific retirement ages offering a broader window of opportunity for couples to retire jointly than other countries that still stick to the old household model in which the husband earns a living and the wife stays at home. In many OECD countries, however, the number of couples who both earn a living and who have reached retirement is still relatively low (OECD, 1995). The importance of the partner in the retirement decision-making process holds, however, not only in case of double-income couples but also in the case of traditional households with one income. The decision to leave work is strongly shaped within the conjugal pair (Szinovacz, in press, 2002; Henkens & Tazelaar, 1997; Henkens & Van Solinge, 2002).

THE USE OF DIFFERENT EXIT ROUTES IS UNRELATED

One of the pitfalls in reforming early retirement programs is that social security (disability, early retirement, unemployment) and early retirement programs often function as substitutes. This is perhaps one of the primary reasons why one may have doubts about the effectiveness of policy reforms in reversing the long-run retirement trend in countries with an extensive welfare state. Reversing the retirement trend cannot be countered by simply focusing on the official retirement program, because sooner or later the other programs will feel the pressure that is caused by tightening the eligibility conditions of official retirement programs. It is well acknowledged that low labor force participation in, the Netherlands, for example, is caused by three types of outflow: early retirement, disability, and unemployment (Heyma, 2001). These three types of outflow are not independent of one another; restrictions in one irrevocably result in an increase in another. Research has convincingly proven that restricting the early retirement outflow will lead to an increase in disability outflow and unemployment (Van Imhoff and Henkens, 1998). This particular state of affairs can be seen in other countries as well. The social security early retirement age is the most critical of plan provisions, but in many countries unemployment and disability programs effectively provide early retirement at younger ages. As Gruber & Wise (1999) stress in their study, the effects of unemployment and disability programs are most evidently in Belgium, France, the Netherlands, and Germany, where labor force departure rates approach or exceed 20% before the official social security early retirement age. And the OECD (2001) is also quite adamant in its verdict on the substitutability of social security arrangements for the 55–64 age group. Disability benefit pathways are a common pathway to retirement, and countries like Finland, Sweden, and the Netherlands are proving this point by showing high levels of disability beneficiaries and relatively low levels of old-age pension and unemployment beneficiaries.

Concluding Remarks

Reviewing retirement behavior and policy across the world is a Herculean task which can only highlight the most remarkable and visible aspects. In addition, in passing one can notice the aspects that are perhaps common knowledge but are not explicitly mentioned or generalized in policy debates. One of the most striking aspects of retirement and policy in all countries may well be the cyclical nature of policy reforms. With the introduction of extensive social security programs, the motive of (social) protection of retirees against income risks during old age was the dominant concern about the possible effects that social security premiums and benefits could have on retirement behavior. With the advent of the 1980s and 1990s, when aging became a visible phenomenon for governments and economic conditions turned adverse, employers and employees effectively used social security as early retirement programs. The solution to neutralizing the effect social security programs had on retirement behavior was to put pensions and social security programs on a more actuarial neutral footing and to limit the eligibility conditions for social security. This era can therefore be characterized as one in which policy makers traded off social protection for individual risk taking.

By reforming social security and pensions, the vulnerability of these programs for the aging process may well be dampened, at the same time the governments abstain from protecting older workers and retirees from income risks which insurance markets fail to cover. Policy makers are often very reluctant to introduce harsh policy measures due to the argument that the most obvious and effective reforms could create new vulnerable groups of retirees and/or hamper the employment prospects of other vulnerable groups on the labor market. Moreover, older workers who are at risk may be forced to extend their working career involuntary, prompted by a lack of financial resources. The emphasis in most countries is, therefore, on introducing painless reforms; measures that may stimulate older workers to retire later, but leave the social protection element largely untouched. In other words, governments want to have their cake and eat it, too, and unfortunately that is a rare event in the real world. This holds true particularly for countries in which the government plays a dominant role in redistributing income through social protection programs and where the connection between work effort and earnings is limited. Especially societies in the European Union redistribute income on a far larger scale than in e.g., the United States, for example, (see Alesina, Glaeser, & Sacerdote, 2001).

A first way to introduce policy changes in a painless manner is to include long transition periods in the pension reform plans. Higher retirement ages are introduced very gradually for instance in the U. K., Germany, Italy, and Japan (OECD, 2001). The transition periods agreed upon tend to be long (sometimes several decades) and many cohorts of older workers will still be able to benefit from the old retirement schemes in the future, which will be reflected in the labor force participation of these cohorts. It is interesting to note that it is the baby-boom generation that will continue to benefit from early retirement schemes while the bill for their retirement benefits will be footed by the younger generations.

A second way policy makers try to initiate a painless reform is to stimulate older workers' participation by giving them fewer obligations and more privileges. The most widely implemented measures tend to be the ones that "spare" older workers such as additional leave, increased holiday entitlements, workload reductions, age limits for irregular work, exemptions from working overtime, or part-time retirement regulations (Remery, Henkens, Schippers, & Ekamper, 2002 for the Netherlands; and Employment Observatory Trends, 1999 for other European countries). These measures are often costly and often reduce the employability of older staff. Furthermore, in evaluating such programs one should be cautious in claiming success too soon. Much of the effectiveness may well be a case of selection bias. Privileges are given to those workers who are inclined to retire as soon as possible. And, in the case a financial bonus is offered if retirement is delayed, these bonuses are happily accepted by those who do not want to retire early anyway (Van Dalen & Henkens, 2002).

The success of raising participation levels of older workers seems to depend largely on the extent to which labor market conditions will make the older worker not some "token employee" but an essential part of the work force. Of course, not just only governments, employers, organizations, and unions need to acknowledge the vital position of the older worker for the present and future work force, but individual employers and employees should also start perceiving this. To date, the urgency of raising retirement ages may be high on the agenda of macro level actors. On the micro level of organizations and older workers the retirement problem is perceived as much less urgent. Many organizations still aim at reducing the number of older workers (OECD, 2001). This may be one of the reasons why much effort is placed on campaigning to put and keep the issue on the agenda. Cynics may argue that the emphasis on these "symbolic" actions (appointing task forces, supporting best practices, educational campaigns, combating stereotypes) mask the policy makers' aversion to policies that hurt their voters.

What does seem clear, is that in order to escape from the cyclical nature of the retirement and social protection debate researchers and politicians have to start thinking seriously about who should carry the responsibility of income risks *during a lifetime*. Furthermore, in making policy reforms more effective, governments should be wary of the selection effects in policy experiments, regulations, or programs. As Nobel laureate Heckman (2001) states in reviewing labor market policies, "Across countries and over time, most active labor market policies are ineffective in promoting long-term wage growth and employment" (p. 730). These lessons may appear like truisms that can perhaps be offered at any occasion where policy evaluations are produced, but in the end most lessons learned turn out to be simple. And the simple "fact" is that designing effective reforms is far more complex than armchair theorists may suggest. The real trouble starts, of course, with translating theory into practice, because the devil is in the details of policy reforms and the contexts in which those reforms are carried out.

ACKNOWLEDGMENT

Computations compiled by Maximiliane Szinovacz are gratefully acknowledged.

REFERENCES

Alesina, A., Glaeser, E., & Sacerdote, B. (2001). Why doesn't the United States have a European-style welfare state? *Brookings Papers on Economic Activity, 2,* 187–277.

Barth, M. C., McNaught, W., & Rizzi, P. (1993). Corporations and the aging workforce. In P. H. Mirvis (Ed.), *Building the competitive workforce: Investing in human capital for corporate success* (pp. 156–200). New York: John Wiley.

Beveridge, W. (1944). *Full employment in a free society.* London: Allen & Urwin.

Beveridge Report (1942). *Social insurance and allied services.* Cmd 6404, London: HMSO.

Blöndal, S., & Scarpetta, S. (1998). *The retirement decision in OECD countries.* OECD Working Paper, No. 202. Paris: OECD.

Börsch-Supan, A. (1992). Population aging, social security design, and early retirement. *Journal of Institutional and Theoretical Economics, 148,* 533–557.

Burgess, S., & Metcalfe, P. (1999). *Incentives in organisations: A selective overview of the literature with application to the public sector.* CMPO Working Paper Series, No. 00/16. Bristol: University of Bristol.

Burkhauser, R. V., & Quinn, J. F. (1983). Is mandatory retirement overrated? Evidence from the 1970s. *Journal of Human Resources, 18,* 337–358.

Costa, D. L. (1998). *The evolution of retirement—An American economic history 1880–1990.* Chicago: University of Chicago Press.

Dahl, S., Nilsen, O. A., & Vaage, K. (2000). Work or retirement? Exit routes for Norwegian elderly. *Applied Economics, 32,* 1865–1876.

Delsen, L. (1990). Part-time early retirement in Europe. *The Geneva Papers on Risk and Insurance, 55,* 119–139.

Denys, J., & Simoens, P. (1999). Belgium. *Employment Observatory Trends, 33,* 9–15.

Durlauf, S. N. (1999). The memberships theory of inequality: Ideas and implications. In E. S. Brezis & P. Temin (Eds.), *Elites, minorities and economic growth* (pp. 161–177). Amsterdam: Elsevier.

The Economist (2002, February 16). *Pensions—time to grow up: A survey of pensions.*

Employment Observatory Trends (1999). *Older workers on the labour market, No. 33 Special issue.* Berlin: Employment & European Social Fund, European Commission.

Feldman, D. C. (1994). The decision to retire: A review and conceptualization, *Academy of Management Review, 19,* 285–311.

Fogel, R. W. (1999). Catching up with the economy. *American Economic Review, 89,* 1–21.

Ghent, L. S., Allen, S. G., & Clark, R. L. (2001). The impact of a new phased retirement option on faculty retirement decisions. *Research on Aging, 23,* 671–693.

Granovetter, M. S. (1988). The Sociological and economic approaches to labor market analysis, In G. Farkas & P. England (Eds.), *Industries, firms, and jobs: Sociological and economic approaches* (pp. 187–216). New York: Plenum.

Greller, M. M., & Simpson, P. (1999). In search of late career: A review of contemporary social science research applicable to the understanding of late career. *Human Resource Management Review, 9,* 309–347.

Gruber, J., & Wise, D. A. (1999). *Social security and retirement around the world.* Chicago: University of Chicago Press.

Guillemard, A. (1999). Work or retirement at career's end? A new challenge for company strategies and public policies in ageing societies. In S. Shaver & P. Saunders (Eds.), *Social Policy for the 21st Century, Proceedings of the National Social Policy Conference, Reports and Proceedings, 1,* 21–40.

Guillemard, A., Taylor, P., & Walker, A. (1996). Managing an ageing workforce in Britain and France. *The Geneva Papers on Risk and Insurance, 21,* 478–501.

Hamermesh, D. S. (2000). *Togetherness: Spouses' synchronous leisure, and the impact of children. NBER Working Paper, No. 7455,* Cambridge, Massachusetts: NBER.

Heckman, J. J. (2001). Micro data, heterogeneity, and the evaluation of public policy: Nobel lecture. *Journal of Political Economy, 109,* 673–748.

Henkens, K. (1999). Retirement intentions and spousal support: A multiactor approach. *Journal of Gerontology: Social Sciences, 54B,* S63–S73.

Henkens, K. (2000). Supervisors' attitudes about the early retirement of subordinates. *Journal of Applied Social Psychology, 30,* 833–852.

Henkens, K., & Siegers, J. (1991). The decision to retire: The case of Dutch men aged 50–64, *European Journal of Population, 7,* 231–249.

Henkens, K., & Tazelaar, F. (1997). Explaining early retirement decisions of civil servants in the Netherlands: Intentions, behavior and the discrepancy between the two. *Research on Aging, 19,* 139–173.

Henkens, K., & Van Solinge, H. (2002, Summer). Spousal influences on the decision to retire. *International Journal of Sociology, 3,* 55–74.

Hernæs, E., Sollie, M., & Strøm, S. (2000). Early retirement and economic incentives. *Scandinavian Journal of Economics, 102,* 481–502.

Heyma, A. (2001). *Dynamic models of labour force retirement.* Doctoral Thesis, Tinbergen Institute, Amsterdam.

Hurd, M. D. (1990). Research on the elderly: Economic status, retirement, and consumption and saving. *Journal of Economic Literature, 28,* 565–637.

Jiménez-Martin, S., Labeaga, J. M., & Martinez Granado, M. (1999). *Health status and retirement decisions for older European couples, working paper.* Madrid: Universidad Carlos III.

Kinsella, K., & Gist, Y. J. (1995). *Older workers, retirement and pensions,* Washington D. C.: U.S. Bureau of the Census.

Lease, S. H. (1998). Annual review, 1993–1997: Work attitudes and outcomes. *Journal of Vocational Behavior, 53,* 154–183.

OECD (1995). *The transition from work to retirement, OECD social Policy Studies No. 16.* Paris: Author.

OECD (2001). *Ageing and income—Financial resources and retirement in 9 OECD countries.* Paris: Author.

Remery, C., Henkens, K., Schippers, J., & Ekamper, P. (2003). *Managing an Aging Workforce and a Tight Labor Market: Views held by Dutch employers. Population Research and Policy Review, 22,* 21–40.

Ruhm, C. J. (1990). Determinants of the timing of retirement, In P. B. Doeringer (Ed.), *Bridges to retirement: Older workers in a changing labor market* (pp. 23–32). Ithaca: ILR Press.

Sherman, S. R. (1985). Reported reasons retired workers left their last job: Findings from the new beneficiary survey. *Social Security Bulletin, 48,* 22–25.

Szinovacz, M. E. (in press). Retirement. In *International encyclopedia of marriage and the family.* New York: Macmillan.

Szinovacz, M. E. (2002, Summer). Couple retirement patterns and retirement age: A comparison of Austria and the United States. *International Journal of Sociology, 32,* 30–54.

Talaga, J. A., & Beehr, T. A. (1995). Are there gender differences in predicting retirement? *Journal of Applied Psychology, 80,* 16–28.

Taylor, P. (2001). *Comparative policy approaches towards older workers.* A Report for Scottish Enterprise, Open Business School, Milton Keynes.

Taylor, P., Tillsley, C., Beausoleil, K., Wilson, R., & Walker, A. (2000). *Factors affecting retirement behavior.* A Literature Review, Research Brief No. 236. Nottingham, England, Department for Education and Employment.

Taylor, P., & Walker, A. (1998). Employers and older workers: Attitudes and employment practices. *Ageing and Society, 18,* 641–659.

United Nations (2001). *World population prospects: The 2000 revision.* Population Division, Department of Economic and Social Affairs. New York: United Nations.

Van Dalen, H. P., & Henkens, K. (2002). Early retirement reform: Can it work? Will it work? *Ageing and Society, 22,* 209–231.

Van Imhoff, E., & Henkens, K. (1998). The budgetary dilemmas of an aging workforce: A scenario analysis for the public sector in the Netherlands. *European Journal of Population, 14,* 39–59.

Wagner, D. L. (1998). *Factors influencing the use of older workers: A survey of U.S. employers.* Washington, D.C.: The National Council on the Aging.

11

Data Analytic Techniques for Retirement Research

Michael J. Zickar and Robert E. Gibby

Researchers who study retirement face challenging statistical problems including time-ordered data, dichotomous dependent variables, and the possibility of discontinuous change. These topics are rarely covered in basic graduate statistical curricula; hence, researchers are either forced to simplify their research questions to fit within traditional ANOVA/regression designs or to find a willing researcher with quantitative expertise with whom to collaborate. The aim of this chapter is to stimulate retirement researchers by highlighting statistical techniques that might be of use when studying the phenomenon of retirement. The purposes of this chapter are to identify these techniques, to present a rudimentary overview of each technique, to demonstrate their potential for retirement researchers, and finally, to highlight follow-up sources for the interested reader who wishes to pursue further research. We review various techniques that have been used in previous studies on retirement as well as suggest several approaches that have not been used yet, but hold great promise.

Longitudinal Techniques

Retirement implies *transition,* which suggests that understanding temporal processes will be crucial to understanding retirement. The transition, either abrupt or gradual, from a life of paid work to a life of more discretionary time is followed with likely changes in physical and psychological functioning, relationship dynamics, financial status, and life perspective among countless other variables of interest. Researchers who wish to study the impact of retirement but want to avoid the complexities of these changes might conduct cross-sectional analyses comparing retired with nonretired individuals matched on as many variables as are of interest. Alternatively, researchers may conduct a simple preretirement and postretirement assessment and then conduct a repeated-measures t-test to determine the impact of retirement. Both of these approaches would greatly simplify the analysis and might provide important initial information under limited resources or limited time. These approaches, however, would fail to answer many important questions. For example, how does the change occur over time? Change might be linear and gradual or it might be nonlinear and drastic. Additionally, traditional approaches to studying change are good at determining the average amount of change experienced by study participants, even though there may be significant variation around that average. The two techniques we will be discussing primarily, hierarchical linear modeling (HLM) and latent growth curve modeling (LGM), move beyond the traditional approaches that focus on analyzing overall change to study individual variation of change. This might be especially important for retirement research in which one might hypothesize that some individuals thrive in retirement and experience increasing life satisfaction whereas others might experience increasing depression or declining levels of life satisfaction. If a sample were equally divided with these two types of retirees, a focus on the average might lead one to conclude that retirement had little affect on changes in life satisfaction. In this case, both the HLM and LGM approaches would be able to identify these individual differences. It would even be possible to use other variables (e.g., social support, commitment to hobbies) to predict the direction of change (positive or negative) in life satisfaction from preretirement to postretirement.

HIERARCHICAL LINEAR MODELING

Hierarchical linear modeling (HLM) has been used in several research areas that involve change over time. Studies have used HLM to investigate and model changes in creativity over the careers of Hollywood film directors (Zickar & Slaughter, 1999), to identify patterns of change in disruptive behavior among children of adolescent mothers (Spieker, Larson, Lewis, Keller, & Gilchrist, 1999), and to model changes in performance (often called performance trajectories) over the beginning of the careers of sewing operators (Deadrick, Bennett, & Russell, 1997). The HLM technique is regression-based and in the longitudinal case (it also is often used for multilevel or nested data) it works by fitting polynomial functions to time-ordered data. The logic of HLM is very similar to using a regression equation to model changes in life satisfaction over time by using time intervals as the predictor variables. By including squared and cubed time terms (e.g., x^2 and x^3), the relationship between time and the outcome variable is not constrained to a straight line; the polynomial function can assume various shapes such as the inverted U or growth with an asymptote.

An advantage of the HLM approach, unlike other approaches such as simple regression, is that different functions of change can be modeled for each individual. Traditional fixed-effects multiple regression approaches to the study of time are able to model the overall pattern of change within a sample well. This capability is useful in that it might be possible to determine that the average person has a moderate increase in life satisfaction soon after retirement and that the modest increase soon decreases to normal levels. Even though that may be the overall trend, it is highly likely that there are individual differences in the trend in reactions to retirement. Some retirees may fare worse over time and regret the day they retired whereas others may view retirement as the beginning of the happiest phase in their life and become increasingly satisfied over time. Under HLM, differences in change can be modeled so that you can conclude, for example, that retirees high in openness to experience tend to increase in life satisfaction after retirement whereas those low in openness to experience tend to react negatively to retirement.

HLM is a regression-based technique that in its standard form has two levels of equations. The first level is the individual level. The dependent variable in the level-1 equation is the variable that is assumed to change over time. Predictors in the level-1 equation would include variables that account for the passage of time (perhaps time frame) as well as any other time-varying factors that might be thought to influence the dependent variable at any given time point. For example, suppose we are interested in how life satisfaction (Y_i) for person i varies over different time periods (each time period is represented by a t). Adapting the Raudenbush and Bryk (2002) notation, the level-1 equation is:

$$Y_{ti} = \Pi_{0i} + \Pi_{1i}a_{ti} + \Pi_{2i}a_{2i}^2 + \ldots \Pi_{Pi}a_{ti}^P + e_{ti} \qquad (1)$$

The e_{ti} term is an individual error term or residual which is assumed to be independent across individuals and is normally distributed with a common variance σ^2. The a_{ti} term refers to the time period at which the observation Y_{ti} is observed. For example, a may signify years since retirement or minutes since the beginning of the experiment. By including polynomial terms (i.e., a to a certain power P), a variety of shapes relating time to the outcome variable are possible. The Π_{0i} term refers to the intercept, which would be the expected value of Y at time 0. The other Π terms are similar to slopes in a regression equation. Π_{2i}, which corresponds to a_{2i}^2, signifies acceleration in the time trajectory. By including this term the time trajectory is allowed to have one inflection point which allows for curves or bumps. By including further polynomial terms (i.e., $P > 2$), the range of possible shapes that the time trajectory can assume increases.

The level-1 equation is similar to what would be obtained if a regression equation were computed for individual i in the sample and then one computed an equation by taking the mean of each separate parameter estimate. Suppose there were 60 people in a sample. In that case, there would be 60 separate level-1 equations estimated, one for each person. Each individual regression equation would represent *intraindividual* change. Overall change for the sample could be determined by computing the mean of the regression terms across all 60 individuals. This equation would represent the overall trend of change across all individuals in the sample. The HLM software estimates and reports both the set of intraindividual parameter estimates as well as the overall equation.

The second equation level represents individual difference variables that might influence the function across time. At the second level, the dependent variable is the slope (and intercept) parameter for level-1:

$$\pi_{pi} = \beta_{p0} \sum_{q=1}^{Q_p} B_{pq} X_{qi} + r_{pi},\qquad(2)$$

where X_{qi} signifies various individual difference characteristics and β_{pq} represents the effect of X_{qi} on the corresponding π term in the level-1 equation. The r_{pi} term is a random error term with a mean of zero and a variance of τ estimated by HLM. The τ variance term is important in that if it is equal to zero it implies that there is no interindividual variation in the parameter π_{pi} after the individual difference characteristics have been accounted for. This can be important in determining whether individuals differ in their change trajectories.

Zickar and Slaughter's (1999) analysis of creative performance demonstrates the logic of using HLM to study longitudinal phenomena. They studied Hollywood film directors to determine how performance (as operationalized by film critic ratings) changed over each of their careers. Their level-1 equation was:

$$Y_{ti} = \pi_{0i} + \pi_{1i}\,\mathrm{FilmNum}_{ti} + \pi_{2i}\,(\mathrm{FilmNum}_{ti})^2 + e_{ti}\qquad(3)$$

where *FilmNum* refers to the number of the film in each director's oeuvre. By including the squared *FilmNum* term, they were able to fit a regression line that allows for changes in slope. The level-2 equations were:

$$\pi_{0i} = \gamma_{00} + \gamma_{01}\,\mathrm{Films/Year} + r_{0i}\qquad(4)$$

$$\pi_{1i} = \gamma_{10} + \gamma_{11}\,\mathrm{Films/Year} + r_{1i}\qquad(5)$$

$$\pi_{2i} = \gamma_{20} + \gamma_{21}\,\mathrm{Films/Year} + r_2\qquad(6)$$

These equations allow for differences in each of the level-1 terms and they use the variable Films/Year as a predictor for each of the level-1 terms. It was hypothesized that directors who had a high number of films directed in a period of time would tend to have less creative films than those who directed fewer films within that time and hence had more time to work on each individual film. Therefore, it was hypothesized that the γ_{11} term would be negative, suggesting that those who directed more films more frequently would tend to have negative slopes in their overall performance trajectory.

Like many other studies looking at creative performance over time (e.g., Simonton, 1997), Zickar and Slaughter (1999) found that the typical director showed initial increase in quality over time but that toward career end, the typical director showed a decrease in creative quality. This finding could be determined by examining the mean of level-1 parameters π_{1i} and π_{2i} across all directors in the sample. However, using HLM, it was also possible to determine that while this performance trajectory described the average film director, there was significant variation across directors (which can be seen in the values of the residual variances in the level-2 equations absent the level-2 predictor), so that some directors showed no decrement in performance at the end of their career, some directors got worse over their career, and for some directors there was no significant change over time. If the data had just been analyzed with multiple regression techniques, researchers might have falsely concluded that the overall model fit all directors equally well.

The real key to using HLM is to identify constructs that explain variation in level-1 parameters. In this case, the Films/Year variable was a significant predictor but contrary to initial hypotheses, directors who had more films directed per year were more likely to have positive growth in creativity over time. Ideally in this study, other variables and constructs would have been considered for inclusion in the level-2 equations. For example, the personality trait "openness to experience" might be related to performance over time in that people high in Openness might be expected to continuously seek out new and exciting film techniques/topics. Those individuals might be expected to not show the decrease in creative performance that is usually observed.

Besides using HLM to analyze longitudinal data, it can also be used to analyze nested data in which individuals are nested within different organizations. Such data are difficult to analyze using traditional techniques such as multiple regression or ANOVA that assume that data are independent of each other. This assumption of independence is most likely untenable if multiple individuals are sampled from the same organization. In that case, all of the individuals in that organization will be exposed to the same organizational and environmental factors; individuals from the same organization are more likely to be similar to fellow employees compared with other individuals from other organizations. The interdependencies of nonindependent data can lead to incorrect standard errors and improper significance tests. Fortunately HLM can conquer the nonindependence problems of clustered data. In this case, the level-1 equation is used to model individual data whereas the level-2 equation is used to model organizational and group-based characteristics. Using HLM in this manner would be an important statistical advance to helping researchers further understand the organizational and environmental factors that relate to retirement (see Hardy & Hazelrigg, 1999). This focus on organizational factors has been a recurrent theme in the retirement literature (e.g., Atchley, 1979; Feldman, 1994; Stetz & Beehr, 2000).

The software HLM (current version 5.04) is a popular, user-friendly program that can be used to do the previously mentioned analyses. With HLM, data can be imported from common statistical packages such as SPSS and SAS. An excellent reference source which is accessible yet thorough is Raudenbush and Bryk (2002). There are also several excellent articles and chapters that provide background on HLM (e.g., Hofmann, 1997; Hofmann, Griffin, & Gavin, 2000). Especially noteworthy among these is Bliese (2002). We think the HLM methodology lends itself especially well to the study of retirement and we urge future researchers to incorporate it into their analytic plans.

LATENT GROWTH CURVE MODELING

Another important statistical tool that has been used to investigate changes over time is latent growth curve modeling (LGM), also known as latent curve analysis (LCA). Although we could not find articles that employed LGM in the retirement literature, we feel it holds great potential for retirement researchers. Despite the lack of research using LGM in this literature, numerous other studies employing LGM have been performed in the related literatures of development, aging, and industrial-organizational (I-O) psychology. For example, Chan, Ramey, Ramey, and Schmitt (2000) used LGM to investigate intraindividual changes in children's social skills and interindividual differences in these changes in home and school settings. Tisak and Tisak (2000) detailed issues related to using latent curve and latent state-trait model analyses with an index of organizational commitment. In addition,

Jones and Meredith (1996) applied LGM procedures to investigate whether or not aspects of personality (i.e., self-confidence, cognitive commitment, outgoingness, dependability, and warmth) changed according to an underlying pattern over either a 30– or 40–year time span. Although these are only a few among the many studies performed with LGM techniques, they indicate the potential of LGM analyses for research on retirement. For example, LGM procedures could be used to analyze how numerous constructs (e.g., life satisfaction and stress) change as individuals transition from full-time work to retirement.

LGM can be thought of as a special case of a structural equation model (SEM) (Hser, Shen, Chou, Messer, & Anglin, 2001). Therefore, the same assumptions that underlie SEM procedures (e.g., normality, independence, and homogeneity of variance) apply to LGM. An additional way to think of the LGM procedure would be to consider it as an extension of repeated measures analysis of variance (ANOVA; Meredith & Tisak, 1990; Tisak & Tisak, 2000). In repeated-measures ANOVA, change over time is only assessed at the group level through the analysis of group means. Therefore, in the repeated-measures ANOVA design, change is thought to operate in the same way for everyone despite the fact that individual differences may exist. Unlike repeated-measures ANOVA, however, LGM analyses provide information for both the group and individual trajectories by taking into account both factor means and variances. Factor means in this case are the group-level parameters; the variances represent dispersion of regression coefficients. It is this ability to take into account change in both group and individual levels of analysis over time that makes the LGM procedure unique among developmental models assessing unfolding over time (Duncan, Duncan, Li, Strycker, & Alpert, 2002).

As mentioned above, LGM is a special case of SEM procedures, and more particularly, a special case of confirmatory factor analysis (CFA). Because they build from a CFA base, LGM procedures can be constructed in different ways according to how development or change in the variable of interest is thought to proceed. More specifically, LGMs are able to model linear and higher order changes over time by utilizing CFAs constructed with either two or more factors representing the repeated measures data. In the simplest case, only two factors are incorporated into the LGM analysis. One factor represents the intercept and one represents the slope. By including only two factors, it is assumed that change unfolds as a linear process. In cases where the researcher is interested in change that unfolds in a more complex manner, models can be constructed that incorporate multiple factors. For example, in the three-factor case of the LGM, change could be thought of as unfolding according to a quadratic model. Due to the complexities of moving beyond linear assessments of change, the present discussion will be limited to the two-factor or univariate case of the LGM procedure. Readers interested in the complexities of moving beyond the two-factor case are referred to Duncan, Duncan, Li, Strycker, & Alpert, (2002).

As its name implies, the two-factor or univariate LGM models repeated-measures data with intercept and growth parameters. Figure 11.1 depicts a typical two-factor LGM built from three repeated measures of a particular variable of interest, shown as the variables *Y1*, *Y2*, and *Y3*. The fact that three repeated measures are included in Figure 11.1 is important because LGMs perform poorly with only two waves of data collection. As an illustration, consider a situation in which a researcher is interested in modeling how stress changes during the retirement process. Further, consider that the researcher has measured the stress of a group of employees two years prior to retirement, at retirement, and two years after retirement. In the two-factor LGM procedure, these variables (*Y1, Y2,* and *Y3*) would coincide with these three assessments of stress, respectively. In addition, the two-factor LGM procedure would represent these three measurements of stress with a slope and intercept factor.

In the two-factor LGM, the intercept parameter, *F1*, is constant across time for any given individual, though the intercepts vary across individuals. Hence, a mean (μ_i) and variance (σ^2_i) can be computed from the collection of intercepts that describe each individual's growth curve. Therefore, Figure 11.1 displays the intercept parameter as fixed at a loading of 1 for all three (*Y1* to *Y3*) repeated measures of the variable of interest. The growth slope factor, *F2*, provides information about the mean (μ_s) and variance (σ^2_s) of the collection of individual slopes of each individual's growth curve. Unlike the intercept factor, the slope factor, *F2*, requires at least two parameters to be fixed to two different values in order for the model to be properly identified

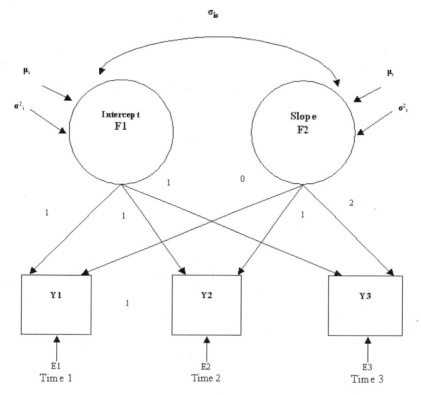

Figure 11.1 Example of longitudinal growth modeling.

identified (Meredith & Tisak, 1990). In Figure 11.1, it is assumed that
the repeated measures were obtained according to equal intervals, and
the slope factor is fixed at a loading of 0 for *Y1*, 1 for *Y2*, and 2 for
Y3. If the repeated measures data had not been collected on equal
intervals, it would have been necessary to reflect the timing of the
data collection in the slope factor loadings. For example, if the time
interval from *Y2* to *Y3* was twice that of the interval from *Y1* to *Y2*,
then the loadings for the slope factor could be constructed to reflect
this set of intervals as follows: 1 for *Y1*, 2 for *Y2*, and 4 for *Y3*. Finally,
as displayed in Figure 11.1, note that the two factors, *F1* and *F2*, are
allowed to covary (σ_{is}) and that error variance terms (*E1*, *E2*, and *E3*)
are specified for each assessment of the repeated measures, *Y1* to *Y3*.

As mentioned previously, and as displayed in Figure 11.1, a unique advantage of LGM procedures is the ability to model both individual and group trajectories for change over time. Another important advantage of LGM is its ability to handle covariates that vary across the same time intervals as the variable of interest (Duncan, Duncan, Li, Strycker, & Alpert, 2002). By including such time-varying variables the researcher is provided information for answering questions about the antecedents and consequences of change in the variable of interest. For example, by including the covariates of self-esteem and life satisfaction in the above stress example, the researcher would be provided information allowing for a clearer understanding of whether or not changes in stress over time were influenced by these covariates. Additionally, LGM procedures allow for multiple samples to be assessed in the same model. Therefore, age cohort, sex, and racial differences, among others can be assessed within the same LGM, allowing for information on whether or not groups develop according to the same trajectory (Duncan, Duncan, Li, Strycker, & Alpert, 2002).

LGMs can be estimated with any of the popular SEM software that is currently on the market. This software includes, but is not limited to, AMOS (Arbuckle, 1995), EQS (Bentler & Wu, 1995), and LISREL (Jöreskog & Sörbom, 1993). The packages vary in their levels of user-friendliness, and therefore researchers are urged to use the program with which they are most familiar. Several references exist that detail the LGM procedure, including a recent book treatment of the technique (Duncan, Duncan, Li, Strycker, & Alpert, 2002). There are also many excellent articles and chapters that provide advanced treatments and further background on LGM (McArdle & Anderson, 1989; Meredith & Tisak, 1990; Willett & Sayer, 1994).

Discontinuous Approaches to Change

The previous techniques rely on the assumption that change over time is continuous and gradual. Polynomial function approaches such as in HLM and SEM fit smooth functions to change data; abrupt changes are difficult to account for in the traditional analytic approaches. Higher-order polynomial functions can allow for rapid change but the change has to fit a proscribed mathematical form. Retirement research might benefit from an approach that treats changes as a discontinuous process, which might be difficult to fit using a prespecified mathematical form. For some individuals, the change from a lifetime of work to a period in which leisure and other nonwork activities are emphasized can be abrupt and life changing. Research that studies transitions from working life to retirement should be able to account for discontinuous change.

Spline regression techniques are able to fit jagged regression lines. Consider Figure 11.2 which presents the hypothetical data from a study of changes in life satisfaction on a yearly basis for employees in relatively unpleasant jobs. Suppose that all these employees retire in Year 3 of the study. Previous to retirement life satisfaction is relatively low, but soon after retirement life satisfaction increases dramatically. Traditional methods of data analysis would be unable to account for such a dramatic increase in life satisfaction in such a short amount of time. A polynomial function might approximate this jagged function reasonably well but still would result in a degree of misfit that might be intolerable.

The basic logic behind spline regression is that the researcher chooses "joints" or "knots" (i.e., places on the x-axis where discontinuity is expected to occur) based on some knowledge of the phenom-

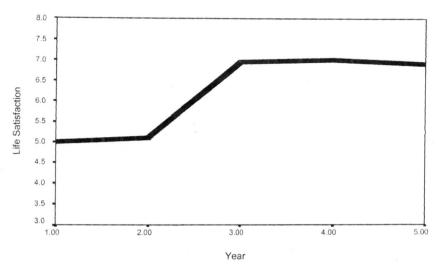

Figure 11.2 Example of discontinuous change.

enon being studied; separate regression lines are estimated between the joints. It is possible to do spline regression without knowing the location of the "knots" in advance, although the methodology then becomes much more complicated (see Marsh & Cormier, 2001). In the retirement case, the "knot" would most likely be the time of retirement. A regression line could be fit to model changes in life satisfaction prior to retirement. Next, another regression line could be fit to model changes in life satisfaction postretirement. These two separate regression lines could then be connected at the knot; this connected line is used to represent the changes in life satisfaction over both pre- and postretirement. Technically, this technique of estimating separate regression lines and then connecting them is called an *interrupted regression analysis*. The advantage of this approach is that there can be breaks and discontinuities in the regression line.

Marsh and Cormier (2001) present a methodology for estimating a spline regression function without estimating separate regression equations. His technique, which can easily be performed with traditional statistical packages, is based on the logic of dummy coding. Dummy codes need to be created for each of the knots in a particular model. For the retirement example, suppose we are merely interested in predicting job satisfaction from length of time since working. The equation would be:

$$Y_t = a_0 + b_0 t + b_1 D_1 (t - t_R) + e_t \ , \tag{7}$$

where t refers to the time elapsed since the beginning of the study. In addition, the variable t_R would signify the time elapsed from the beginning of the study until retirement. The a and b terms are the traditional regression intercept and slope terms. D_1 is set to 0 when the amount of time from the beginning of the study is less than the time at retirement (i.e., when $t < t_R$). D_1 is set to 1 when the amount of time from the beginning of the study is greater than the time of retirement (i.e., when $t > t_R$). By including the dummy code variable D in the equation, abrupt changes in the slope can occur at the specific point of retirement.

Although spline regression has been infrequently used in research related to retirement, the technique is more common in economic and political research (e.g., Speyrer & Ragas, 1991). Marsh and Cormier

(2001) report an analysis in which the approval rating of a politician is modeled over time with spline regression. At initial approval, hopes and expectations are high and, hence, approval is also high. Over time, though, the approval rating might fall as the politician turns toward addressing issues thereby ignoring public opinion. When re-election efforts begin again, the politician's efforts are more geared toward public approval and hence approval rises again. In this case, the abrupt change in slope would appear at the commencement of reelection efforts. A spline regression equation with a joint at the time when the reelection campaign began would be able to nicely fit these data. Other regression models might be able to approximate this change though they would underestimate the sharp change in slope that oc-curred.

We urge retirement researchers to consider using spline regression techniques when studying changes pre- and postretirement. Statistical packages that conduct multiple regression analyses can be used to conduct spline regression analyses. In addition, the logic that is used to apply this technique to multiple regression can also be used to extend HLM to include discontinuous change (see Raudenbush & Bryk, 2002). For more complete treatment of spline-based regression techniques, we recommend Marsh and Cormier (2001).

Other Techniques of Interest

Although retirement research implies a process that unfolds over time, there may be research questions that involve more static phenomena, and hence require different analytic techniques than those reviewed under the longitudinal section. In addition, specific challenges present in all kinds of research, namely missing data and good measurement, are addressed. This section highlights some important analytic tech-niques that might be of use for retirement researchers.

LOGISTIC REGRESSION

At one level, the decision to retire is a dichotomous phenomena (ei-ther you decide to retire, scored "1," or you do not, scored "0"). Therefore, it is plausible that retirement researchers may be interested in using the retirement decision as the dependent or outcome variable.

Traditional methods used in prediction research (e.g., multiple regression) are unable to handle dichotomous dependent variables; traditional regression models require continuous dependent variables with approximately normal distributions. In addition, predictions from traditional regression models will exceed the boundary of plausible values (i.e., between 0 and 1), leading to impossible conclusions. There is a temptation to create surrogate variables (e.g., intentions to retire instead of actual retirement) that avoid the problems associated with dichotomous variables. For example, in the turnover literature some researchers have created "intention to quit" measures which are continuously scaled and avoid many of the problems of the dichotomous turnover item. Although this resolves some of the statistical problems of dichotomous variables, it must be remembered that intentions are different from actual behavior.

The logic behind logistic regression (LR) is similar to traditional regression methods though the mathematics behind LR is more complicated. Traditional regression equations use a linear equation to represent the relationship between the predictor variables and the outcome variable. In logistic regression, a mathematical transformation, the natural log, is taken of the predictor variables. This transformation linearizes the relationship between the predictor variables and the outcome variable. In addition, this transformation bounds the predicted value to a number between 0 and 1. Therefore,

$$ P = \frac{e^{(a + \Sigma b_j X_j)}}{1 + e^{(a + \Sigma b_j X_j)}} \tag{8} $$

where a is the intercept, b_j is the slope term corresponding to predictor X_j, and e refers to the base of the natural logarithm (i.e., roughly 2.718). P refers to the expected probability that an individual will retire (or engage in whatever outcome variable is being studied), which is conditioned by their standing on the various predictor variables. This expected probability ranges from 0 to 1. One of the difficulties in LR is interpreting the magnitude of the slopes. In traditional regression, the slopes have intuitive meaning in that they correspond to the change in Y expected due to a 1-unit change in X, while controlling for all other predictor variables in the model. In LR the slope corresponds to the change in log odds expected due to a 1–unit change in the corresponding predictor variable. Because the metric is in log odds, the results are often difficult to interpret and require more consideration.

Just as in traditional regression, significance tests can be computed for each slope to determine whether that variable aids in the prediction of the outcome variable. Instead of R^2, though, LR uses the negative log likelihood statistic to determine the overall fit of a model. A chi-square statistic associated with the negative log likelihood can be used to test the incremental predictive ability of additional variables much like a significance test can be associated with the R^2 statistic in traditional regression analyses. Unfortunately the chi-square statistics are only able to determine whether a set of predictors helps predict significantly above and beyond that of a set of predictors entered in a previous step. Nagelkerke (1991) provided a method of computing an effect size measure similar to that used in multiple regression. The Nagelkerke R^2 is similar to the R^2 measure in multiple regression and is interpreted as the percentage of variance accounted for by a set of predictors.

There have been many retirement researchers who have used LR to determine factors related to the decision to retire. For example, Parnes and Somers (1994), using LR, found that older men who had good health, a strong commitment to work, and a distaste for retirement, were most likely to shun retirement. Stetz and Beehr (2000) used LR in their study of how retirement rates for female workers were related to type of industry, environmental munificence, and unemployment rates. In one of their analyses, they used LR to test whether industry munificence related to individual decisions to retire (scored dichotomously). In the first step, they entered the control and demographic variables of marital status, age, health limit, education, race, and occupational prestige. They found that as a whole this set of variables resulted in a significant chi-square, which means that those variables *as a whole* were significantly related to the decision to retire. Significance tests were reported for each of the individual terms in this set; however, these significance tests were not interpreted due to the correlated nature of the predictors. After it was established that these demographic variables were significantly related to retirement decisions, four variables related to munificence were entered in a second step. The chi-square testing the improvement of this second step beyond that of the first step was statistically significant, indicating that munificence variables add in the statistical prediction of retirement decisions. They found that workers in munificent industries were more likely to retire compared with those in less munificent industries. In concluding this, it was important that they entered the demographic variables in the first step. It had been well documented in prior research that those control variables were important factors in retirement decisions. By showing that munificence predicts above and beyond those previously studied factors, the researchers can be more confident that munificence is an important factor that needs to be considered in predicting retirement.

Fortunately, LR can be easily conducted within most common statistical packages. We recommend the book by Pampel (2000) as an introduction to LR; Zelterman (1999) provides a more detailed text with a section on LR but also discusses other techniques that can be used to model dichotomous dependent variables. Researchers need not shun inherently dichotomous outcome variables.

ITEM RESPONSE THEORY

Good research requires good measurement. There has been a revolution in psychometrics and educational measurement since the 1960s that has slowly worked its way from researchers in psychometric research areas into more applied areas. Item response theory (IRT) is a collection of measurement techniques that rely on specific statistical formulae to model how respondents react to psychological test items. Social and behavioral scientists typically use many of the techniques developed through the old method of psychometrics, classical test theory (CTT), to evaluate tests and scales used in research and practice. Concepts such as reliability, item-total correlations, and the Spearman-Brown prophecy formula are all based on the traditional test theory model. Despite the many accomplishments of CTT, many limitations of this framework have been noted. For example, in CTT, each scale has a reliability that is used to characterize the measurement precision of the entire test. This concept fails to recognize that tests have differential capabilities in discriminating among different levels of examinees' abilities.

Item response theory (IRT) relates characteristics of items and characteristics of individuals to the probability of affirming, endorsing, or correctly answering individual items. The cornerstone of IRT is the *item response function* (IRF). This function is a nonlinear regression of the probability of affirming item i on a latent trait, θ. Figure 11.3 presents a graphical representation of an IRF. It is possible to predict how a person with a particular θ would be likely to respond to the item. For example, someone with $\theta = 0.0$ would be expected to affirm this item with approximately .50 probability whereas an individual with $\theta = 1.0$ would be expected to affirm this item with approximately .90 probability. Although the IRF is limited to dichotomous items (e.g., right or wrong; true or false), other models called polytomous models can be used to model more complex item formats such as Likert-type formats (see Zickar, 2002).

Although IRT should provide better measurement and evaluation of psychological characteristics compared with CTT, the real advantage, and the advantage that should have the most benefit to retirement

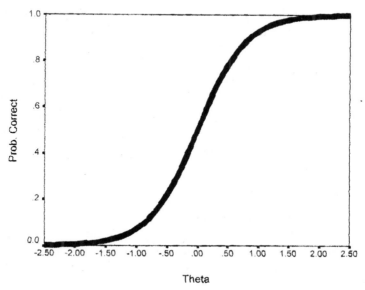

Figure 11.3 Sample item response function.

researchers, relates to the psychometric tools allowed by IRT. In fact, IRT has allowed the possibility of several different psychometric tools that were technically infeasible prior to its introduction.

Tools such as computerized adaptive testing (CAT), appropriateness measurement, and differential item functioning (DIF) are really the main accomplishments of IRT. CAT has revolutionized educational measurement by allowing test developers to create a large bank of items that are used by a computer program to generate a test that is optimized to best measure the characteristics of an individual respondent. This allows test developers to achieve high levels of test reliability while also minimizing the number of test items to which each individual has to respond. For retirement researchers, this could be of great advantage to those who wish to collect data on a large number of constructs but would like to minimize the time taken to complete the research instrument. See Wainer (2000) for an excellent book devoted to CAT.

Appropriateness measurement is used to identify individuals who might be responding to items on a particular scale in a method that is inconsistent with the psychological theory used to develop the scale items. For example, some individuals might fail to respond correctly to the scale because they cannot read the language in which the scale is written, they misunderstand the directions, or they lose interest or become fatigued. By identifying these respondents, the researcher can choose to eliminate them or perhaps follow up with the respondent to determine if there were actual problems in the scale administration. By doing this, researchers can improve the quality of their research data, which is especially important when using self-report data. For background on appropriateness measurement, the reader is referred to Meijer and Sijtsma (2001).

The final tool, differential item functioning (DIF) analysis, has revolutionized detection of item bias in the educational testing realm. In short, in a DIF analysis, the researcher is testing whether IRFs differ significantly across distinct groups. For example, in the testing realm, one might examine whether there are significant differences across racial or gender categories. Items that have significant differences should be eliminated if the test is designed to be free of bias. The use of DIF analysis has many applications outside of the educational testing realm. For example, Zickar and Highhouse (1998) used

DIF analysis to determine whether an experimental manipulation of item framing had an effect on how people responded to items about risky behavior. In terms of retirement research, DIF analyses could be used to determine whether there are significant differences in how retired versus nonretired workers respond to various items or to examine gender/age differences in item interpretation and item response. In addition, DIF analysis is an excellent way to determine whether instruments translated into new languages function in the same fashion (see Hulin & Mayer, 1986). As with much of IRT research, now that it has moved outside of the realm of educational assessment, the potential and possibilities of IRT and DIF analysis are really wide open. For an excellent discussion of DIF analysis, the reader is referred to Camilli and Shepard (1994).

An excellent book-length introduction to IRT is Embretson and Reise (2000). One of the impediments to the use of IRT has been the need for that specialized software. The two most popular IRT programs are BILOG (Mislevy & Bock, 1991) and MULTILOG (Thissen, 1991). BILOG is used for estimating dichotomous models and MULTILOG is used to estimate polytomous models. Whereas in the past the IRT programs were not considered user-friendly, WINDOWS versions of the software programs were being released in the Fall of 2002, which should be a big advance for substantive researchers who want to take advantage of the power of IRT. We urge researchers to consider IRT techniques to develop new psychological scales and to further understand constructs measured by existing scales.

MISSING DATA

Unfortunately missing data is present to some degree in almost all research efforts. Oftentimes, the consequences for missing data are slight in that sample size may be reduced by a small amount for certain analyses. In other cases, the effects of missing data can be severe. In analyses that require complete responses to all items (often called *listwise deletion,* in that any case that has missing data in any of the list of variables used in that analysis is deleted for that analysis), a missing response to one item can exclude that person from further analysis. In an analysis of many items, the sample size can be reduced by a large amount. In these situations, researchers are often faced with dropping cases with missing data or imputing responses to the missing items. Both choices have potentially negative consequences. The former approach reduces the amount of data for a particular analysis and hence has reduced statistical power. The latter approach uses some statistical mechanism to guess the likely response for the participant who skipped the item. Like most guesses, the statistical imputation may often be incorrect.

In some cases the loss in statistical power may be tolerable. In that case, analysis can proceed as usual. However, if imputation is desired, several options and decisions must be made. There are several methods of imputation. A simple approach would be to use the mean or modal response for that item for all other individuals in the sample. Roth, Switzer, and Switzer (1999) refer to this technique as "item mean substitution." Alternatively, if the missing item belongs to a unidimensional scale, the mean of all other items for that particular person can be substituted for the missing item. Roth, Switzer, & Switzer, (1999) refer to this as "person mean substitution." Both of these techniques are statistically simple to implement, though, the techniques are crude. For example, it may be that the mean of all other respondents would be a bad choice for a respondent if that respondent is extreme on other similar measures. Also, the mean for other items in the same scale for that person may be a bad choice if there is something unique about the item that was skipped.

Another technique called *regression imputation* uses additional information to guess at the likely response. In this case, a regression equation is computed with the item that was skipped as the dependent variable; other variables that were not skipped are used as the predictor variables. This approach works by using information about the individual's answered responses; relationships between those variables and the skipped variable are also used to generate the prediction. This technique is considered an advance over the item-mean and person-mean substitution techniques because it uses information from both the individual who skipped the item and the rest of the sample that did not skip the item. One limitation that Switzer and Roth (2002) point out is that this technique does not work well when there is a high level of missing data for a single individual. We would argue, though, that data from someone who skips a large number of responses should be discarded if possible.

A final method used for imputation is based on expectation maximization (EM) principles. This process does not attempt to "fill in" the missing responses of individuals; instead, it attempts to determine how study results would differ if there were no missing data. Specifically, this method uses an iterative process. Initially, results are computed after deleting cases that have missing data for the particular analysis. Next, results are computed using the output from the first step to estimate the likely values for the missing data. Missing values are then recomputed given this updated information. The procedure iterates until further steps result in little change from previous steps. This approach differs from the other approaches in that the real focus is on estimating study results as if there were no missing data. One Monte Carlo comparison suggested that the EM approach provided the best results in a structural equation modeling context (see Gold & Bentler, 2000). For more information about this technique, readers should consult Little and Rubin (1987).

Several studies have shown that when the amount of missing data is slight (e.g., less than 5% of all responses) the choice of missing data technique makes little difference (see Raymond & Roberts, 1987). Therefore, the payoff for using the more advanced computational methods might be slight for most cases. In cases of large amounts of missing data with little possibility of collecting additional data, some of the advanced techniques like the EM approach should be tried. Of course, the best solution to dealing with missing data is to prevent it in the first case.

COMPUTATIONAL MODELING AND COMPUTER SIMULATION

Computational modeling and computer simulation techniques (we use the terms synonymously) are important research tools that are rarely considered by organizational users. To pursue this technique, a researcher must develop a theory that can be translated into mathematical or statistical formulas. Typically, the model would allow for user-specified input conditions (e.g., unemployment rate, pension plan) that can be varied to test the effects of those conditions on some output variable (e.g., retirement rate). Computational modeling is an excellent way to test the ramifications of complex theories that may be difficult to test in real-world situations.

Computer simulations are excellent tools because they allow researchers to pursue questions that might be implausible or impossible to conduct due to ethical, practical, or other limitations. For example, a retirement researcher might be interested in how retirement rates for a particular company are impacted by unemployment rates. Traditional research techniques might be limited to correlating unemployment rates with retirement rates or perhaps using a multiple regression equation with nonlinear terms to try to determine the relation. The limitation, though, is that the researcher is limited to the range of unemployment rates observed in the time frame of the study. Extrapolating beyond those data points would be statistically dangerous. If the researcher were interested in predicting retirement rates that fall outside the range of observed values, they would be unable to proceed. By generating a computational model, a researcher can evaluate hypothetical situations by varying an almost unlimited number of conditions and influences.

Of great interest to retirement researchers is the computational modeling research on organizational withdrawal done by Kathy Hanisch and colleagues (Hanisch, 2000; Hanisch, Hulin, & Seitz, 1996; Seitz, Hanisch, & Hulin, 1997). They developed a computational model of a "virtual organization" that relates organizational characteristics (e.g., base rates of withdrawal behaviors, size, organizational policies), individual characteristics (e.g., distributions of age, gender, tenure), and environmental characteristics (e.g., unemployment rate) to organizational withdrawal behaviors (e.g., turnover, retirement). The program WORKER (Seitz, Hanisch, & Hulin, 1997) uses the principles of fuzzy logic and fuzzy calculus to create data from conditions specified by the researcher. The body of findings generated by WORKER have been impressive.

First off, Hanisch (2000) used WORKER to test the plausibility of various theories of organizational withdrawal (e.g., progression of withdrawal, spillover) by simulating results over a 20-year time frame. She found, for example, that early retirement rates vary quite differently across the various models of withdrawal. Munson and Hulin (2000) used WORKER to compare predictions generated from the different theories to work withdrawal data from a sample of female members of a large university. Data were collected across eight time periods for these workers. A correlation matrix of withdrawal behavior measures (e.g., missed meetings and absenteeism) was computed for the actual data and also from data generated by WORKER. By comparing the expected correlation matrices for various models, they were able to determine which one most closely fit the observed correlation matrix. Although retirement was not one of the types of withdrawal behavior considered in their study, it is an excellent example of how a computational model can be used, along with real data, to test various theories.

An excellent book on computational modeling in organizational research is the volume edited by Ilgen and Hulin (2000). This book presents theoretical discussion of these methodologies as well as ten examples of computational modeling research endeavors. This book is essential in providing technical advice to those who might be interested in writing their own computer simulations but do not have programming skills. Programs such as SPSS, SAS, and EXCEL can be used to generate many basic simulations that might help answer questions in the retirement area that would be difficult to answer using empirical approaches. The slim book by Taber and Timpone (1996) is also useful in providing a readable background on computational modeling methods.

Conclusions

The topic of retirement is a demanding one to study and requires consideration of alternative techniques and methodologies than traditional data analytic techniques such as regression and ANOVA. Traditional methodologies will always remain the mainstay of retirement researchers but in many cases they will have limited relevance. In this chapter, we provided a brief introduction to several techniques that we think retirement researchers could greatly benefit by considering. We believe the techniques of HLM and LGM hold great promise for retirement researchers by allowing modeling of both interindividual and intraindividual variation. In the past, research has focused on overall change which is an important first step in an area of research. However, studying how individuals differ in their directions and rates of change is an important next step. We also encourage researchers to explore the possibilities of discontinuous change (e.g., spline regression) when studying retirement longitudinally. It is unclear whether spline regression models will fit significantly better than more simple approaches but it seems worth the effort.

Although it might be tempting for statistical and theoretical reasons to study intentions to retire instead of actual retirement, we believe it is important to study actual retirement even if it is a dichotomous outcome variable. LR is the appropriate analytic technique in that case. This technique is similar procedurally to multiple regression, a technique with which most researchers are familiar. It has already been applied several times in retirement research.

Good research requires good measurement. Item response theory has revolutionized the field of psychological measurement even though it has had little impact in retirement research. IRT has great potential for helping retirement researchers to refine their existing psychological scales and to help guide them in decisions when developing new scales. In addition, the psychometric tools of adaptive testing, appropriateness measurement, and differential item functioning should provide endless uses for researchers with the ingenuity to think of new uses for them.

Missing data techniques now exist that allow researchers to estimate likely values for respondents who skip a few items. Some of these techniques are statistically sophisticated and can help in situations in which there is little hope in obtaining additional respondents due to availability, cost, or other considerations. Although we urge caution in their use, these techniques can help economize research by utilizing respondent data that might otherwise have to be discarded.

Finally, computational modeling is another technique that can be used by retirement researchers to answer questions they might not be able to investigate using other methods. Hanisch and colleagues have already demonstrated the utility of using computational modeling to investigate the dynamics of retirement and other withdrawal behaviors in the organizational context. Their research suggests that, in addition to generating novel results, the process of creating a computational model is rewarding because it requires more precise theorizing than most of us are used to doing.

Social and behavioral scientists often have an unproductive fascination with complex statistical techniques. Using complex methodology can make it difficult to communicate with others who might be unfamiliar with the technique. In addition, there is a danger in that it is easy to get lost in the statistical details of the analysis while forgetting the theoretical and practical reasons for which the analysis was conducted initially. Researchers are urged to use the simplest methodology as possible in all cases. Having said that, there is also another danger in that complex statistical analyses are often avoided because of the often-formidable difficulty of learning the new technique. We view this error as equally dangerous as the first one. We urge researchers to investigate and consider complex techniques to determine their applicability to their research questions. Nevertheless, we believe some of the techniques discussed in this chapter have the potential to more fully answer questions about retirement than would be possible without them.

REFERENCES

Atchley, R. C. (1979). Issues in retirement research. *The Gerontologist, 19,* 44–54.

Arbuckle, J. L. (1995). *Amos for Windows. Analysis of moment structures. Version 3.5.* Chicago, Illinois: SmallWaters.

Bentler, P. M., & Wu, E. (1995). *EQS structural equations program manual.* Encino, California: Multivariate Software.

Bliese, P.D. (2002). Multilevel random coefficient modeling in organizational research: Examples using SAS and S-Plus. In F. Drasgow & N. Schmitt (Eds.) *Modeling in organizational research: Measurement and analyzing behavior in organizations* (pp. 401–445). San Francisco: Jossey-Bass.

Camilli, G., & Shepard, L. A. (1994). *Methods for identifying biased test items.* Thousand Oaks, California: Sage.

Chan, D., Ramey, S., Ramey, C., & Schmitt, N. (2000). Modeling intraindividual changes in children's social skills at home and at school: A multivariate latent growth approach to understanding between-settings differences in children's social skill development. *Multivariate Behavioral Research, 35,* 365–396.

Deadrick, D. L., Bennett, N., & Russell, C. J. (1997). Using hierarchical linear modeling to examine dynamic performance criteria over time. *Journal of Management, 23,* 745–757.

Duncan, T. E., Duncan, S. C., Li, F., Strycker, L. A., & Alpert, A. (2002). *Modeling intraindividual variability with repeated measures data: Methods and applications.* Mahwah, New Jersey: Erlbaum.

Embretson, S. E., & Reise, S. P. (2000). *Item response theory for psychologists.* Mahwah, New Jersey: Erlbaum.

Feldman, D. C. (1994). The decision to retire early: A review and conceptualization. *Academy of Management Review, 19,* 285–311.

Gold, M. S., & Bentler, P. M. (2000). Treatments of missing data: A Monte Carlo comparison of RBHDI, iterative stochastic regression imputation, and expectation-maximization. *Structural Equation Modeling, 7,* 319–355.

Hanisch, K. A. (2000). The impact of organizational interventions on behaviors: An examination of different models of withdrawal. In D. Ilgen & C. L. Hulin (Eds.). *Computational modeling of behavior in organizations* (pp. 33–60). Washington, D. C.: American Psychological Association.

Hanisch, K. A., Hulin, C. L., & Seitz, S. T. (1996). Mathematical/computational modeling of organizational withdrawal processes: Benefits, methods, and results. In G. Ferris (Ed.), *Research in personnel and human resources management* (Vol. 14, pp. 91–142). Greenwich, Connecticut: JAI Press.

Hardy, M. A., & Hazelrigg, L. (1999). A multilevel model of early retirement decisions among autoworkers in plants with different futures. *Research on Aging, 21,* 275–303.

Hofmann, D. A. (1997). An overview of the logic and rationale of hierarchical linear models. *Journal of Management, 23,* 723–744.

Hofmann, D. A., Griffin, M. A., & Gavin, M. B. (2000). The application of hierarchical linear modeling to organizational research. In K. J. Klein & S. W. Kozlowski (Eds.), *Multilevel theory, research, and methods in organizations* (pp. 467–511). San Francisco: Jossey-Bass.

Hser, Y., Shen, H., Chou, C., Messer, S. C., & Anglin, M. D. (2001). Analytic approaches for assessing long-term treatment effects: Examples of empirical applications and findings. *Evaluation Review, 25,* 233–262.

Hulin, C. L., & Mayer, L. J. (1986). Psychometric equivalence of a translation of the Job Descriptive Index into Hebrew. *Journal of Applied Psychology, 71,* 83–94.

Ilgen, D. R., & Hulin, C. L. (2000). *Computational modeling of behavior in organizations: The third scientific discipline.* Washington, D. C.: American Psychological Association.

Jones, C. J., & Meredith, W. (1996). Patterns of personality change across the life span. *Psychology & Aging, 11,* 57–65.

Jöreskog, K. G., & Sörbom, D. (1993). *LISREL 8: Structural equation modeling with the SIMPLIS command language.* Chicago: Scientific Software International.

Little, R. J., & Rubin, D. B. (1987). *Statistical analysis with missing data.* New York: John Wiley and Sons.

Marsh, L., & Cormier, D. R. (2001). *Spline regression models.* Thousand Oaks, California: Sage.

McArdle, J. J., & Anderson, E. R. (1989). Latent growth models for research on aging. In L. E. Biren & K. W. Schaie (Eds.), *The handbook of the psychology of aging* (3rd ed; pp. 21–44). San Diego, California: Academic Press.

Meijer, R. R., & Sijtsma, K. (2001). Methodology review: Evaluating person fit. *Applied Psychological Measurement, 25,* 107–135.

Meredith, W., & Tisak, J. (1990). Latent curve analysis. *Psychometrika, 55,* 107–122.

Mislevy, R., & Bock, R. D. (1991). *Bilog's users' guide.* Chicago: Scientific Software.

Munson, L. J., & Hulin, C. L. (2000). Examining the fit between empirical data and theoretical simulations. In D. Ilgen & C. L. Hulin (Eds.). *Computational modeling of behavior in organizations* (pp. 69–83). Washington, D. C.: American Psychological Association.

Nagelkerke, N. J. D. (1991). A note on a general definition of the coefficient of determination. *Biometrica, 78,* 691–692.

Pampel, F. C. (2000). *Logistic regression: A primer.* Thousand Oaks, California: Sage.

Parnes, H. S., & Somers, D. G. (1994). Shunning retirement: Work experience of men in their seventies and early eighties. *Journals of Gerontology, 49,* S117–S124.

Raudenbush, S. W., & Bryk, A. S. (2002). *Hierarchical linear models: Applications and data analysis.* Thousand Oaks, California: Sage.

Raymond, M. R., & Roberts, D. M. (1987). A comparison of methods for treating incomplete data in selection research. *Educational and Psychological Measurement, 47,* 13–26.

Roth, P. L., Switzer, F. S., & Switzer, D. M. (1999). Missing data in multiple item scales: A Monte Carlo analysis of missing data techniques. *Organizational Research Methods, 2,* 211–232.

Seitz, S. T., Hanisch, K. A., & Hulin, C. L. (1997). *Worker: A Computer Program to Simulate Employee Organizational Withdrawal Behaviors,* University of Illinois at Urbana-Champaign and Iowa State University.

Simonton, D. K. (1997). Creative productivity: A predictive and explanatory model of career trajectories and landmarks. *Psychological Review, 104,* 66–89.

Speyrer, J. F., & Ragas, W. R. (1991). Housing prices and flood risk: An examination using spline regression. *Journal of Real Estate Finance and Economics, 4,* 395–407.

Spieker, S. J., Larson, N. C., Lewis, S. M., Keller, T. E., & Gilchrist, L. (1999). Developmental trajectories of disruptive behavior problems in preschool children of adolescent mothers. *Child Development, 70,* 443–458.

Stetz, T. A., & Beehr, T. A. (2000). Organizations' environment and retirement: The relationship between women's retirement, environmental munificence, dynamism, and local unemployment rate. *Journals of Gerontology: Series B: Psychological Sciences and Social Sciences, 55B,* S213–S221.

Switzer, F. S., & Roth, P. L. (2002). Coping with missing data. In S. G. Rogelberg (Ed.), *Handbook of research methods in industrial and organizational psychology* (pp. 310–323). Malden, Massachusetts: Blackwell.

Taber, C. S., & Timpone, R. J. (1996). *Computational modeling.* Thousand Oaks, California: Sage.

Thissen, D. (1991). MULTILOG: Multiple, Categorical Item Analysis and Test Scoring Using Item Response Theory (Version 6). Chicago: Scientific Software.

Tisak, J., & Tisak, M. S. (2000). Permanency and ephemerality of psychological measures with application to organizational commitment. *Psychological Methods, 5,* 175–198.

Wainer, H. (2000). *Computerized adaptive testing: A primer.* Mahwah, New Jersey: Erlbaum.

Willett, J. B., & Sayer, A. G. (1994). Using covariance structure analysis to detect correlates and predictors of individual change over time. *Psychological Bulletin, 116,* 363–381.

Zelterman, D. (1999). *Models for discrete data.* New York: Oxford University Press.

Zickar, M. J. (2002). Modeling data with polytomous item response theory. In F. Drasgow & N. Schmitt (Eds.), *Measuring and analyzing behavior in organizations: Advances in measurement and data analysis* (pp. 123–155). San Francisco: Jossey-Bass.

Zickar, M. J., & Highhouse, S. (1998). Looking closer at the effects of framing on risky choice: An item response theory analysis. *Organizational Behavior and Human Decision Processes, 75,* 75–91.

Zickar, M. J., & Slaughter, J. E. (1999). Examining creative performance over time using hierarchical linear modeling: An illustration using film directors. *Human Performance, 3/4,* 211– 230.

12

Concluding Observations and Future Endeavors

Terry A. Beehr and Gary A. Adams

There is much that we already know and much yet to be learned about retirement decisions and retired life. With the aging of America and many other countries, if the average age of retirement remains constant, we soon will have perhaps the largest proportion of our society classified as retired than we have ever had. This is one of the issues driving retirement-related research, theory, and applications.

We as a society have taken little action regarding the impending dramatic increase in people reaching retirement age. The consequences of an aging society, both those that are known and those that are as yet little understood, will inevitably be upon us in the next couple of decades, however. Retirement only became an institution in the West during the middle of the 20th century, but now it is widely perceived as a right for people who have been active in the workforce for a certain period of time. The status and recognition that come to individuals with paid employment disappear or change when that employment is given up for any reason. The factors that lead people to a decision to give up their status, lifestyle, daily companions, and even income must be strong. Why do we do this? Well, obviously one reason is the lure or positive characteristics of retirement. If we are giving up much, then we must be doing it at least partly to obtain something else. Little research seems to have addressed this issue, however—the lure of retired life. There is much left to be learned about retirement, and we need to learn it.

Without solid knowledge, we make less informed decisions. That knowledge comes best from rigorous, reasoned research. As a process, retirement seems to require longitudinal research methods. What do people do and decide to do over time during critical change points in their lives? Some decisions are of a continuous nature. For example, we can decide how much of our retirement assets to put into the stock market, versus bonds, real estate, certificates of deposit, bank accounts, or other elements of a portfolio. We can keep none, all, or any portion of our savings in these forms. On the other hand, some retirement variables that need research are, or approximate, dichotomous choices: to retire or not would be the classic example. Even though it is possible to partially retire (e.g., by working part-time in another job with bridge employment), this decision seems less like a continuous variable (i.e., there are fewer conditions that people actually seem to choose). The most appropriate research methods and statistics, therefore, may vary for different issues in retirement.

Many parties could use information based on retirement research because there are many actors making decisions about retirement. There are micro, meso, and macro issues involved in decision-making. Much psychological research on retirement has focused on micro-level or individual decision making. We know that finances play a part in individuals' decisions to retire, and health probably plays a role, but there is much left unknown about these decisions. A little research has been done, but more is needed on factors such as gender and joint (couples) decision making, working conditions, social conditions, life and work goals, and expectations about a retired future that might affect individuals as they ponder retiring.

The employing organization and the society or government often try to understand individual motivations in order to make policies that will lead to outcomes they prefer. While the individuals engage in their decision making, organizations (meso-level) approach retirement issues from their own perspectives and with their own needs and goals. We do not view organizations as sentient decision makers, but their "behavior" (as evidenced in their policies, procedures, and other "actions") implies decision making about retirement of their members. The "organizational" decisions are, of course, made by individuals in decision making positions who are supposed to act as stewards on the behalf of the organization. That is, the goals and criteria for success could involve getting the organization to have the "right-sized" work force, cutting costs by eliminating the highest-priced employees, getting rid of those who might be considered obsolete, and so forth. While the individual is looking for a well-earned retirement, organizations are more likely looking for a well-deserved competitive strategy.

At the macro level, government, acting as a steward for society's welfare, has still different goals. These goals can be in a constant state of flux, with turnover among congressional and executive decision makers altering national priorities from time to time. In the U.S., the goals at the macro level might include keeping the social security system solvent, providing a livable income for seniors, preventing discrimination against older workers, maintaining or improving the nation's productivity, maintaining or reducing unemployment levels, and encouraging a myriad of behaviors by aging workers.

Overall, decisions are made about retirement at all three levels (individual, organizational, and societal), and these decisions are made with different goals in mind. To some extent, people making decisions at the higher levels are trying to control what happens at the lower levels. That is, government sometimes makes decisions trying to control what organizations and individuals do, and organizations make decisions trying to control what individuals do. But each makes decisions for its own purposes, even though information and understanding of how to achieve those purposes is incomplete. To complicate matters, still other entities are involved in retirement decisions and retirement life. Insurance companies, retirement planning consultants, and health organizations are examples. These organizations are acting in their own interests and/or in the interests of the individuals. Their effects on retirement further complicate attempts to understand, make predictions about, and control retirement. Information is needed to make decisions at all levels, and thus many of the chapters note the need for more research on retirement. These complexities can lead to ineffective policies or unintended consequences. Examples of the latter occur (1) when organizations offer early retirement plans that are accepted by more people than anticipated, or are accepted by specific people the organization does not want to retire and (2) when part-time employment offers intended to keep retirees working for the company instead encourage more people to retire so they can work part-time.

Retirement policies of organizations and society are often aimed at controlling individuals' retirement decisions, (i.e., getting individuals to retire earlier or later). One could interpret these attempts as efforts to force people to retire (or remain in the workforce), even though U.S. law forbids forced retirement. The assumption is that if the conditions are arranged just right, people will decide to retire; with complete knowledge, conditions can be arranged so that people will make the voluntary decision to retire. If we have a philosophical inclination, we might ask whether there is any such thing as free will or voluntary retirement if others can determine our decision for us in this manner.

One way to get information about causal variables in people's decisions to retire is simply to ask them. We can ask retirees why they retired, and we can ask elderly employees why they have not retired or what conditions will induce them to retire. Human beings often have only imperfect knowledge of their own motives, however. They are likely, for example, to provide answers to such questions that seem hypothetically more rational or more socially desirable; they might tell us how they think they would or should react but not how they really would react if placed in the situation. The common research method, therefore, is to find relationships between individual, organizational, and societal conditions and people's actual retirement decisions, and to infer motivation and causation from these relationships. We can ask employees what they will do after retirement and what will make them happy in retirement, but again the answers to such questions need to be confirmed with other kinds of research. Even some concrete retirement plans, both plans about when to retire and about what to do after retirement, do not get implemented. As of this writing, the U.S. stock market is in a serious downslide, and many of us know people who once had plans to be retired by now but have not followed through, apparently due to changing economic conditions. In addition, people who intended to do a lot of traveling, playing golf, or other specific activities after retirement do not always engage in these activities as much as their preretirement thoughts indicated.

A very specific conclusion by some of the authors in this volume is that we still do not know as much about women's retirement decisions and behaviors as we do about men's, due to less research on that topic. On average, women tend to have more interrupted work histories than men, a factor that can lead to a less financially viable retirement. Fortunately, the retirement knowledge gap between the sexes is diminishing with new research on women and on gender differences regarding retirement. For couples, predictors of retirement decision making are probably still more complex, because couples' retirement decisions are at least loosely coupled. If, on the average, women's work histories cause them to be financially less ready for retirement at a similar age as men, and if on the average women tend to be younger than their male partners, one might expect some conflicting pressures on their decisions to retire at any one time. Thus couples' retirement decision making and behaviors are not yet well understood.

A final issue that no doubt affects retirement, but is often overlooked in theories and research, concerns social and cultural norms. We researchers might examine finances, health, the nature of occupations, social connectedness, and other individual-level variables, but all of our studies of the decision to retire find that very large percentages of variance in these decisions is still unaccounted for. Norms are an explanation for retirement decisions that are usually neglected in our research and theories. When I talk to people about their decisions, one comment in their answers often is that "it was just time to retire." Where does one get the idea that it is time to retire? It is likely to be at least partially influenced by the societal (and maybe organizational) culture of which we are a part. If it is "normal" to retire at age 65, then maybe that is what we "should" do. If we see everyone else retiring at a given age and if we hear others comment approvingly about it, then it may become our own goal or standard for when we should retire. We probably have had many different cultural norms for work over the last century. During the Great Depression, having more than one family member employed (thereby taking a job from a totally unemployed family) might be something that one didn't boast about publicly. If women's "place" was once thought to be in the home and a man's to provide income, then a man whose wife worked might have felt somewhat uneasy about it. During times of high unemployment, there might be some thought that a person working past "normal" retirement age is keeping a more needy, younger person from a job. For whatever rational or irrational reasons, we do develop norms about appropriate workplace behaviors, and it would be unusual if there were no norms for retirement behaviors. This topic is not, however, the subject of much research or even theoretical speculation at present.

Obviously, there is much yet to be learned about the process of retirement. The importance of acquiring more knowledge about retirement is clear to researchers and policy makers at all levels. Retirement has proven to be an interesting and yet vexing research topic that should attract the curious, the adventurous, and the concerned.

Index